JOHN SIMPSON CHISUM

JOHN SIMPSON CHISUM
CATTLE KING OF THE PECOS REVISITED

CLIFFORD R. CALDWELL

SANTA FE

Sunstone books may be purchased for educational, business, or sales promotional use.
For information please write: Special Markets Department, Sunstone Press,
P.O. Box 2321, Santa Fe, New Mexico 87504-2321.

Book and Cover design ═ Vicki Ahl
Body typeface ═ Garamond
Printed on acid free paper

Library of Congress Cataloging-in-Publication Data

Caldwell, Clifford R., 1948-
  John Simpson Chisum : cattle king of the Pecos revisited / by Clifford R. Caldwell.
     p. cm.
  Includes bibliographical references and index.
  ISBN 978-0-86534-756-4 (softcover : alk. paper)
  1. Chisum, John Simpson, 1824-1884. 2. Chisum, John Simpson, 1824-1884--Family.
3. Ranchers--Pecos River Valley (N.M. and Tex.)--Biography. 4. Ranch life--Pecos River Valley
(N.M. and Tex.)--History--19th century. 5. Cattle trade--Pecos River Valley (N.M. and Tex.)-
-History--19th century. 6. Pecos River Valley (N.M. and Tex.)--Biography. 7. Pecos River
Valley (N.M. and Tex.)--Social life and customs--19th century. 8. Pecos River Valley (N.M.
and Tex.)--Genealogy. I. Title.
  F392.P3C35 2010
  976.4'905092--dc22
  [B]
                                    2010002943

Published in

WWW.SUNSTONEPRESS.COM
SUNSTONE PRESS / POST OFFICE BOX 2321 / SANTA FE, NM 87504-2321 /USA
(505) 988-4418 / ORDERS ONLY (800) 243-5644 / FAX (505) 988-1025

TO

Harwood P. Hinton Jr., PhD
who has helped me immeasurably

But search the land of living men,
Where wilt thou find their like again.

—Sir Walter Scott

CONTENTS

ILLUSTRATIONS

FOREWORD

John Simpson Chisum was a towering figure on the western cattle frontier. At the height of his operations as the "Cattle King of the Pecos," Chisum employed 100 riders and ran 80,000 head of "Jinglebobs" on an enormous range that he pre-empted in New Mexico.

Born in Tennessee in 1824, he was prophetically nicknamed "Cow John" as a boy. The Chisum family moved to Texas, where John became a merchant and county official at Paris in northeast Texas. But by the 1850s the range cattle industry was developing in Texas, and at thirty Chisum plunged into the colorful business that was destined to captivate the American public. He bought and traded and sold livestock, led cattle drives, and was designated a beef supplier for Confederate troops. He was paid $40 per head in Confederate money, and following each sale he bought more cattle. By war's end Chisum had converted the ultimately worthless currency to livestock, and in time he would complain, "I'm in great trouble because I cannot dispose of my stock as fast as it increases."

A couple of years after the Civil War he moved from West Texas to an isolated range along the Pecos River in eastern New Mexico. By this time Chisum had devised the "Long Rail" brand, a straight line burned on the left flank from hip to shoulder. The Long Rail was easy to alter with a running iron, but Chisum's cattle also wore the distinctive "jinglebob" earmark. A slice of a pocketknife left the bottom two-thirds of the ear dangling and swinging "just like an earring."

Chisum's sprawling rangelands and vast herds of cattle and horses were tempting targets for rustlers and Indian raiders. But many of his riders were as good with a gun as a lasso, and Chisum often struck back. He was reputed to run roughshod over small ranchers, he was widely suspected of shady dealings, and he was connected to the infamous Lincoln County War. But through ambition and relentless effort Chisum became one of the great cattle barons of the Old West.

I first wrote about John Chisum more than a decade ago in *Historic Ranches of the Old West*. I visited his famous South Spring ranch headquarters in New Mexico, along with his grave in Paris and other sites. I studied the articles on Chisum by Harwood P. Hinton. These three articles were published in the *New Mexico Historical Review* in 1956 and 1957, and Dr. Hinton continued to research Chisum, an investigation which has lasted for more than half a century. Dr. Hinton is the leading authority on John Chisum, and I have been privileged to discuss with him his work on the cattle king and to hear him reflect at great length on Chisum. I could not resist asking if he intended to write a biography, but he feels that Chisum is too elusive for proper biographical treatment.

Nevertheless, a biography of this important westerner is long overdue, and western author Clifford R. Caldwell at last has provided this book-length study. Caldwell consulted with Harwood Hinton, and he pored over the work of other authors who have written about Chisum. He traveled to all of the Chisum sites, he combed numerous archival collections, and he demonstrated special command of the Lincoln County War and Chisum's role in this notorious conflict. Caldwell has put together the historic saga of an enigmatic legend of the range cattle frontier, and it is a pleasure to read about Chisum's adventurous life.

—Bill O'Neal, Carthage, Texas

ACKNOWLEDGEMENTS

Much of the credit for this book goes to the earlier researchers, historians and authors whose hard work made this project possible. Most notable on that list of names are Dr. Harwood P. Hinton Jr., Maurice G. Fulton, Robert N, Mullin, Philip J. Rash, and J. Evetts Haley. I was shown the path by the likes of these men and am grateful to have benefited from their labor. In particular, Dr. Hinton's manuscript *John Simpson Chisum: 1877–1884* provided much of the research validation I needed, and served as a valuable guide in assembling my work. Hinton's generous personal assistance provided the encouragement and inspiration I needed to shoulder this daunting enterprise. Among the dear friends whose special assistance proved to be invaluable are Skipper Steely and James Owens. Both Skipper and James have shared their research work openly, adding to the accuracy and completeness of this book. Skipper Steely's unpublished manuscript *Forty Seven Years* provided untold details concerning the Chisum family, John Chisum's early life, and the formation of Lamar County, Texas. Skipper's *Forty Seven Years* is a magnificent, well researched and sourced manuscript that should be published and shared with all. James

Owens' aid in locating and gathering many of the photographs, and tracking down numerous pesky details, was incalculable.

Archivist James Bradshaw of the Haley Library & History Center in Midland, Texas devoted many hours of his time aiding me in my research. His generous efforts contributed mightily. Mark Dworkin, editor for the Wild West History Association Journal, deserves a sincere thank you for his professional assistance, and for taking the time to offer some much needed editorial assistance. In addition, his constant encouragement has helped me to bring this book to a successful conclusion. All have given freely of their time and knowledge.

I also wish to thank the following people who provided valuable aid during the writing of this book:

Nancy Dunn, Artesia Historical Museum & Art Center, Artesia, New Mexico.
Elvis E. Fleming, Historical Center for Southeast New Mexico, Roswell, New Mexico.
John LeMay, Historical Center for Southeast New Mexico, Roswell, New Mexico.
Charles O. "Butch" Sanders, Baltimore, Maryland.
Holly Angeline Stevens, Special Collections Archivist, Gee Library, Texas A&M University, Commerce, Texas.

INTRODUCTION

Perhaps it has already been said best over a half century ago, by noted historian Dr. Harwood P. Hinton Jr. when he penned "A definitive biography of John Chisum may never be written, for there is quite a paucity of information not only concerning his life but also his stock dealings, which spanned the Southwest for thirty years."[1] Like the saga of other legendary personalities of the American West, such as Billy the Kid, the story of the life and times of John Chisum has become so contaminated with hypothesis and folklore that what remains of his story is little more than "a blurred picture of a misrepresented and uninterpreted individual, living in the shadows of a bygone era," as Hinton has so aptly put it.

The earlier works of Philip J. Rasch, Maurice G. Fulton, Robert N. Mullin, J. Evetts Haley and the often maligned Walter Noble Burns provided much of the bones of the story. Hinton added the flesh later. In due course Dr. Hinton's work on John Chisum became the wellspring from which all future authors would draw when their stories included *The Cattle King of the Pecos* in much the same way that Frederick Nolan's in depth studies on John Henry Tunstall, Billy the Kid and the Lincoln County War have become the resource that new writers on these subjects look to when in doubt. But new research did not cease after Nolan's work, as it seems to have on John Simpson Chisum. Chisum continues to play a bit part, often as little more than a walk-on actor, in practically everyone's newly written chronicle of the American West. Yet hardly a musty, mildewed page of the Chisum archives, sparse though they may be, has been turned in quite some time.

John Simpson Chisum stands tall among the legendary cattlemen of the 1800s as a major force in the formation and development of the cattle business so closely identified with Texas and New Mexico. A charismatic leader of men, he stood up to the corruption and monopolistic trade practices in Lincoln County, New Mexico in the 1870s. With practically no land holdings whatsoever he crafted a cattle empire for himself along the Pecos River. He never traveled the famous Chisholm Trail to Kansas, nor was it actually named for him as so many believed. In his personal manner, he was always neatly groomed, polite and generous to a fault. A true visionary of his time, he was a shrewd businessman and accomplished self-promoter, but he was not always a sharp financial manager. On several occasions during his life he wound up strapped for cash, unable to make good on his debts. Although he was instrumental in opening up the Pecos River area of New Mexico to large scale ranching and diverse agriculture this fact is seldom recognized. Chisum's cattle reached distant markets, and his impact was widespread, but unlike men like Charles Goodnight who survived to write much of their own history John Chisum's accomplishments remain narrowly defined.

Along with legendary cattlemen Charles Goodnight and Oliver Loving, Chisum pioneered the famous Goodnight-Loving Trail. But John Chisum's cattle trail began further east, in Denton County. It ran through Central Texas to near the present day village of Trickham in Coleman County, then meandered across the arid open country of West Texas fording the Pecos River at Horsehead Crossing.[2, 3] The trail then turned north through New Mexico and on to Fort Sumner. His efforts led to opening up the Pecos Valley of

New Mexico to cattle ranching. In his later years he was active in the Roswell, New Mexico community.

Myth and legend have clouded the true picture of the man, his accomplishments, his flaws and his contributions. His own prolific efforts at self-promotion, although they served him well during his life, further obscure our vision of the truth of the man. Regrettably, had it not been for his role in the Lincoln County War history might have painted a more accurate picture of John Chisum. Some have asserted, perhaps legitimately, that the Lincoln County War was nothing more than a continuation of the lesser known Pecos War.

In *John Simpson Chisum, The Cattle King of the Pecos Revisited* you will learn more about John Chisum the man, his background, the events that led up to the Pecos War, and the part he played in the Lincoln County War. This book incorporates the traditional knowledge of Chisum that earlier historians such as Dr. Harwood P. Hinton Jr. and Skipper Steely labored long to compile and updates that with more recent discoveries. You will gain a broader understanding of Chisum, with greater insight into the origin of some of the myths about his life that have been perpetuated for decades.

1

JOHN SIMPSON CHISUM

THE BEGINNING

*An invincible determination can accomplish
almost anything ... and in this lies the great
distinction between great men and little men.*
—Thomas Fuller

It was in the spring of 1880 on a stopover at Fort Sumner during his return trip to the South Spring ranch that John Chisum had an unexpected encounter with William Bonney, soon to be known by the handle that history would forever identify him with, Billy the Kid.[4] The Kid, still fresh after scores of desperate shootouts during the Lincoln County War and boasting a handful of notches on his gun had now taken to cattle rustling for a living. Billy brazenly approached Chisum and demanded payment for services he claimed that he had previously performed for the cattleman while in Lincoln County.

Not many years earlier Chisum led a thousand head of gaunt, wild eyed Texas Longhorn cattle that were desperately pawing their way up the steep muddy banks of the Pecos River at Horsehead Crossing. The scene must have been awe inspiring in its frontier majesty. Chisum knew if he could successfully drive his livestock up that bank and on to market, he would reap a windfall profit. But here was an obstacle—there were always obstacles on the frontier. This time the obstacles took the form of a desperate young outlaw who had boldly chosen to face down the veteran Cattle King.

The old cattleman must have thought of the overwhelming odds he had faced years before, when he established his ranching operations along the isolated banks of the Pecos River. If he did think of such things, it probably helped him to remain undaunted. Neither the inhospitable territory nor the ceaselessly hostile Indian raids had slowed his progress, even as they depleted his herds and placed his family and cowhands in constant peril. The local trade monopoly held by the Murphy/Dolan consortium did not check his progress. Perhaps he was thinking about how the murderous Lincoln County War had not slowed down the determined growth of his cattle empire. He knew he would have to find a way to overcome this challenge, and in the end, somehow, like he always did, he would prevail.

Boldly and confidently the unarmed Chisum once again relied on his inner strength and intellect when he replied, "You know just as well as I do that I never hired you to do anything for me." After a brief pause to contemplate, Billy replied "Aw, you ain't worth killing." Once again, Chisum didn't simply survive, he prevailed.

John Chisum left a trail across the American West so wide that a blind scout could follow it. Although his track can be picked up effortlessly, the gaps, and sketchy information about the man, leave us with only half of the story.

Chisum did nothing in a small way. Possessing an entrepreneurial spirit, he saw opportunities and boldly seized them. The dogged cattleman stopped at practically nothing to achieve success. Yet, historians have generally failed to fill in the gaps between the major events in which he played a pivotal role. This has, in part, been a result of the profound scarcity of information about the man and his life. Spanning the period of his legendary cattle drives of the 1860s to the Bosque Redondo and on to the Lincoln County War...and ultimately to his tragic and untimely passing...all without so much as a pause in between. Had it not been for the 1970s movie *Chisum*, produced by Andrew Fenady, in which John Wayne played John Chisum those with a casual interest in the man might have had a much better understanding of him without trying to reconcile the movie with his life. In an unlucky twist of historical circumstance the totally unrelated Chisholm Trail that is named for Jesse Chisholm and covered roughly the same path as the Kansas Trail, the Abilene Trail, or McCoy's Trail, would be forever confused with John Chisum's cattle trail west to New Mexico.[5] His life story seems to have been unfairly and narrowly defined by his association with the iconic Billy the Kid and a singular, epic cattle drive across the barren expanses of West Texas. This picture of the man is akin to simply claiming that Henry Ford assembled cars. Yes, Ford did that, but he practically invented the modern day assembly line process and was a decisive figure in American industrial history.

John Simpson Chisum as a Younger Man.
Courtesy of The Haley Memorial Library and History Center, Midland, Texas.

It seems that popular attention has been focused on the role of the cowboy, rather than the cattleman, in the building of the American west. This is unfortunate. Although the nomadic life of the cowboy may appeal to our romantic side, it was the cattlemen like Chisum who made the lifestyle of the cowboy possible by opening vast tracts of previously desolate and inhospitable lands. These early cattle kings were rough, rugged men, risk takers and visionaries. They saw what was possible. They transformed their vision through hard work, at unprecedented risk, into wealth on the hoof. John Simpson Chisum was such a man. A truly charismatic individual, he became a major force and influence in the formation and development of the cattle business in the West. He was among the cult of self-made men who, as Joseph G. McCoy put it in his 1870s account of such giants of the cattle trade were "men who in their youth received a thorough drilling in adversity, and thus not only learned the intrinsic value of a dollar but how to make and take care of one, invariably make earth's most successful business men."[6]

John's niece Sallie Chisum would later say that "My Uncle John was one of the best men that ever lived, big hearted and generous.... He was a plain, bacon and frijoles sort of man—no frills.... Though he never had a fight in his life, he was a brave man."[7] Well groomed and neatly dressed, his moustache always trimmed, he was a man of medium build and height, wiry and muscular, and could most often be found wearing a soft gray hat and flannel shirt with his trousers tucked into his boots. Dr. Hinton makes reference to A.M. Gildea's description of Chisum as being "a medium sized hombre with shrewd eyes, his face sunbaked to the color of leather, but unless his appearance and methods of working cattle were deceptive he was a man of forceful action." Chisum's nephew Will later described his Uncle John in the following way:

> In height, he was about five feet eight inches, firmly built and had dark brown hair and a heavy mustache.[8] His gray-blue eyes were sun squinted and deeply set in a face which

seemed thin due to a long jaw and prominent chin and nose. When on the ranch, Chisum was repeatedly mistaken for an ordinary cowboy by his rough attire, but when traveling or visiting in distant cities, he appeared in clothing befitting his prominence. In considering his nature and drives, the Pecos stockman seems to have been inconsistent and paradoxical.[9]

He was, it is claimed, most particular about his footwear, and he bought the best, soft leather boots available. Chisum never wore a gun, although it was usually considered to be a part of one's normal attire at the time.[10] When asked by one of his cowboys why he went about unarmed Chisum replied…"You carry the guns, I'll carry the brains." But contrary to popular legend, Chisum kept a firearm, usually a Colt Single Action Army .45 revolver within reach whenever riding horseback or traveling by buggy. True, he did not wear his revolver holstered and affixed to a cartridge belt and strapped around his waist in cowboy fashion, but it is foolish to believe that he went about weaponless. His nephew Will Chisum disposed of this persistent contention when he said, "I never saw him buckle a gun on, but [he] carried it in a holster, buckled to the right side of his saddle horn. I never saw him shoot at anything."[11] In *Cattle Kings* author Lewis Atherton contends "tradition insists that Chisum hired thugs to do his fighting for him."[12] A case may be made that he did have in his employ a cadre of men who had reputations as being accomplished gunhands, like James Highsaw for example.

Claimed by some to have been a man of few words, he was nevertheless strongly opinionated, and could on occasion be outspoken and forcible in his tone. Hinton writes of Chisum that he "was slow to anger…. he dealt with friend and foe with consummate tact and diplomacy. Whether in the parlor of a lady, the office of a capitalist, or lounging with cowboys around a campfire in the evening far out on the prairies, he appeared ever at ease."[13] He rarely missed an opportunity to promote himself. As he traveled the west he made a point of stopping at the local newspaper office in each town he visited to introduce himself and announce his presence.[14] Many have formed strong opinions about John Chisum. Oftentimes they are broadly divergent. It would seem that if one had spent any time with the man almost certainly the formation of a strong opinion would have resulted. He was not forgettable. Not in a domineering way and not by him having overpowered the encounter, but by his force of personality which has almost unanimously been echoed by those who knew him. He engaged you with his humor, which fit him naturally and comfortably, laughing loudly as if he hadn't a care in the world. Chisum's breeding, and soft spoken knowledge, shown through his often rugged attire. Known to have been flirtatious with the ladies, he traveled comfortably in groups of both genders.[15]

Another observation about Chisum was made by Miss Mary V. Daniel, whose home he often visited during the latter years of his life. She offered that "John loved money ... was very dictatorial and was accused of cutting corners when to his advantage."[16] This comment is typical of those voiced by Chisum's critics, and suggests that many of his decisions were influenced by his drive to obtain wealth. But for all the carping John Chisum suffered at the hands of his detractors, he was widely admired and respected for the regard and esteem with which he treated his employees. When Chisum would occasionally accompany a herd west to New Mexico he always seemed at ease with the cowboys. His style and manner quickly won over those who worked with him. In the western tradition, he asked no questions about a man's past; he was concerned only with a man's ability to handle cattle and take orders. Former Chisum cowboy Abneth McCabe is quoted by Lily Klasner as having said..."no one else laughs as easily or as heartily as he does. You would think he never had a care or a sorrow in his life...."[17]

The following incident is said to be one that was the topic of Chisum's own frequent storytelling. I shamelessly borrowed it from an earlier account since it illustrates the humor and matter of fact attitude Chisum's men so appreciated about him. Following a cattle drive three horses had been stolen from the remuda. John Chisum and a dozen of his cowboys set out in pursuit. The next evening they finally caught up with one of the thieves and captured him. The men promptly administered the usual prescription of frontier style justice. According to Chisum's own telling… "We asked him no questions. Vegetation was scant there, but we took the highest we could find and dragged him up until his head was within two inches of the limb…. The buttons of his clothing gave way, and when we left him he was almost as naked as when he was born."[18]

Another account of Chisum that provides some insight into the man, and his quick wit, comes from J. Frank Dobie's book *Cow People*. Like most cowmen, John Chisum did not care for soup. Chisum was dining at the Brown Palace in Denver, Colorado where meals were served at regular hours. Dinner was in the evening instead of noon. The meal was served in courses, soup first, and waiters who filled the bowls at each place before the guests dispensed the broth. Three different waiters tried to serve Chisum soup, and each time he declined…increasingly raising the volume of his protest after each successive attempt. Later that evening, after the meal and evening conversation, Chisum retired to his room. In those days the Brown Palace hosted many guests who suffered from tuberculosis, as did similar establishments in the more favorable climates of Colorado. Hotel attendants would administer evening injections to the guests who were so afflicted. Chisum had neglected to lock his door that night. He was awakened to the sight of an attendant who had mistaken him for a guest with tuberculosis and was standing over him with a hypodermic needle. Startled, but without rebuke, he said…"Well, damn your soul, you are getting that soup into me after all."[19]

One of the many observations concerning John Chisum, and perhaps the one that I find most revealing, is the account of Pecos stockman J. Smith Lea. Lea was an early resident of Lincoln County, New Mexico and credited with having named the town of Roswell.

Lea wrote this some years ago while preparing a lengthy statement that contained recollections of his association with Chisum. In this he says… "Chisum was one of the smartest men I have ever known, although he did not have that appearance and was rather inclined to make people believe that he was not so bright. He was never afraid of anything or anybody, and if he ever got mad, no one ever knew it, and he would never, to save his life, change a position he had once taken." Paradoxical, as Hinton put it in his chronicle, which contains the foregoing account by Lea. From Lea's narration we are left to believe that John Chisum was "dumb like a fox" as well as profoundly "stubborn." But stubborn later manifests as resolute when Chisum faces the staggering odds of successfully completing a series of epic cattle drives through the hostile landscape of West Texas.[20] Equally, "dumb like a fox" would seem to mean cunning, and that is an apt description of Chisum.

John Chisum did not invent the cattle business in Texas. Cattle ranching has been a major Texas industry for nearly three centuries. As early as the 1690s the Spaniards brought livestock to Texas. Ranching as such dates from the 1730s, when herds were grazed along the San Antonio River to feed missionaries, soldiers, and civilians in the San Antonio and Goliad areas. As the Spanish missions declined, ranching shifted to private stock raisers like Tomás Sánchez de la Barrera y Garza, Antonio Gil Ibarvo, and Martín De Léon. Some modern scholars place the birth of the Texas ranching industry in the southeastern Texas and southwestern Louisiana area. From there cattle raisers drove their herds to markets in New Orleans. The Spanish government also encouraged the cattle industry in the Coastal Bend area with liberal land grants. Huge tracts were given to those like Tomás Sánchez at Laredo, who owned seed stock of horses, cattle, and sheep and had enough tenants and ranch hands to occupy the land and manage livestock.[21] There were grants as large as the Cavazos (San Juan de Carricitas) grant in Cameron County, which consisted of 4,605 acres. Some grants were even larger. Though few are still owned by the descendants of the original grantees, many ranches in South Texas predate the American Revolution.

The Texas cattle industry was not founded entirely on *free range* ranching.[22] Entrepreneurs such as Thomas and Dennis M. O'Connor, Richard King, Mifflin Kenedy, Charles Schreiner and scores of other ranchers operated on their own land from the onset. Other Texas cattlemen who bought land after the Civil War included the Coggin Brothers, Charles Goodnight, William T. Waggoner, C. C. Slaughter, S. M. Swenson, and William D. and George T. Reynolds. Most ranches consisted of some form of a headquarters house or a collection of buildings that were centrally located from which the ranchers could access the surrounding open range. In the settled parts of Texas in the post- Civil War era, ranchers owned the land on which they built their improvements. As the frontier advanced westward, cattlemen set up their operations on land for which they did not have ownership and title, often purchasing a small section of ground on which they constructed the *home ranch* or headquarters building.[23] Before the advent of barbed wire in 1874, few stockmen acquired large expanses of land for grazing their cattle.[24] Their primary need was a good site from which they could work their stock and control the range. Even the foreign capitalists who invaded the open range country during the cattle boom of the 1880s bought just enough land having live water to hold the range.[25]

History has recorded that John Chisum's role in establishing a cattle trail across West Texas and along the Pecos River into New Mexico was secondary to the immense part he played in opening up New Mexico to cattle grazing, ranching, and farming. This fact is seldom fully recognized. The part that Chisum played in the Lincoln County War was a complex one, and has not generally been treated with the depth of analysis and understanding that it deserves by many historians. Some have alleged that the Lincoln County War was merely a continuation of John Chisum's Pecos War. But to the extent that the Lincoln County War was the result of a complex set of circumstances, and a divergent collection of personalities that came together in a catastrophic way, the suggestion that the war was a continuation of Chisum's Pecos War is a colossal oversimplification.

It is important to note that Chisum was seriously ill with smallpox during much of the Pecos War and that in all likelihood his brother Pitser, and Robert Wylie, took leadership roles in many of the encounters during that affray.[26] The Pecos War, a running battle with the smaller cattlemen of Seven Rivers that had begun a few years earlier, is inexorably linked to the Lincoln County War and was in large part brought on by John Chisum and his battle for grazing land along the Pecos River. Without a doubt enemies were made and relationships strained during the Pecos War period. Alliances were formed, often based solely upon which side of the recently concluded Civil War one had fought on. Some were comrades at arms and some were sidekicks on cattle drives. Some men may have come together based on their ethnicity or religion while others were brought together by their relative wealth and status. Few managed to remain neutral. Even the notorious "Buckshot" Roberts, who labored to remain detached, was ultimately drawn into the fight and forced to choose sides. Although Chisum did not play a role in the actual shooting war in Lincoln County, which began with the murder of John Henry Tunstall and concluded with the death of Billy the Kid, he was a pivotal figure in this saga and it had a profound effect on his life and enterprise.

So where do we begin with the saga of the Cattle King of The Pecos? John Simpson Chisum was born August 16, 1824 in Hardeman County, Tennessee and was the son of Claiborne C. and Lucinda Armstrong Chisum. The family name had actually been spelled Chisholm originally. The mutation in spelling to Chisum took place while the family was still in Tennessee, but not until about 1815.[27] John's parents were cousins.[28] Father Claiborne was born in Grainger County, Tennessee and was the son of James Stewart and Elizabeth Gibbons Chisum. Claiborne's parents had married on January 26, 1794 in Hawkins County, Tennessee.

Before moving to Texas, Claiborne and his father, James,

had moved to western Tennessee as surveyors of the new lands purchased from the Chickasaw Indians by the Federal government. They often received land in payment for their services.[29] The Chisum family had settled there by late 1829. Claiborne purchased 800 acres near his father in March of 1830 and took his family to live at the new location. Upstream from the Chisum family group was the John and Polly Johnson family. They would later accompany the Chisums to Texas.[30]

In stark contrast to so many early immigrants who came to Texas around the time of Independence the Claiborne Chisum family was not without resources. Quite the opposite was the case. In Tennessee they had been substantial landholders and had moved west with a large, extended family and a considerable number of slaves. Neighbors such as the Leven Moore family had already successfully established themselves in Texas. Abner Kuykendall's move may have influenced John Johnson, who was related to the Kuykendalls.[31] To point out any singular reason for the Chisums and Johnsons to have cleared out of Tennessee and selected Texas as their destination is almost impossible. They had families, and did not simply pull up roots and aimlessly wander west hoping to apply their skills in the new republic. Friends, family or news articles gave them a basic direction in which to travel and a location to center their hunt for land as they were preparing to leave Tennessee.[32] Johnson's son, James M., who was also married to a Chisum girl, was given power of attorney to sell Johnson's home. Pitser Miller, a local Bolivar, Tennessee attorney and friend, was given the same duties for Claiborne Chisum.[33]

Skipper Steely, regional writer and historian, suggests that westward expansion for the Chisums was not just desirable, but due to the large families they produced was an economic necessity.[34] John was one of the five Chisum children who accompanied their parents and a group of relatives to Red River County, Texas during the summer of 1837.[35] The Chisums were among the first Presbyterian families in the western half of Red River County.[36] Young John, age thirteen, is said to have driven one of the four Conestoga wagons drawn by a four-horse team.[37]

In 1816 Claiborne Wright and his family, along with two married slaves, Jin and Hardy Wright, joined George and Alex Wetmore and William Mabbitt who had settled near Pecan Point in what would later become Red River County. By the mid-1820s more settlers had begun to move out onto the prairies and by 1833 James Clark had settled at the site of present day Clarksville. Red River County was formally delineated by an act signed by Republic of Texas President Sam Houston on December 14, 1837, which divided the Red River District into two counties, Fannin and Red River. Red River County originally included all or part of lands later belonging to Lamar, Hopkins, Delta, Franklin, Titus, Morris, Cass, Marion, and Bowie counties.

Steely claims the Chisums and Johnsons traveled to Memphis, across the Mississippi River, through Little Rock, down the Southwest Trail to Washington, Arkansas and across to Jonesboro. By late November the Chisum group forded the Red River at Ragsdale's Ferry. Giving further evidence to the fact that the Chisum party was not a caravan of poor immigrants, their load was so large that it took three days to complete the crossing.[38]

The journey had been particularly difficult for the pregnant Lucinda Chisum. She became ill and died while the Chisum contingent was establishing temporary residence during the winter and spring of 1838.[39] In the spring of 1838 Claiborne Chisum purchased about 2,085 acres of land west of present day Paris, Texas from a man named R.B. Jarman.[40] They moved onto the land which was situated near the Latimer family place southeast of Jonesboro.

The following is an excerpt from T. U. Taylor's *The Chisholm Trail and Other Routes*[41] and provides some perspective about Claiborne Chisum:

Claiborne C. Chisum was a typical pioneer of the Texas stamp; he was ever ready to help a neighbor or defend his home and country from the red warrior. Claiborne Chisum was on that historic punitive expedition that was organized in the early months of 1841 to follow and punish the Indians for raids on Bowie and all counties to the west as far as Parker. The members of this expedition were volunteers from Arkansas, and the counties of Bowie, Red River, Lamar, Fannin and others to the west, John Chisum (Cow John) was only seventeen years old at this time, and stayed at home in Paris, TX to guard the family hearthstone. There were seventy in the expeditionary force under the command of General Tarrant, for whom Tarrant County was later named.

Although far from the first dwelling in the Paris vicinity, Claiborne Chisum built the first permanent residence of any kind to be erected within the corporate limits of the city of Paris, Texas. It was a large, double log dwelling with an upper floor and an open hall between the lower rooms.[42] He was considerably active in early efforts to organize the town and the county, and to protect the safety of the people who resided there.

Among the many challenges faced by the early settlers was their encroachment onto lands that had previously been the domain of various tribes of Native Americans. Peaceful cohabitation soon became impossible as the flood of Anglo settlers overran the Red River Valley. Indians were being displaced, their habits and routines disrupted and their native lands systematically annexed. Not surprisingly, angry clashes with mortal consequences became more commonplace. Indian depredations in the Red River Valley rose to an even more serious level in 1837 when a four year long wave of continuous raids and encounters began. That year Daniel Montague and a group of sixteen men attacked a party of Shawnee, Kickapoo, Cherokee and Delaware Indians on May 15, 1837.[43] The attack took place near the community of Warren. During the fighting several Indians were killed as well as one of Montague's men named Billy Amos. For a time afterwards the earlier peace treaties were once again respected, but after several months Indian raids in the Red River Valley began anew.[44] Between the summer of 1837 and fall of 1844 thirty-four settlers lost their lives during Indian fights in the area. A total of sixteen expeditions were mounted seeking to engage the hostiles. Most were dispatched along the Trinity River. Claiborne Chisum was placed in charge of the second such foray on June 8, 1838, taking a party of six men into the field.[45] Claiborne also served in Brigadier General John H. Dyer's Fourth Brigade, Sims Regiment, Edmondson's Company from September 6, 1838 until January 7, 1839.[46]

Soon the division of Red River County into three smaller counties, with one Representative in the Congress of the Republic of Texas from each, would lead to the establishment of Lamar County. The Chief Justice of the county ordered elections on the first Thursday in June, 1841, for the permanent location of the county seat which was to be within five miles of the center of the territory of the county. The first court site of Lamar county was at Mount Vernon, where court was held from June 28, 1841, to June 26, 1843. On July 24, 1843 the records show that the court met at Mount Vernon but transacted no business. It met again in October with the same result. The last recorded meeting was January 22, 1844. No actual courthouse was ever built at Mount Vernon. A man named Mat Click had a tavern there, and local historians have surmised that the sessions were probably held at the tavern during the winter while summer sessions were held outdoors in the shade of a large Osage orange tree that once stood near that site. It is thought that enough people in Lamar County were dissatisfied with Mount Vernon as the location of the county seat that it was moved to the village of Pinhook (sometimes spelled Pin Hook) after a petition and subsequent vote in 1844.[47] Rather than Pinhook, T. H. R. Poteet and Dr. William T. F. Cole suggested that the new town be called Paris. The name change was approved. There seems to be no real consensus concerning the selection of the name "Paris" for the town among local historians and genealogists, although strong opinions do exist. George Wright donated 50 acres in the northwest corner of his property and the first courthouse was built at the new county seat of Paris in 1844.

Unlike many early cowmen whose youth was spent handling livestock, John Chisum did not begin ranching until about the age of thirty, and then largely on a partnership basis. The first thirteen years of his life were spent in western Tennessee on his grandfather's plantation, where his parents had resided from John's birth until their move to Texas. Contrary to what some believe, the nickname *Cow John* has nothing at all to do with John Chisum's success as a stockman and Cattle King. His family gave him that nickname quite early in life. John had an uncle named John as well as a cousin by that name.[48] The appellation lessened any confusion, and it stuck with him his entire life, later proving to be prophetic.

Events of John Chisum's early years remain largely a mystery. Based on what limited history of the Claiborne Chisum family we have one can extrapolate or surmise a great deal from the family's movements, marriages, and pioneering activities during the years on the Red River. There is, however, no autobiography, no oral history that was transcribed from the accounts of family members, and no memoirs to draw from. In her book *My Girlhood Among Outlaws* Lily Klasner claims that Chisum probably led the life of a normal boy of the period, performing chores around the farm and working with livestock as any boy of his age and station would have performed. John Chisum is said to have kept a diary for some years, but either he or someone who came to possess it destroyed it.[49] Although the details of much of Chisum's boyhood years in Tennessee and on the Red River in Texas are lost to time we know that in October 1846 he was hired to supervise the construction of the Tarrant to Sulphur River Road. But the twenty two year old Chisum resigned after only three months on the job.

Construction for a new courthouse building for Lamar County began at Paris in 1847. In Ed Gibbons's story in the *Paris Press* of September 16, 1878, he tells of the building of this new structure, which was the first brick courthouse in Paris. It was in the center of the square, now the plaza, and was a two-story building. Part of the money for building it was obtained from the sale of lots from the fifty acres donated for a town site by George W. Wright. Epps Gibbons and Claiborne Chisum took the contract for building the structure. The courthouse building was the first such structure to be built in Paris.[50] John helped in the construction by hauling bricks made by Epps Gibbons to the masons working on the building. Gibbons fired the bricks in a kiln at the brickyard near his home in the northwest part of town. The Gibbons' home was on what is now West Cherry Street, west of Fourteenth and the brick yard was north of Cherry between Fifteenth and Fifteenth and a Half Street. Ed Gibbons would later claim that the foundation was laid in 1846 and the building was completed in 1847.[51] He added that Epps Gibbons and Claiborne Chisum both had hired hands working on the courthouse, including John S. Chisum, James Chisum, Ed and John C. Gibbons. All worked as common laborers, and Z.M. Paul was the mechanic. On July 4, 1847 Mr. Gibbons told how the town celebrated in the new courthouse, and that the first piano ever brought to Paris was played for the occasion. Unfortunately, there is no record of the cost of the building since the county records for that period have long since been destroyed or lost.

John Chisum ran for county clerk in 1850 but was defeated by John R. Craddock.[52] He made money hauling water to town and contracting for the construction of buildings and bridges. By the age of twenty-seven Chisum remained undecided about his future direction. In a letter dated September 29, 1851 to a relative in Tennessee his indecision becomes apparent when he penned… "I am selling groceries in Paris for M. M. Grant, but I can't tell what I will do next year."[53] The foregoing refers to the grocery business of Monroe M. Grant in Paris.[54] Later he apprenticed as a store clerk for a man named Cheatham. It has been claimed that Chisum became a full partner with Cheatham in the general merchandise store business.[55]

At age twenty-eight Chisum decided to run again for county clerk. This time he defeated John Craddock and won the election of 1852.[56] Chisum served in the new courthouse building in Paris, Texas that he had had a hand in constructing. Although by all reports he did an excellent job of bringing the county records up to date and organizing the business of the office, it became apparent to John that this was not a line of work he favored.[57] His preference was to be outdoors, free of the routine of an office job, traveling about as he pleased. This developed into a lifelong pattern of behavior for Chisum, particularly after he later settled in New Mexico in the late 1860s. He also sought to obtain considerable wealth. Some feel that he was literally driven to personal success and the accumulation of wealth from a very early age. In *Forty Seven Years* Steely opined that Chisum probably did little actual work during his tenure as clerk, with most of the chores falling to his assistant Jacob Long.[58] Chisum spent much of his time involved in land speculation, especially when it was for sale at a bargain on the steps of the courthouse.[59] By 1853 Chisum had begun to develop an interest in Denton County and had contracted to purchase acreage north of the town.

Chisum was vigorously involved in courting a local Paris girl, simultaneously wrestling with direction and the prospect of marriage. By his own admission he fancied himself as a "ladies man" while young and in his prime. Lily Klasner wrote that Chisum claimed to have courted a number of girls, but this one was "a fine looker … a better class country girl, full of health and vigor and life."[60] Klasner, as well as others, report Chisum's heartthrob as Sue Holman.[61] Others claim that her name was Frances Waters (Wafer).[62] The somewhat factually unreliable novel *Three Ranches West* gives John's sweetheart's name as Jenny Wells.[63] Apart from the foregoing uncertainty, the ascendancy of information would seem to point to the identity of John Chisum's romantic interest as having been Sue Holman. Miss Holman came from a local family that, like the Chisum clan, was not without means. Although there was competition for the hand of Sue Holman in the form of a "dude from the city" as Chisum put it, John was determined to prevail in his courtship efforts.[64] In a letter to a cousin in Tennessee dated September 29, 1851 he remarked, "I can't tell how soon I may marry, but I think soon." Sadly for John, she turned down his frequent attempts to win her favor. Miss Holman had chosen "the dude from the city." Years later, when John heard reports of Sue living in California on the edge of poverty, he was furious.[65]

Some who study the life of John Chisum believe that the loss of favor by Sue Holman had a profound and lasting impact on him. Some believe that it was the prospect of a rugged lifestyle, on the move and without roots, that cost him her favor. Lily Klasner stated that Chisum himself claimed responsibility for the rift, having pressed the point of a timely marriage with Miss Holman and having lost the debate.[66] In any case, John Chisum was devastated. He did not seek reelection to the clerk's post in 1854. The loss of her hand is thought to have contributed to that decision.

The incident may truly have had enduring implications, since he never married. But most believe that he was too busy and driven to take the time for affairs of the heart. It must be reaffirmed that John Chisum did enjoy the fellowship of women, and was often in their company. When asked about his lack of a spouse he is quoted as having said, in a humorous way, "none of them had courted him hard enough." Another factor may have been the decided shortage of women on the western frontier. I mention this to discourage readers from forming any hasty judgements about John Chisum. It seems clear that he enjoyed the company of women, but was married to his cow business. Evan Ball writes in her introduction to Lily Klasner's book *My Girlhood Among Outlaws* that "It was readily admitted that John Chisum indulged in decorous flirtations with young women, but most of them, including Lily, understood his attentions." It was a country where, as Sam Jones said, "They was maybe thirty to thirty five young men to every girl; when a new one come to the country the cowboys married her before she lit offen her hoss."[67] Another source claimed that he remained a bachelor because... "he was plain too hard to get along with."[68] Ms. Ball opines that it was rumored that if she had wished to do so Lily Klasner could have married John Chisum. It is quite clear from reading Klasner's accounts of John Chisum in her book *My Girlhood Among Outlaws* that she held a special fondness for the man. Although a bachelor, Chisum's life was anything but the lonely and pitiful existence of a forlorn skinflint. He traveled often and extensively. He lived well, and enjoyed the benefits of his growing empire. He devoted the majority of his life to the cattle business, and the quest for financial and personal prosperity.

John Chisum always felt a strong responsibility for his brothers, and it has been claimed that his first thoughts were always for their welfare.[69] I question some aspects of the depth of Chisum's loyalty to brothers Pitser and James in particular, since he was quite willing to leave both of them behind to manage the difficult and often dangerous job of looking after the ranch and livestock while he traveled around the country deal-making. On the other hand, John was the consummate entrepreneur, and in his soft spoken and folksy way he was a more effective emissary of the Chisum cattle empire than either Pitser or James. Pitser, who had been a sergeant in the Confederate Army, was best at managing the force of often difficult and rowdy cowboys. James, who some have described as not being very "quick," excelled at matters dealing with the farming aspects of the operation. Nonetheless, it cannot be denied that John's devotion to his brother Thomas Jefferson "Jeff," who was afflicted with epilepsy, seemed particularly affectionate. I believe that Lily Klasner said "everywhere he went he managed it so that Jeff was well cared for when not under his watchful eye."[70]

In the Lamar County, Texas census of 1860 a mulatto family lived next door to Jeff Chisum. The mother, Sarah Chisum, was listed as a domestic and her six children were Levi, Harrison, Martha, Clinton and Thomas. No other Chisum families lived nearby. For years there has been speculation that Jeff fathered Sarah Chisum's children, but thus far no concrete proof has been uncovered by researchers who have been diligently trying to lay bare any solid clue. In 1863 Jeff Chisum was involved in a rather heated altercation with a man named Turner Edmundson.[71] Edmundson, the former mayor of Paris, was a big, rough character who provoked Jeff Chisum's fury in a dispute over a boundary line. Edmundson beat the frail, epileptic Jeff Chisum fiercely. When Jeff recovered he went to town with his shotgun and killed Edmundson. Soon after Jeff left Paris for good and joined with his brothers John and Pitser on the cattle drives to New Mexico in the mid 1860s. He died at age thirty-seven, at Puerto de Luna, New Mexico in 1866.[72]

Some have claimed that John Chisum resigned his post as clerk in 1854.[73] More recent research seems to disprove this however. As cited earlier, Chisum simply did not run for reelection in 1854. This was in part a result of his recently failed relationship with Sue Holman. During 1854 he left Paris for Denton County to go into the cattle business, taking on a silent partner named Stephen K. Fowler.[74] Fowler, who is sometimes reported as a "New Orleans Man" and in other accounts as a " New York Man," put up the sum of $6,000 as his share of the ten year partnership.[75] On examination, both characterizations of Fowler are accurate ... New York and New Orleans. Fowler was born in New York in 1826. By 1850 he was living in New Orleans and working as a clerk for harbor master Francis Quarles.[76] In the end, this investment would yield Fowler a handsome profit of $50,000 in only a few short years.[77] Chisum had filed on land in northwestern Denton County, purchased a partnership herd of cattle, and entered the cattle business with the Half Circle P brand. Chisum also managed herds for neighboring families and various partners and shared in the calves, taking one in five as his fee for oversight. By the end of 1854 he had collected a herd of 1,200 head of cattle.[78] Chisum eventually drove 500 head of cattle to Shreveport, and others to his Denton County land which was located about six miles east of the Wise County line.[79]

John Chisum had become an active cattle dealer in search of new opportunities and markets. He had driven his first small herd to a packinghouse in Jefferson, Texas. There would be many more cattle drives that followed.

2

THE TEXAS CATTLEMAN

Nothing in the world can take the place of persistence.
Talent will not; nothing is more common than unsuccessful men
with talent. Genius will not; unrewarded genius is almost a prov-
erb. Education alone will not; the world is full of educated derelicts.
Persistence and determination alone are omnipotent. The slogan 'press
on' has solved and always will solve the problems of the human race.
                                        —John Calvin Coolidge

In the spring of 1854 John Chisum went to
Colorado County, Texas and bought cattle for a
mere $6 a head. Further, that stunningly low price
included the calves. He collected approximately 1,200
head in all and drove them to an area of excellent
grass and water on the Clear Creek near Bolivar, some
twelve miles north of Denton. Chisum located his
operation along Clear Creek, which has its mouth
at the Elm Fork of the Trinity River and runs in a
shoestring fashion and ultimately tapers off into
Williwalla Creek northwest of Rosston in Cooke
County. The settlement of Bolivar itself was referred
to as the Clear Creek settlement. Within the colony
the Reverend Hiram Daily, who had bought the land
from the original owner, William Crawford, laid out a
town site in 1859. Chisum had plans to file claim on
this land by means of continuous use, the common

method of the day in Texas.[80] He had expected the United States Army to offer him some protection from the hostile Indians that still inhabited the region and preyed on settlers. Those tribes included the Anadarko, Caddo, Tehuacana, Tonkawa, Waco, Cherokee, Choctaw, Delaware, Shawnee and a few others. To his surprise, he learned that the troops at Fort Worth,[81] which he believed to have been established as a permanent fort, were to be reassigned to a new post called Belknap[82] on the Salt Fork of the Brazos River on June 24, 1851. This move placed the nearest military protection one hundred miles away from his cow camp at Bolivar. Chisum quickly learned that he would receive little or no help on the frontier from the United States Army, and it was going to be pretty much up to him to figure out how to make a go of it. Undeterred, in the summer of 1854 he set about collecting and building his herd and constructing a large house from which he would base his operations for several years to come. Travelers on the trail west occasionally stopped at Boliver to resupply. By this time Chisum had gained a reputation as being a generous man, and his home was the frequent site of social gatherings. His ranch house, called "the Great White House" for the fact that it had been painted white, was located about three miles above Bolivar.

The Chisholm Trail and Other Routes speaks of John Chisum's Bolivar ranch:[83]

> ...the ranch house is on the crest of a hill and the terrain slopes gently to the west, south and east. The long ridge falls gently to the south and from the ranch house a watcher could spot a redskin half a mile away. Its location was a natural defense against the Indians. Grass was free and all John Chisum needed was enough land for house, garden and feed stuff for a few horses for ready use, water was a necessity and well diggers were few. Finally, he found a man that was anxious to make a trip overland to California. Chisum offered to pay his way over the Overland Trail if he would dig all the wells; the offer was accepted....

John Simpson Chisum Standing by Chair.
Courtesy of The Historical Center for Southeast New Mexico at Roswell.

Although still a bachelor, women frequently attended these gatherings. He always had a housekeeper. Chisum insisted that the dwelling be kept neat and tidy, and that the business of the household be managed efficiently. Among the first to occupy the prestigious post of housekeeper was a mulatto slave girl who appeared to be about sixteen when Chisum bought her. Popular myth has it that he bought the attractive teenage girl, named Jensie, from a wagon master named Joseph Baines.[84] Baines had come from Arkansas, and was on his way to California with his family and several slaves. It's claimed that Chisum paid Baines somewhere between $1,400 and $2,000 for Jensie.[85] Unfortunately, none of these stories can be confirmed. But records show that Chisum purchased Jensie in 1858 in Gainesville, Texas from his first cousin Frances Johnson Towery and her husband Tom V. Towery. Cooke County, Texas court ledgers document this fact. The records further establish that Jensie already had three children when Chisum bought her (Phillip[86] born about 1851 or 1852, Harriet born 1855, and Almeady born April 13, 1857). In an 1876 interview Jensie's daughter Almeady claimed that John Chisum bought her mother in 1849 from his niece Miss Towery. But in 1849 the twenty five year old John Chisum was still clerking in Paris, Texas and John Johnson, Jensie's owner of record, would not die for three more years.[87] Almeady also thought that Jensie was sold to Chisum for $1,500. Neither of these claims fit the facts.

From an aggregation of all of the various records that have been uncovered to date it is clear that Jensie had belonged to John Johnson, Frances Johnson's father, and was mentioned in his will.[88] When he died on September 27, 1852 Jensie went to his daughter Mary Ann Johnson Stell,[89] Frances Johnson Towery's sister. By the time John Chisum bought her she had become the property of Frances Towery, and had the three children already mentioned. Some, including descendents of Jensie herself, believe that the father of some if not all of Jensie's children was a Towery.[90] Frances and Tom Towery used Jensie and the children as collateral for a note of $814. The note was for 100 head of cattle the Towerys were buying, probably to sell in California, which is where they were planning on going, along with a small party of other adventurous souls from the Paris, Lamar County, Texas area.[91] In 1855 the Rhine brothers organized a cattle drive to California.[92] In 1857 Cy Holman, former Lamar County sheriff, and his brother-in-law George Wright, arranged another such trip. Yet another group left Lamar County on April 26, 1858 bound for California with William Bell in charge of that expedition.[93]

Chisum promised to give back the Jensie Johnson family in ten years, plus any increase in children, after the loan was paid. The

Towerys would eventually move to New Mexico with Chisum before going on to California where they settled in Visalia. They never collected on the promise of John Chisum to return Jensie. Jensie remained John Chisum's housekeeper until 1862. Later, while in New Mexico, Frances Towery managed the household for Chisum and remained in that capacity until Chisum's niece, Sallie took over the reins on December 24, 1877.

Still, popular myth has perpetuated the story that Chisum fathered Jensie's youngest child, Almeady. Some continue to believe that he may have been the father of Harriet as well. Earlier historians and researchers seemed to have believed this, in part based on twentieth century interviews with children of Almeady and Harriet.[94] In their defense, they did not have knowledge of more recently discovered documents. In recent years a preponderance of historians and researchers no longer believe that John Chisum fathered any of Jensie's children.

Texans suffered a particularly cold and difficult winter during 1854-1855. Christmas was the only time the cowboys left the range that year, and they rendezvoused at the Boliver store to celebrate briefly. Once the celebration was over they all headed back out across the bleak Texas prairies to look after the struggling but ever-increasing Chisum cattle empire. By the spring of 1855 word had spread of John Chisum's "Great White House" in Boliver, his band of cowboys, his burgeoning herd of cattle and his congenial hospitality. The Chisum cattle empire, now known as the Long Rail outfit, continued to prosper. The Long Rail was Chisum's new brand, replacing the Half Circle "P." The Long Rail mark was somewhat unique in that it was a horizontal line across practically the entire side of the cow, making it difficult to mistake.[95] As was customary at the time, Chisum also marked the left ear of his cattle with the soon to become famous Jinglebob Ear. By starting at the bottom center of the left ear and inserting a knife in the middle of the calf's ear, he cut straight up to the tip. This allowed one part of the ear to remain with the muscle in it standing erect and the other part dangling like the Jinglebobs on a spur when viewed head on.[96] This distinctive marking was easy to spot and impossible to mistake. By 1856 the Long Rail brand and the unique Jinglebob ear had become well known throughout Northwest Texas.

In those days the nearest bank was in Austin. Chisum is said to have carried his money in a wallet hung on the horn of his saddle. According to the account of a Coleman County, Texas old timer named Dick Fiveash, "John Chisum would send (Bill) Franks to Austin after money to pay off his men, and Franks would return with his saddlebags full of gold and silver; or he would be sent to Austin with the money received from the sale of a herd of cattle, to be placed in the bank."[97] In this year (1856) Chisum met Felix McKittrick, an experienced cowboy who wore a long barreled Colt and would become a close acquaintance.[98] Ike Fridge described McKittrick as being a tall, blond haired man who was a nondrinker.[99] Together they scouted the country further to the west, looking for good grass and abundant live water to support the ever-growing Jinglebob herd. In August of 1856 Troops A and F and United States Cavalry under Major Van Dorn had just relocated Camp Colorado to Mukewater Creek, about six miles north of the Colorado River and on the route between Fort Belknap and Fort Mason in what is now Coleman County. Chisum took this as a good sign, and made plans to set up an operation around what is now Trickham near Mukewater Creek. The Coggin Brothers also located there, along Home Creek, moving a sizeable herd to the area in 1860.[100]

The first town settled in Coleman County was Trickham. It is in the extreme southeastern part of the county, on the path of John Chisum's old cattle trail near its entrance into the county. It is hard to determine just when the first little store was established on the Mukewater, but it was sometime during the late 1850s, and most likely about the time Camp Colorado was established.[101] For the convenience of his trail drivers the Chisum store was about a mile below the army post. Emory Peter ran the store with the help of a man named Bill Franks.[102, 103] George W. Teague was the bookkeeper.[104]

John Chisum never lived in Coleman County, but for a number of years maintained both the store at Trickham and a ranch headquarters on Home Creek. He also kept a series of corrals in Cooke and nearby counties to aid in the distribution of his cattle. Chisum's herd ranged all the way from the Concho down the Colorado and over all the southern part of Cooke County. In May 1874, John Chisum sold his store at Trickham to Leonida L. Shield. Shield had been born in Mississippi and had come into Coleman County from Hunt County. He enlarged the old building, which for so long had been the center of all activities in that part of the county, into one of generous proportions in which he installed a general mercantile business, the first of its kind in the county. Leonida Shield also bought cattle and marketed them for a number of years. Shield operated the store until it was destroyed by fire in 1892.

The history of the earliest development of Trickham has been recounted by one of its first residents, Dick Fiveash.[105] Fiveash was born in Erath County in 1862 and moved with his parents to Coleman County in 1864. They settled on the Mukewater, about a mile south of where Trickham is now. His father built a log cabin to live in. There were very few people in the county at that time and his uncle, Bill Williams and his family, who came with them, were the only neighbors. Uncle Bill, who was a real pioneer, became known all over the county as Mukewater Bill. According to Fiveash "He had lots of fights with the Indians and owned a bridle, which was made out of the hide of an Indian he had killed."[106] There was a lot of wild game in the county then, and he recalled seeing the valleys of the creek black with buffalo. Provisions could only be had in Austin, and it generally took two weeks to make the trip. Prices were high and flour was $20 a barrel.

In 1857 John Chisum's father, Claiborne, died. The elder Chisum had married Cynthia Ann Henderson Latimer after John's mother Lucinda had passed in 1837. The division of his estate was made more complicated by the fact that Claiborne had left no will. The court appointed Ed Gibbons and Zachariah Rice as administrators.[107] At the estate sale John purchased 500 head of sheep and an ox wagon. Ben and Nancy Chisum bought the family carriage. The estate of Claiborne Chisum was appraised at over $45,000 in total.[108] Claiborne's daughters Lucinda and Nancy filed suit against Claiborne's third wife Cynthia, and her son Daniel Latimer, Jr., as well as her children by Claiborne. The lawsuit lasted about two years and by 1870 Daniel Latimer, through sheriff's sales to pay the debts of James, Pitser and Jefferson, gained control of most of the Chisum estate.[109] The arguments concerning the settlement became so heated that at one point James Chisum took a shot at his stepmother, slightly wounding her.[110] Cynthia received property valued at $15,216.99 along with the family home. Each of the seven children were awarded property valued at $4,347.68. The final settlement was not made until four years later in 1861.

The fact that John Chisum left behind considerable unpaid obligations in Texas when he removed to the Pecos in New Mexico is a point often overlooked by historians. This was, however, not uncommon at the time. Ranchers required large sums of cash, or working capital, to purchase their herds, maintain the stock, buy supplies and pay the cowhands during the period of time that the cattle were grazing and producing calves. The income from a cattle operation does not occur until the cattle are sold. In the meantime the rancher's debt mounts.

John Chisum's cattle empire was expanding. He had established a hugely successful business. By 1860 Chisum was running 36,000 head of cattle, which he valued at $50,000, owned six slaves, and was already considered a major cattleman in North Texas.[111] He also had 11,000 head of sheep, which were probably managed by Tom Gibbons, a brother of Ed, and were pastured northwest of Bolivar.[112] In January 1861 the not unexpected news of the dissolution of the Union, and the secession of Texas, reached Boliver. Chisum is not known to have ever publicly claimed that he either supported, or opposed slavery. His family had come west with a large number of slaves, and John had always owned slaves. Although his position seems to have remained unspoken, the fact of his ownership alone would seem to quantify his standing on the matter. At the same time, however, his silence on the topic did give him the opportunity to appear neutral in the company of either Confederate sympathizers or Federals. His family is said to have generally treated both hired hands and slaves well. Outwardly, it seemed there was little differentiation between the two groups in their day to day lives.[113] Unlike other family members, Chisum had no plans of getting involved in the fight. He put business ahead of the war. There is evidence that he traded cattle with a broker in New Mexico who supplied the Union forces prior to the cessation of hostilities, and only a short time after he had driven several herds of cattle to supply points on behalf of the Confederate forces.

It has been claimed that subsequent to a visit paid him by Governor Elisha Pease[114] and the notoriously unpopular Texas Ranger Colonel James M. Norris,[115] he was exempt from service.[116] However, an examination of the papers of Governor Pease reveal no record of any such meeting having taken place.[117] Nonetheless, Chisum did agree to do two things, thereby having chosen sides in a de facto fashion. First, he reluctantly agreed to trail cattle east to Shreveport and on to Vicksburg to supply the poorly organized and not yet fully formed Confederate Army. Next, given that the United States Army had abandoned all forts in Texas and withdrawn its troops, settlers on the frontier were without protection. Chisum agreed to dedicate some of his cowboys to looking after the safety of the settlers within a radius of one hundred miles of Boliver. He was eventually commissioned Regimental Quartermaster and Commissary of State Troops under the 21st Brigade by General William Hudson on October 17, 1862.[118] This appointment enabled the cattleman to continue his operations and to avoid service in any armed conflicts during the war.

Following through on his first promise, on December 15, 1861 John Chisum, Dan Dansby, nineteen year old D.R. "Reese" Hanna and five other men moved seven hundred and fifty head of cattle out of the Clear Creek Valley toward Vicksburg in the east. A black cowboy named Giles Chisum drove the chuck wagon and served as cook.[119] Reese Hanna was trail boss. Felix McKittrick, whose wife had just recently passed away, remained behind with twelve men to look after the ranch.[120] A near stampede took place a few days out of Vicksburg, but the men ultimately arrived with the herd largely intact. It took two full days to push the cattle into low flat barges to cross the Mississippi.

Chisum was, by all reports, the best man anyone had ever seen at tallying a herd of cattle. It is claimed that he could keep an accurate count of a herd passing by while logging the stock into three or four categories.[121] Once the loading was complete, the Confederate colonel in charge tried to settle the account with Chisum in Confederate paper money. But Chisum had insisted at the onset of the war that he be paid $40 per head,[122] in gold coin. He declined the paper currency, and reinforced his demand the he be paid in gold.[123] This angered and frustrated the colonel, but payment was eventually made in the manner that had been contractually prescribed.[124] Chisum's cowboys were chiefly sympathetic to the cause of the Confederacy, and some quit and joined the Confederate Army when the drive was over and they had been paid. Perturbed at the loss of his cowhands, Chisum left for home with only cowhand Dan Dansby, a four year old black boy they had picked up along the trail,[125] a shot up saddle tramp named Ike Fridge, Giles Chisum the black cook and an old carpenter.[126]

In total John Chisum took two more herds of cattle to Little Rock and one to Shreveport. He quickly used the money that he made to buy land in Denton County.[127] Chisum arrived back at Boliver early in 1862 to discover that the drought had been the most severe he had ever seen, and that Indians had repeatedly raided his ranch. They had stolen most of the horses and set the prairie grass on fire, laying waste to the land. It was like looking out over a black ocean of parched earth dotted with the carcasses of dead cattle. Chisum wrote a letter to James Waide[128] on March 7, 1862 in which he describes the condition of things in Boliver "I got back from Vicksburg a few days since. I find the Prairies all burnt off and we have had no rain hear since last spring.... All my hands are gon, [sic] all my horses are gon. [sic] I am left behind in charge of 6 other stocks besides [my]own...." [129] Most of the men were gone, having joined the Confederate Army or moved on to other ranching operations. Some claim that Jensie had taken Phillip, Harriet and Almeady to Gainesville, although evidence shows that Chisum left Jensie and the children in Bonham in about 1863. [130] Explaining that life would be too difficult on the frontier without the protection of his armed cowboys, Chisum set Jensie and the children up in a boarding house in Bonham.

Felix McKittrick had left the ranch. Some reported that he had joined up with Quantrill's outfit. Many men of the Eleventh Texas Cavalry merged with Quantrill's Camp during the winter of 1862-1863. Likewise, members of the Fifth Texas Cavalry joined after the battle of Pea Ridge. Some of the Fifth Texas Cavalry, who had in part been formed in Lamar and Red River counties, also merged. [131] Actually, McKittrick joined Darnell's 18th Regiment of Texas Cavalry as a captain, but may for a time have been associated with Quantrill's noted band of Missouri raiders. [132]

In the summer of 1862 the renowned Texas cattle king Oliver Loving paid John Chisum a visit. Loving had also lost all of his horses to the raiding bands of Indians. Loving, however, had it on good information that United States Troops at Fort Bent were paying the Indians to cross over the Red River and steal horses and cattle from Texas ranchers. [133] Loving convinced Chisum that Colorado was where all of his horses had gone. Chisum hatched a plan to get his remuda back, and a dozen heavily armed Jinglebob cowboys rode north in the fall of 1862. Under cover of darkness they raided the Comanche camp where they discovered the horses were penned up in rope corals and took back the animals.

Loving also recovered most of his horses, and on a subsequent visit to the Big White House told Chisum that he and Charles Goodnight were going to take their cattle west to the Pecos River and drive them north into New Mexico Territory. In the summer and early fall of 1863 Chisum and other cowmen in the Denton area started moving their herds to the territory that Chisum had scouted around Mukewater Creek six miles north of the Colorado River and on the route between Fort Belknap and Fort Mason in Coleman County. With the black cook Giles Chisum and a team of big bay mules pulling the chuck wagon, and the five equipment wagons pulled by teams of oxen leading the way, the procession headed west. Jim McDaniel or John Chisum took turns riding ahead to pick the location of the coming night's camp. Just behind the wagons were David Waide and the horse wranglers, with the remuda of spare horses. Christopher Fitzgerald and Bob Johnson rode point, Newt Anderson and Patrick O'Farrell rode swing, Jim Spoon[134] and John McGee rode flank with Matt Smith and Ike Fridge eating grit and riding drag. This was not glamorous work, and most days were monotonous. The cattle plodded along at a leisurely pace of ten to fifteen miles a day.

By November 1863 Chisum cowboys had moved about 1,500 head of cattle to a point near the confluence of the Concho and Colorado Rivers in West Texas. M. C. Smith, Sr., who participated in this drive, later wrote "Chisum selected a place for his ranch buildings in a monte of pecan trees.... We began building log huts and pens. Jim Spoon, John McGee, Bob Johnson, Henry Settles, Fitzgerial, Felix McCittric and myself were left to improve the ranch; the other hands going back to Denton County. Ours was the outside ranch; our nearest neighbor was twenty-five miles."[135] Once they had reached their destination and set up their operation on Home Creek Chisum severed all ties with his silent partner, Fowler. This marked the culmination of his first and only partnership business arrangement.[136] From that point forward Chisum managed his own business affairs, or in the case of his later agreement with Hunter, Evans and Company managed livestock for others but did not take on any partners.

Chisum soon had 18,000 head grazing along the Colorado. The town of Trickham was established near his new herd location. It became the first town settled in Coleman County. Trickham is in the extreme southeastern part of the county and on the line of Chisum's cattle trail.

In J. Evetts Haley's book *Charles Goodnight, Cowman and Plainsman* Haley comments that "After the war (Civil War) Chisum entered into a strangely contradictory career, and his motives and character are still matters of reminiscent conjecture. "[137] Goodnight was not especially fond of Chisum, and that certitude comes through in the legendary cattleman's memoirs as well as Haley's interpretation of them. It would seem that Goodnight's disfavor for Chisum centered around the divergent beliefs, and apparently the ethics, of the two men. Goodnight was a devout Baptist, a stern disciplinarian and structured businessman. He did not drink, and did not tolerate such behavior from his men. He ran a tight operation, but was well respected by his cowboys. Chisum, the Presbyterian, earned the respect and fondness of his men as well but he saw no harm in drinking and celebration on the part of his cowboys. The two men soon entered into a business arrangement that proved to be quite beneficial to both. Although their pact lasted several years the association was not without conflict.

In 1864 Charles Goodnight returned to Palo Pinto County. He and other cowmen spent the next year there as they sought out a new range along Elm Creek in Throckmorton County, a place where Indians ran off nearly 2,000 head of cattle in September 1865. Immediately after the Civil War Chisum drove three small herds to Little Rock and sold them to a packing house that was owned in part by himself and Fowler. The processing facilities at this packing house were crude, the beef spoiled, and the business was soon bankrupt.[138]

By 1864 Chisum had already moved a small herd to New Mexico, well ahead of the first drive of Goodnight and Loving.[139] John's brother Pitser made the first drive to New Mexico with him, and remained there to investigate the market and report back to John.[140] During this time he worked at a slaughterhouse at Fort Stanton.[141] John's younger brother Thomas Jefferson "Jeff" Chisum also went along on one of the drives. It's unclear how long he remained in Texas after the killing of Turner Edmundson but given that Jeff died in New Mexico in 1866 it is fair to presume that his stay in Denton County was brief.[142]

Cattle markets in Texas were poor at that time. Along with Chisum, Charles Goodnight and other ranchers from West Texas and the Coleman County area trailed herds to the various Indian Reservations and Army posts in New Mexico and Arizona during 1865 and 1866. They were able to make a quick sale, and secure a higher price for the beef by moving them west.

In the spring of 1866 Charles Goodnight and Oliver Loving organized a cattle drive from Fort Belknap southwest to the Pecos River at Horsehead Crossing and up the Pecos to Fort Sumner. There they sold their steers to feed the Indians beef through the government subcontractors, the Patterson Brothers, at eight cents a pound. This netted Goodnight and Loving $12,000 in gold after expenses.[143] Eighteen cowhands, including Bose Ikard, the notorious Robert Clay Allison, and 'One-Armed' Bill Wilson participated in that cattle drive.[144] The route that Goodnight, Loving and their cowboys laid out became known as the Goodnight-Loving Trail and was soon one of the most heavily used pathways in the southwest.

John Chisum was not with Charles Goodnight and Oliver Loving on their first drive to New Mexico. He had made his first departure in 1864 as previously cited, and had mounted additional forays to New Mexico before joining Goodnight and Loving in the fall of 1866.[145] Others had also preceded Goodnight and Loving, including James Patterson and Robert K. Wylie. Patterson may actually have made the first drive from Texas to the New Mexico Territory.[146] John Chisum, acting on the advice of his cousin Tol Chisum who had written him a letter about his travels to the region, sent Pitser to the territory to investigate first hand.[147] Pitser is believed to have traveled with James and Tom Patterson on one of their early cattle drives to New Mexico. Pitser also worked for James Patterson and Bill Franks butchering beeves at Fort Sumner and had a partnership herd with Bill Franks. Robert K. Wylie, who would later be a neighbor of John Chisum on the Pecos River in New Mexico, and would eventually sell the Cattle King his herd, had also worked for James Patterson. Wylie had headed up his own cattle drive to New Mexico in the fall of 1865.[148] This particular journey proved to be an eventful one for Pitser as he was robbed of $2,500 along the way.[149]

It should be noted that the Civil War did not end until April 9, 1865. James Patterson, the agent with whom John Chisum traded, brokered cattle to the Union Army as well as the Indian reservations. Chisum was, in essence, supplying beef to feed combatants on both sides of the Civil War at the same time.

The drive most often noted by historians is the one that began in August 1866. That is when Chisum, Goodnight, Loving, and a group of small ranchers trailed a herd of cattle to the Bosque Redondo Indian Reservation in New Mexico with cattle enough to provide food for the soldiers and the 8,000 hungry Navajos being held there.[150] Chisum had secured the supply contract for the delivery of 10,000 head of cattle from a New York firm.[151] Ironically, he never received any payment for the fulfillment of that contract due to the failure of the New York concern with whom he had made the deal. This particular drive began at Trickham, Texas on the first day of August 1866. With John Chisum in the lead, astride his mule as was his preference, the procession commenced. A herd of about a thousand Texas Longhorn cattle slowly stretched out across the prairie. Frank Chisum, one of the two black boys that John had bought in Denton County from Doctor Hiram Daily and his wife Sarah, was now old enough to wrangle horses and go along on the cattle drive.[152, 153, 154]

After a couple days on the trail the Middle Concho River dwindled to a mere trickle. The group hit the last good water hole on the fifth day out. The cattle were already starting to get restless and show signs of weariness. Chisum had calculated that it would be three full, hard days without water before they reached the Pecos River. What had started out as a fairly easy trail drive across the flat open country of West Texas was now becoming an arduous journey. The men were growing weary and the cattle were having a tough time managing without water or sufficient grass upon which to graze. They scouted ahead to Wild China Ponds and found no water there. The men now began driving the cattle by the cool of night in an effort to conserve the remainder of the herd's stamina.[155]

After a couple more night's ordeal they found themselves about twelve to fifteen miles from Castle Gap on the Pecos.[156] The valley ahead was about ten miles wide, with few trees, but with what appeared to be good grass. The scouts reported that there was evidence that the Goodnight/Loving herd that had gone before them had run into some Apache Indian trouble ahead.[157] Chisum was afraid that as soon as they grazed the cows into the valley they would catch the smell of water and the cattle would stampede for the Pecos River. Accordingly, as if scripted by Chisum, the cattle detected the scent of water in the air just before daybreak. As if dazed, they began to trot. The cowboys tried to hold back the herd, but the cattle headed towards the Pecos River at a flat run. Now nearly senseless from thirst, the cows covered ten or twelve miles of sandy ground and dove into the river. The ford at Horsehead Crossing was dangerous, as the river was swollen from late summer rains, so they pushed the cattle across as quickly as possible.[158] At Horsehead they drove the cattle up the east bank of the river, pushing them north. They remained on the east side of the Pecos until they reached Popes Crossing and the point where the Delaware River meets the Pecos, just over the present day New Mexico border.[159] There they made the crossing to the west bank, and remained on the west side as they continued north towards the present day town of Carlsbad and beyond.[160]

Eventually a small village would spring up at the Horsehead Crossing, comprised largely of cowboys who were resting up from a long trip east or west. A cemetery grew on the west bank, and those graves can still be found by careful search.[161]

Chisum and his herd arrived in the spring of 1867 at Bosque Redondo, near present day Fort Sumner, New Mexico. The trail through the wilderness that they had cut began near Boliver, Texas and continued through the new camp near Trickham. From that point it headed down through Buffalo Gap, southwest of present day Abilene. The route next continued southwest to a point below San Angelo, then turned westward through the largely uncharted lands of western Texas, curving to meet the Pecos River at Horsehead Crossing between present day Imperial and Girvin. For a brief distance the trail paralleled present day Interstate 10 near Bakersfield, then headed northwest, following the Pecos River. It ran north along the river, crossing to the west side at Popes Crossing then continued along the west bank past the present day towns of Carlsbad, Artesia, Seven Rivers, and Roswell finally terminating near Ft. Sumner. In the 1860s few Mexicans, and even fewer white men, had set foot in that country. The new cattle route that Chisum charted was actually never named, although some contemporary historians refer to it as Chisum's Western Trail. By 1873 Chisum would eventually move 26,000 head of cattle over that route.[162] I suppose this is effective in differentiating it from Jesse Chisholm's Trail, commonly called The Chisholm Trail, which for the most part was not even in Texas nor did it begin as a cattle trail. But the route would eventually be known as the Goodnight-Loving Trail. Although John Chisum never traveled the actual Chisholm Trail he did take a herd in a northwesterly direction across Indian Territory in 1866, crossing the Red River at Fish Creek northwest of Gainsville. The drive culminated on the Smokey River where he sold the cattle. Cattle were moving north from Jack County as early as 1858 when Oliver Loving made a drive to Denver and eventually all the way to Chicago.[163]

Author Georgia B. Redfield in an article in *The Cattleman* about 1942, describes the trip:

> Although it was early spring, it was as hot as any mid-summer day of the year 1867 when nine hundred head of gaunt beef cattle staggered over an unbroken trail, on the last lap of a three-day waterless drive... 'They won't ever make it to Sumner,' said one of the cowboys... 'We'll make it,' replied the dauntless Chisum with a grim tightening of the tired lines of his mouth and jaw, which in every crisis of his life characterized his refusal to accept defeat.

Upon arrival at their destination there was a great celebration among the cowboys. Chisum broke open the barrels of bourbon whiskey, as was his custom. A grand sort of intoning of the masses took place to mark their successful arrival and deliverance from peril. The gala along with the consumption of spirits drew much criticism from Charles Goodnight, a devoutly Christian man who frowned on rowdiness and libation. As mentioned earlier, Goodnight was quite direct in later years concerning his general dislike for John Chisum.

Once they had arrived at Four Mile Bend, just below Bosque Grande, Chisum made a deal with government broker James Patterson for the sale of 900 head of cattle. Patterson had made an agreement with the firm of Stadtahr & Company of New York to supply the beef to the Navajo and Mescalero reservations nearby. Chisum was to receive $28,000 for the lot, but before he was paid Stadtahr & Company went broke. Undeterred, John Chisum headed back to Texas to gather another herd and bring them west to the Pecos. Pitser remained behind to look after the new cow camp at Bosque Grande.[164] In order to establish his operations along the Pecos Chisum later purchased James Patterson's trading post at Bosque Grande and added more buildings and corrals.[165]

It was at the end of the third cattle drive to Fort Sumner, in the summer of 1867, that Oliver Loving was ambushed by Apache Indians along the banks of the Pecos River not far into New Mexico Territory.[166] Loving and 'One-Armed' Bill Wilson had ridden ahead to scout the region. Goodnight warned them to travel only by night so as to avoid Indian attack. After the second night Loving became impatient and began traveling by day, ignoring Goodnight's advice. The first day their scout brought them to the Rio Sule, or Blue River, which flows out of the extreme east end of the Guadalpue Mountains. After crossing the Sule the land leveled out into a sort of flat plain for about sixteen or eighteen miles. At a point about four or five miles from the Pecos River Wilson observed a large body of Indians charging them from the southwest. They immediately quit the trail and took the shortest path towards the Pecos and the shelter of its high banks.

When they finally reached the river they found a small sand dune, covered with mesquite brush and tied off their horses. According to Wilson's later account, their attackers numbered about six hundred. The hostile party soon surrounded them. Loving and Wilson managed to stand off the band until near sundown using their guns, each one having two six shooters, with Wilson also having a six shot rifle and Oliver Loving having a Henry rifle that held sixteen cartridges in the magazine. When the darkness of night finally provided the men cover, the reluctant Wilson crept off to seek help leaving the seriously wounded Oliver Loving behind at Loving's insistence. 'One Armed' Wilson did finally find help, and returned to the site with Goodnight and a group of cowboys some days later. When the men arrived they discovered that Oliver Loving had already limped away and found help, but he would ultimately succumb to his wounds.

The long forgotten location is near a place that is now called Cass Draw, situated along the Pecos River several miles north of Loving. Charles Goodnight himself wrote of this location, and made note of the place on a trail map he sketched in his own hand for J. Evetts Haley. That map now resides at the Haley Memorial Library and History Center in Midland, Texas. The notation reads "7 miles below Carlsbad where Loving had gunfight."

Loving was shot through the right arm and the bullet lodged in his side, but he survived the Indian attack. Severely wounded, he demonstrated his extreme grit and determination by making his way out of the fix with the assistance of some passing Mexicans. He was able to reach Fort Sumner and receive medical treatment. Unfortunately he died from a gangrenous infection that set in some weeks later. Loving's partner Charles Goodnight traveled to Santa Fe to purchase a readymade coffin for Oliver Loving. Chisum and Goodnight buried Loving temporarily at the Army Post cemetery at Fort Sumner. Much like the electrifying story told so inaccurately in the movie *Lonesome Dove*, on February 8, 1868 John Chisum, Charles Goodnight, and about twenty of their cowboys made their way down to the Horsehead Crossing and back to Texas. They were following

Loving's last wishes by returning his body to Weatherford, Texas for his final resting place. He is buried in the Greenwood Cemetery in Weatherford.

Site of Oliver Loving's Last Stand Near Carlsbad, New Mexico.
Courtesy of James Owens, Hobbs, New Mexico.

Grave of Oliver Loving. Courtesy of James Owens, Hobbs, New Mexico.

Chisum wintered the 600 to 900 steers near Bosque Grande,[167] below Fort Sumner and about forty miles north of present day Roswell.[168] In the spring he sold the herd and contracted to furnish additional cattle. In the late 1860s Chisum lost two entire herds of cattle on the Pecos to Indian raids. These were cattle that he had contracted to sell to Goodnight. The "free grazer" John Chisum had no problem with his cowboys gathering a herd of cattle in West Texas to replace the stock that had been lost to the Indians without regard for brand. This process, which came to be known as "mavericking," was commonplace at the time.[169] Goodnight refused any such stock from Chisum and took him to task over it. Both men remained congenial afterward, going their own way and continuing their business dealings.[170]

The Civil War was now long over. The frantic post war demand for beef had all but passed and the army had resettled the Navajos in Arizona. The market for cattle vanished in 1868. But new markets for Chisum's beef would soon emerge.

3

JOHN CHISUM

CATTLE KING OF THE PECOS

The look of success, when it is worn a certain way, would infuriate a jackass.

—Albert Camus

Chisum continued to drive cattle from Texas to New Mexico. He made a verbal agreement with Charles Goodnight, who was now ranching in Colorado, to supply him with cattle for markets there and in Wyoming. For three years Chisum delivered 10,000 head annually to Goodnight's cowboys at Bosque Grande for the price of one dollar a head over the prevailing Texas market. Historian and author Morgan Nelson reaffirms that James Patterson, who had preceded Chisum and Goodnight to New Mexico, sold John Chisum the site at Bosque Grande. Chisum used this area as his base of operations. The site, which contained Patterson's trading post and an assortment of other improvements, was actually the first building in Roswell according to Nelson.[171] Patterson later sold, or more accurately traded, John Chisum cattle for the site at South Spring that would later become the Cattle King's new base of operation. Goodnight's men would take over the herd at Bosque Grande and drive them north to Colorado, Kansas and elsewhere.[172] Within two years, at the height of Chisum's prosperity, he moved five thousand head of cattle to Tucson, six thousand head to the San Carlos Apache Reservation in Arizona, four thousand to the Gila River and six thousand to Dodge City. Each season he had three or four herds on the move to different market locations. In 1871 his successful agreement with Goodnight ended. By then Chisum had made plans to relocate his operation to New Mexico permanently.

In 1868 Chisum faced some legal difficulties, and was accused of being a partner in the beef packing and cattle trading firm of Wilber, Chisum and Clark. However, John Chisum had never entered into any such agreement with these men. John C. Wilber of Springfield, Missouri and William H. Clark of Little Rock, Arkansas raised these allegations about Chisum's involvement with them, which were soon widely known and publicized. On May 2, 1868 Chisum wrote a rather forceful letter to the Dallas Herald refuting their claims.[173]

In early 1870 John Chisum's brother Pitser worked as a dry good merchant in Lincoln County for a time with Missouri native Thomas H.B. Collier.[174] Collier later moved on to Colorado.

Legal difficulties were not the only challenge Chisum had to face. Indian raids remained a constant threat along the Pecos River. On September 29, 1870 John Chisum, Frank Rhodes[175] and a man identified simply as Sloan were attacked by about fifty Indians at Dagger Bend on the Pecos where they lost fifty-six head of horses and mules.[176]

By 1872 Chisum had all but abandoned his base in Texas and established his headquarters in New Mexico. Chisum cattle initially ranged at various locations in Lincoln County, first along the Black River and later down at Three Rivers and on the Pecos near Bosque Grande. Jinglebob cows roamed the range near Fort Stanton, where Chisum is claimed to have controlled 1,600 sections of land.[177] By 1873 Chisum had removed his cattle from the Black River Range to the Pecos. His cattle now grazed for nearly 150 miles up and down the Pecos River and fifty miles on either side, extending from the *Eighteen Mile Bend* below Fort Sumner to the mouth of Salt Creek.[178]

As the winter of 1874 approached, Chisum, now referred to by some as the *Cattle King of the Pecos*, had finalized his deal with James Patterson on a forty acre spread called the South Spring Ranch.[179] The South Spring was located three miles to the south of present day Roswell.[180] John Chisum is claimed by some to have purchased the property for $2,500 but he actually traded James Patterson twenty-four hundred head of cattle for the forty acres and improvements located on the South Spring.[181]

South Spring Ranch.
Courtesy of The Haley Memorial Library and History Center, Midland, Texas.

James Patterson had acquired the property from J.M. Hudson the preceding year. Patterson owed John Chisum $7,000 and Hudson owed Patterson $3,000.[182] Patterson took the ranch and improvements from Hudson and settled that debt. Patterson then made the transfer of the ranch to Chisum on December 15, 1874. Patterson conveyed a total of forty acres of land, working cattle, equipment, dwelling house and furniture.

Chisum made the ranch his headquarters. The old house on the ranch was built of adobe and was much larger than most similarly constructed homes of the day. It was practically square, with four rooms on each side and enclosed in the middle area with a courtyard. The builder of the structure had obviously fabricated it with the thought in mind of making it a suitable fort, from which attacks by Indians could be beaten back. Imbedded in the walls were long planks to prevent anyone from sawing through and thereby gaining access to the interior. The roof was flat, and had a two or three foot tall parapet, or *pretil* as the Mexicans called it. You could conceal yourself behind the parapet and defend against attack.

It has been claimed that an old man named Pedro Sanchez originally built the home. After the death of John Tunstall in 1878, Chisum tore down the old adobe house at the South Spring Ranch and built a new home. What became the catalyst for his actions was his decision to turn the ranch over to his brother Pitser, who had decided to get married after many years as a bachelor. John's brothers Pitser and James had come to New Mexico with him and managed the majority of the work on the ranch. John bought Pitser's interest and gave him $25,000 and a portion of the ranch, then set about building the new structure. Later named "The Long House," it was a simple adobe structure with nine rooms in a row and porches running all along the east and west sides. The huge spring of clear water on the ranch provided an ample supply of water for more than just the daily needs of living. He sowed eight hundred acres of alfalfa and constructed an acequia that ran underneath the hall in the middle of the building. This helped to keep the house cool during the hot summer. The acequia ran into a ditch that Chisum kept full of fish. He used to enjoy sitting on the porch early in the morning, or in the cool of the evening, watching the fish and feeding them cracker crumbs. The house was surrounded with prodigal amounts of shrubbery and flowers. John Chisum was especially fond of roses, and he had literally hundreds of rose bushes planted on the grounds. He brought in cottonwood trees from Las Vegas by pack train and planted them in two rows along the lane leading to the house.[183] To add to this, he brought in fruit trees from Arkansas, and planted a huge orchard containing apple, peach, pear and plum trees.[184]

There were other buildings on the complex, including a camp house for the cowboys and a large single room building for dances or special occasions. It was a remarkable complex for its day, all built on a grand scale. Locals sometimes referred to the place as Chisumville, and it is said that he endeavored to establish a post office there. J.J. Hagerman purchased South Spring Ranch, now located on Old Dexter Highway just south of the town of Roswell, in 1892 after Chisum had passed away and the estate had gone into bankruptcy.[185] Most of the buildings on the ranch today were built by Hagerman when he remodeled the structures at the turn of the last century.

During 1874 John Chisum was the successful bidder for the supply contract for beef to the Apache Indians, landing that deal at $2.19 per hundredweight for southern New Mexico and $1.98 for the Mescalero.[186] Marauding Indians plagued his operations, and he ran up a loss of approximately $150,000 during the six years between 1868 to 1874. As an example, Chisum claimed that in June 1872 Indians stole 120 horses valued at $100 each and thirty draft mules valued at $150 each. In April 1873 Indians got away with seventy horses and thirty-five mules, totaling approximately $13,500. Then in July 1873 another seventy-five horses and twenty-five mules were stolen, valued together at $9,510. In August 1873 Indian raiders came right up to the corral at Bosque Grande and made off with 125 horses. Next they raided the store, making off with about $33,550 in livestock and merchandise. After filing his claim with United States Indian Inspector

Erwin C. Watkins for alleged losses from Indian depredation, Watkins commented, "I think the evidence shows conclusively that in the matter of horse stealing, Mr. Chisum is far ahead of the Indians and that a balance should be struck in their favor," Watkins's report showed that John Chisum had been systematically robbing the Indians of their horses and using his cowboys to do the dirty work.[187] This, coincidentally, was the same Indian Inspector Erwin C. Watkins who on November 9, 1875 submitted a report to Washington, District of Columbia, stating that hundreds of Sioux and Cheyenne Indians associated with Sitting Bull and Crazy Horse were hostile to the United States. In so doing, Watkins set into motion a series of events that led to the Battle of the Little Big Horn in Montana the following year.

Chisum Cowboys at the South Spring Ranch.
Courtesy of The Haley Memorial Library and History Center Midland, Texas

Along with Inspector Watkins, others claimed that John Chisum was just as much a horse and cattle thief as the Indians. He provided his ranch hands with horses and guns, and paid his men a fair price for stolen animals. In what might be termed a somewhat self-serving statement considering the fact that it was made in 1878 by Chisum's former employee and now staunch adversary Jessie Evans, Evans claimed that Chisum was stealing horses from the Mescalero Indian Reservation and had taken about 140 or 150 head of horses since 1873.[188] He further alleged that Chisum encouraged his men to steal the horses, and offered to pay them a fair price for the animals.[189]

Smaller ranchers grazed their herds side by side with Chisum along the Pecos River. It is claimed that Chisum's cowboys were all too often intentionally careless in marking cows and calves with the Long Rail brand at roundup. Among the cowboys employed by Chisum was Jessie Evans. This was not the same Jessie Evans from North Carolina who would go on to become one of the four founders of the Comanche Pool in Oklahoma in 1880.[190, 191] He was the Seven Rivers outlaw Jessie Evans[192] who had arrived in New Mexico in about 1872 from Texas.[193] Evans would go on to head up a large, powerful and effective gang of thieves who, like other smaller ranchers in the area, preyed on Chisum's cattle. Evans would be a staunch adversary of John Chisum's until he left New Mexico for Texas in 1880.

Not all of the losses Chisum claimed were a result of Indian raids. By 1872 a Texan named John Hittson[194] had become convinced that he was losing livestock to Comanche Indians, who then traded or sold the animals to Comancheros.[195] The Comancheros in turn sold the stolen cattle to ranchers in New Mexico. Hittson's solution was to organize a large group of cowboys and gun hands to go to New Mexico and take back the livestock. Hittson undertook the most ambitious operation of securing powers of attorney from many other Texas ranchers. He then employed approximately ninety gunmen and moved into New Mexico in classic "Texan" fashion to reclaim animals bearing Texas brands from possessors lacking bills of sale.[196] Despite considerable turmoil, and some bloodshed, Hittson's forces drove several thousand cattle out of New Mexico before legal difficulties ended the operation in late 1872. Hittson eventually sold the cattle, with no reimbursement flowing to the Texans who had granted powers of attorney. Although charges later were made that Hittson had profiteered, and that the proceeds of the sale were used to finance an office building built in Denver by Hittson's sons-in-law, the expenses of his raid quite likely equaled the value of the cattle recovered. By disrupting the Comanche's New Mexico market for cattle, the Hittson raid reduced the incentive for the Indians' cattle-stealing forays. It is believed that John Hittson took about 4,000 to 6,000 head of cattle from the area around Puerto de Luna in July 1872 alone.[197]

The Hittson group did not just drive cattle back to Texas, they conducted numerous bloody raids in New Mexico while gathering and trailing the appropriated cattle. In one such raid, Hittson's men shot and killed a rancher named Simpson who was trying to protect his herd.[198] Citizens of Loma Parda were so concerned that they organized to prevent the incursions by the Texans. They did manage to fight off a small party of the raiders, but sixty of the Texans returned in a couple of hours and severely pistol-whipped one of the men, Julian Baca. A neighbor, Toribo Garcia, was shot and killed when he came to the aid of Baca. Town marshal Edward Seaman arrived on the scene and was immediately assaulted by a Texan then shot in the head, killing him instantly.

But Hittson did not originate the technique of securing powers of attorney from Texas ranchers to market their cattle. John Chisum had done precisely the same thing some years earlier, and drew great criticism for having done it. But New Mexico Territorial Attorney Thomas Catron hauled Chisum into court to account for what he described as stolen cattle and failed to make good the allegations when Chisum produced the powers of attorney to support his position.[199] This episode in the log of the Cattle King's dealings served to taint his reputation, and many would continue to view his actions as sharp practice.[200] Chisum detractors would, for the remainder of time, be quick to remind us that his failure to live up to his moral obligations indicated that among his contemporaries his word was not as good as his bond.[201] Although I am less inclined to judge Chisum on the strength of this one incident it does go together with other ethical shortcomings revealed throughout the course of his life that tend to form a somewhat darker picture of the business side of man than is often portrayed.

Catron's pursuit of Chisum was relentless. The Cattle King would later be unceremoniously tossed into jail in Law Vegas, New Mexico over the Christmas holiday of 1877 where he would pass his time writing a lengthy defensive statement documenting and explaining his actions.

Indian depredations along the Pecos continued right through the Hittson affair and well beyond. In 1873 Chisum cowboy Jack Holt was shot to death by Indians at a place about eighteen miles from Loving Bend of the Pecos. In August 1873 Indians stampeded 125 head of horses from the Bosque Grande ranch house. In 1874 Ben Turner, a member of the Horrell gang, was killed on the Hondo Road. The same year Joe Haskins was killed by Horrell partisan Edward "Little" Hart.[202] Bob Beckwith was held up and deprived of his horse and sidearm by the Horrell party near Roswell. On December 20, 1874 a man named Lucero was caught rustling by Chisum cowboys and flogged, but not killed. On July 3, 1875 Chisum cowboy Newt Huggens (Huggins) was killed by raiding Indians near Bosque Grande at a place now known as Huggens Arroyo. Although some have claimed that it was cattle thieves, not Indians, that did the killing the incident was witnessed by Alejo Herrera who confirmed that it was indeed Indians.[203]

In spite of his troubles, Chisum's fame as Cattle King of the Pecos grew. On April 11, 1875, *The Grant County Herald*, at Silver City, New Mexico, elaborated:

We hear of cotton being king, of railroad kings. But J. S. Chisum of Bosque Grande is our stock king of New Mexico.

We remember upon one occasion, when finding our stock king in a deep reverie, of asking him why he was in such a 'deep study?' Chisum looked up and said: "I'm in great trouble because I cannot dispose of my stock as fast as it increases."

4

CHISUM'S PECOS WAR

Everybody, sooner or late, sits down to a
banquet of consequences.
—Robert Louis Stevenson

By 1875 John Chisum had 80,000 head of cattle grazing along the Pecos River. The cattle count had increased considerably. This took place in part naturally, but also because Chisum had been unable to trail herds to market on a routine basis. The disruption was primarily caused by the continued Indian raids on his horse remuda that crippled Chisum's ability to get his beeves to market.[204]

Efforts of the United States Cavalry soon improved the situation with respect to the Indians. Herds of cattle once again began to move. The drives followed already well-marked trails to the west, along the Hondo River for nearly sixty miles. The path then turned slightly southwest and followed the Ruidoso River through the White Mountains flanking the southern edge of the White Sands until they reached the Organ Mountains. From that point the path continued up the southeastern slope to San Augustine Pass, then down the western side and across the open plain to the Rio Grande. Fording the river below what is now Las Cruces, the drives headed almost due west through Cook's Canyon and on to the beef markets in Arizona.[205] In 1875 Chisum was the successful bidder with Ewing and Curtis of Tucson, who had the contract to furnish beef to all of the Indian agencies in the Territory of Arizona.[206] In the summer of that year Chisum cowboys drove more than 11,000 head along the trail to Arizona to fill this contract. Also in 1875 Jinglebob cowboys herded 20,000 beeves north to Colorado, Kansas and Missouri.[207]

Proving conclusively that he was not a politician, John Chisum made an unsuccessful run for a seat on the New Mexico Legislature in 1875. When votes were counted for House of Representatives the tally showed John P. Risque won 163 votes, John B. Patron 114, John S. Chisum ninety three and John M. Ginn sixtythree.[208] Chisum returned his focus to the cattle business. Ironically, of the foregoing aspiring politicians vying for the seat in the House of Representatives all but John M. Ginn would be dead by Christmas of 1884.

In November of 1875 Chisum transferred a massive herd of over 60,000 head of cattle to the St. Louis beef commission house of Hunter, Evans, and Company.[209] However, most of the cattle were not his. In turn, that company assumed Chisum's considerable indebtedness of over $200,000, which was accrued chiefly from cattle brought from Texas. From his headquarters at South Spring River near Roswell he helped Hunter and Evans gather cattle to supply more markets. Hunter and Evans were running stock in the Cheyenne Reserve and Cherokee Outlet in the Oklahoma Territory. The Newman brothers, Zeke and Tom, who were friends of Hunter and Evans were also running cattle there at the same time. In the winter of 1878-79, they had a ranch on the Niobrara River in Nebraska. This was, in part, what caused Hunter and Evans to locate there.

Hunter and Evans had several different names, depending on who they were partnering with and where their operation was located. In Texas, they were Hunter and Evans and Company. In the Indian Territories it was Hunter, Evans, and Newman. According to William Hunter McLean in his book *From Ayr to Thurber, Three Hunter*

Brothers and the Winning of the West in Nebraska they were known as Hunter, Evans and Hunter. The second Hunter being David Hunter, the younger brother of Robert Dickie Hunter.[210] David Hunter was ranch manager. In Kansas, it was Hunter, Evans, and Evans. This Evans was Jessie Evans the stockman from Texas…not the outlaw. Hunter and Evans placed him in overall charge of the herd purchased from John Chisum. Evans was later a major player in the Comanche Pool, a conglomerate of ranches in Kansas. He was a neighbor of W. R. Colcord and his son Charles Colcord. W. R. was John Middleton's father in law and was one of the folks who recommended Henry Brown to be city marshal of Caldwell, Kansas. That was a recommendation Colcord later regretted. The Colcords got to know Middleton and Brown when they arrived at their cattle camp in present Woods County, Oklahoma, with one of the Chisum herds.

Chisum Ranch Roundup 1888.
Courtesy of The Historical Center for Southeast New Mexico at Roswell.

A portion of the herd that tallied 60,000 which John Chisum had sold to Hunter, Evans and Company became the seed stock for one of the largest cattle operations on record. Each western state has in its early history a celebrated cattle spread that overshadowed all others. Kansas had the Comanche Pool, which was located near Medicine Lodge. It was the largest cattle ranch in the state's history. Four men—Jesse Evans, Wylie Payne, Richard Phillips and Major Andrew Drumm, started the Comanche Pool in 1880. Prior to 1880 millions of head of cattle were driven from Texas to markets in Kansas, but the Indian authorities at the new Army post at Sheridan's Roost in Oklahoma forbade the cattle from passing through on the old trails.

The idea was to gather all the local cattle into one great herd and divide the expenses, as well as the profits, in direct proportion to how many each owner had placed in the pool. When the expenses were totaled it averaged out $1.00 per year, or 9 cents a month, to keep each head of stock. They started business with 26,000 head of cattle, 10,000 of which had come from Hunter, Evans and Company who had purchased much of John Chisum's herd just a few years earlier. The peak population of animals was reached some five years later when 84,000 were tallied in the pool.

The operation covered an amazing 4,000 square miles and needed an army of cowhands to patrol it. It stretched from near Waynoka, Oklahoma on the south and bordered the west and north sides of Comanche County, coming within a few miles of Medicine Lodge on the east. Headquarters for this great spread was at Evansville in the eastern part of Comanche County, where a warehouse was built to store the wholesale food and clothing sent out from Kansas City. The ranch house and main headquarters were built among the rolling hills twenty-eight miles southwest of Medicine Lodge. Warehouses were maintained in different parts of the ranch territory, to hold supplies sent out from Kansas City to outfit the three principal horse camps. The blizzard of 1885–1886 struck Oklahoma with a vengeance, resulting in the unbelievable loss of all but the last

13,000 head of cattle. Thus there were—71,000 dead beeves when reconciled to the previous fall tally of 84,000. The small ranchers were completely wiped out and the remaining owners moved their stock to Montana.[211]

From this catastrophe perhaps one of the few humorous stories that can be salvaged from the fading memories of the open expanses of prairie littered with the bleaching bones of the once magnificent Comanche Pool is that of legendary cowman Charles Colcord and his toothbrush. J. Marvin Hunter tells this story in his book *The Trail Drivers of Texas*. Charles Colcord was one of the original organizers of the Comanche Pool. Colcord, who later became a millionaire oil man, met J. Marvin Hunter at a reception many years ago and reminded Hunter that it was he who brought the first toothbrush to Medicine Lodge, Kansas. Colcord told the story of how the punchers all wanted to borrow his ivory handled toothbrush till pay day. After payday finally rolled around, for a short time afterwards, each rider had an ivory handled brush sticking out of his top vest or shirt pocket. Thus this style of adornment was introduced on the Kansas plains by then humble cowboy Charley Colcord.

In Lincoln County, local horse thieves and renegade Indians continued to attack John Chisum's cowboys, stealing his horses and looting his herds and remudas. Neither Lincoln County authorities nor the army at Fort Stanton offered any measurable help. Chisum had set about trying to secure all the good grazing land he could along the banks of the Pecos near Roswell. In 1876 he had staked his claim to miles of the best grassland available. Fifteen thousand calves were born under his brand that year, and more stock was continually streaming in from Texas.[212] But taking over the best grazing land along the Pecos River had placed Chisum at odds with the small ranchers and farmers in the vicinity of nearby Seven Rivers who relied on those same lush meadows to nourish their herds.

Seven Rivers was a community that some claim had been settled by a caravan of thirty Texans and their families in 1870. Perhaps more accurately, the William Heiskell Jones family of

Virginia actually settled the community in about 1870, originally called Dogtown because of the abundance of prairie dog colonies that could be found there. Situated where seven arroyos fed into the Pecos River, it became an important trading post on the cattle trail. Other ranchers, men like Hugh Mercer Beckwith from Alabama, had also settled there with his large extended family. Hugh Beckwith, whose given name is sometimes oddly cited as Jose Enriquezor or Henry, had opened a store near Santa Fe earlier in 1849.[213] He married Refugia W. Rascon y Pino on December 22, 1849.[214] At the onset of the Civil War Beckwith operated a saloon near Fort Stanton. After his tumultuous time at Seven Rivers during the Pecos War he moved to Fort Stockton, Texas about 1880 and opened a hotel. He later moved south to Presidio, Texas where he had another hotel. Beckwith died there in 1892, reportedly beaten to death by robbers.

Indigenous Seven Rivers farmers and ranchers soon became accustomed to picking up a few head of Chisum's cattle when they cut out their own herds at roundup. Chisum alerted his cowboys and range riders to pay particular attention to this ever increasing menace. About this time Chisum learned that obvious alterations to his Long Rail brand were appearing in the small herds of cattle periodically turned in by local ranchers at Fort Stanton. Unrecorded markings that were crafted from Chisum's brand manifested themselves as the *pitchfork/* * the "*lazy P attached to a rail*, and the *pigpen*. All were noted at the military slaughter pens.[215] One prominent local rancher, Lucien Bonaparte Maxwell, carried the cattle rustling to a new low when his men shot a Chisum cowboy named Tabb in the back while he and cowboy Ike Fridge were checking Maxwell's herd for Jinglebob brand cattle. Tabb was the new assistant clerk that had just been assigned to understudy the bookkeeper Emory Peter at the South Spring Ranch headquarters.[216] Next, the thieves shot another Chisum cowboy named Charles Rankin. Rankin was also shot in the back while he was leaving Puerto de Luna where he had been sent for supplies. Ike Fridge, twice lucky, narrowly escaped being shot once again. The Beckwiths boasted that they had come to Seven Rivers with one milk cow "borrowed" from John Chisum and now had one thousand six hundred head of beeves roaming their pastures along the Pecos River. Clearly whatever efforts that had been made to slow the steady drain on Chisum's herd by local Indian tribes were offset by the ever increasing draw by local cattle rustlers.

Robert Kelsey Wylie, who was a friend of John Chisum from the Concho Country of Texas, had followed Chisum to New Mexico in 1872 and settled along the Pecos River at Eighteen Mile Bend, several miles above the Chisum Ranch.[217] During a brutal storm that hit the region during the winter of 1872-1873 his cattle had become completely scattered, and hopelessly intermingled with Chisum's herd. The storm had been so severe that when it finally ended Wylie claimed that he was unable to spot a single cow on the horizon with his telescope from the steps of his ranch house. He reached an agreement with John Chisum whereby he became a partner in Chisum's operation and Chisum paid him $60,000 for his now commingled livestock. Wylie then located his camp about six miles north of present day Carlsbad. This move managed to firm up Chisum's control of nearly two hundred miles of grazing land along the Pecos River.

Violence in the region was widespread during the 1870s, and it did not always involve John Chisum or his cowboys directly. On occasion, however, it occurred in his front yard. So prevalent were the killings that the local slang term *Pecosed* was coined to describe the death of someone who had come to a violent end along the Pecos River in New Mexico. One man who met such an end was Barney Gallagher. Gallagher came to the Pecos River region of New Mexico in pursuit of "Texas" John Slaughter. John Horton Slaughter was actually born in Louisiana on October 2, 1841. He formed a cattle business in Texas with his brother in 1874 and trailed beeves to New Mexico, Kansas and beyond. Barney Gallagher and a colleague of his named Boyd had cheated Slaughter at San Antonio, Texas in a poker game in an establishment on Commerce Street. Slaughter spotted the ruse, called Gallagher out on it, then picked up his pot of winnings at gunpoint and left. The enraged Gallagher trailed Slaughter all the way to New Mexico to settle the score. He caught up with "Texas" John, who at the time was trailing cattle near John Chisum's South Spring ranch. Armed with his customary sawed off shotgun Barney Gallagher challenged Slaughter, riding directly towards him with the scattergun cocked and at the ready. As the men closed the distance it seemed to all who witnessed the event that Gallagher would get the best of Slaughter. In a flash Slaughter produced a pistol from the holster that he kept attached to his saddle horn and shot Gallagher through the heart. None of the witnesses to the incident recall a second shot being fired. Gallagher fell dead. John Chisum's nephew Will Chisum would later describe the spot where the brazen Gallagher was buried as being near the irrigation ditch and about a hundred yards from the old adobe ranch house at the South Spring.[218]

One of the first open clashes between the small local ranchers and John Chisum's men occurred in October 1876 at the Wylie camp about eighty miles below the Chisum Ranch at South Spring. A man named Isaac W. Yopp was in charge of the camp at the time.[219] Yopp became involved in a confrontation with two cowboys while he was questioning them about the disappearance of some cattle. Yopp drew his revolver and fired three shots at the first man, Thomas Benton "Buck" Powell. Powell grabbed his Winchester and shot Yopp in the mouth. At first the wound took him out of the fight, but the intrepid Yopp quickly resumed firing at Powell. Powell's Winchester jammed, so he grabbed Yopp's revolver and shot him with it. This time Yopp's wound was fatal.

"Buck" Powell was a known outlaw and cattle thief, and at the time of the Yopp incident he was believed to have been in the employ of James J. Dolan. Dolan was the business partner of Lawrence G. Murphy, and together they ran the store and trading operation in nearby Lincoln. Murphy and Dolan had a close alliance with the smaller, local ranchers in the Seven Rivers and Lincoln area and bought whatever "stray" cattle the rustlers were able to come up with. By 1877 Lawrence G. Murphy had purchased the Fairview

Ranch near Seven Rivers from a man named Blake. He set up William Scott "Buck" Morton as foreman of this ranch, having bought the place for the express purpose of preying on Chisum cattle pastured along the Pecos. Murphy adopted the "Arrow Brand," which was nothing more than the Chisum "Long Rail" brand with an arrow tip and fletching. They cut the "Jinglebob Ear" and made a "Lop Ear" out of it, thereby re-marking Chisum cattle once they had rustled them. Murphy had managed to accumulate what was locally referred to as "the mystery herd." The herd was a mystery in that no matter how many cows were cut out and sold, or sent to slaughter, the size of the herd never seemed to be diminished.

On January 12, 1876 John Chisum was treated to his first stagecoach robbery. While traveling from Silver City to Mesilla in the company of long time friend and attorney Thomas Conway three masked men held up the stage that was traveling along a route near Cook's Canyon. Chisum was carrying $1,000 in cash, which he quickly stuffed down into his boots. The robbers escaped with about $4,000 in silver bars that were being shipped from H.M. Porter and J.F. Bennett to the Kountze Brothers in New York City.[220] Chisum escaped with his cash, managing to dupe the robbers with his boot trick and by surrendering a small handful of bills as a diversion.

Soon after the Yopp shooting Chisum learned of suspicious activities around the Beckwith Ranch. In November 1876 Pitser Chisum, Jim Highsaw (sometimes spelled Hysaw) and a group of Chisum cowboys discovered a few gallons of severed Jinglebob cow ears buried in the Beckwith corral.[221] In mid February 1877 Chisum and Highsaw traveled to El Paso to retrieve stolen cattle. On March 28, 1877 Chisum cowboy and gun hand Jim Highsaw, who was known to be "quick as lightning on the draw and cool under any circumstances," rode into a public corral on the Loving Bend of the Pecos River and confronted Dick Smith with what Highsaw believed was solid evidence of Smith's cattle rustling activities.[222, 223] When Smith went for his gun the faster Highsaw beat him to the draw and shot him fatally. Two other known Seven Rivers cattle thieves, Charley

Perry and Jake Owen, stood by and did nothing to help Smith. A gang of Seven Rivers ranchers including Bob and John Beckwith, Wallace Olinger, William Johnson, Andy Boyle, Milo Pierce, Lewis Paxton and Buck Powell pursued Highsaw and caught up with him at the Chisum ranch. Insults were exchanged, as well as a few rifle shots, but ultimately the Seven Rivers men rode off without Highsaw.

In a later report to U.S. District Attorney Thomas B. Catron of Santa Fe by Seven Rivers rancher Andrew Boyle it was claimed that Dick Smith was "shot in the back five times with a Colt's improved .45 cal. six-shooter."[224] The two witnesses, William H. "Jake" Owen and Charles Perry, testified that "Smith was killed by revolver shots in the head, back and breasts fired by Highsaw."[225] Highsaw was indicted for the killing. When John Chisum failed to support his defense Highsaw fled to Texas. It is interesting that John Chisum did not raise a hand to help protect his valued employee Highsaw when he was charged with the killing of Smith. This is a pattern of behavior on the part of John Chisum frequently observed throughout his lifetime.

In Texas Highsaw continued to affirm his status as a dangerous gunman. By all accounts he was not an ordinary cowboy, but was someone to be feared by all. Author Bill Oden wrote of Highsaw:

At San Angelo, Texas between June 1883 and spring 1884 "Jim Highsaw" (spelled Hysaw), a sort of desperado, and Jim Spears, the Sheriff, had trouble. Highsaw ran him into a store and was going to kill him but his Winchester hung.[226]

The Texas Rangers attempted to run Highsaw to ground but they gave it up as impossible. He returned to New Mexico and went to work for the XIT, and later the Crooked Seven in the Pecos Valley.[227] He managed (or owned) the 89 Brand Ranch in the Pecos Valley and operated the Mason Ranch in Blackwater Draw. In 1888 Highsaw was the foreman at one of the XIT cow camps when Sheriff Nowlin of Chaves County, New Mexico undertook to arrest him as a fugitive. There was an exchange of gunfire, and Sheriff Nowlin was apparently wounded by rifle fire from one of the XIT cowboys known locally as Williams but who was actually Highsaw's brother George W. Hysaw.[228] Jim Highsaw followed the sheriff's buggy all the way back to Roswell but made no attempt to overtake or attack the sheriff. Before Highsaw left Roswell he sent the Sheriff a threatening letter:[229]

> For what crime was Highsaw sought by Texas Rangers at Blackwater Draw? (Point in New Mexico near the Texas line, Blackwater Springs being in the Panhandle; not the Agua Negro spring near which Morton, Baker, McCloskey were killed).

The Highsaw shooting of Dick Smith further exasperated the already tense situation between Chisum and the local Seven Rivers *little fellows*, as the smaller ranchers were referred to by the Cattle King. On hearing of the killing of Smith, Chisum is said to have commented that he had six more Seven Rivers thieves to kill: Nathan Underwood, Louis Paxton, Charlie Woltz, Hugh Beckwith, Bill Johnson and Buck Powell. This killing of Dick Smith by Highsaw, taken together with John Chisum's declaration of vengeance against these six men, was by some accounts the spark that ignited *The War of the Pecos*. Chisum supporters sometimes called this the *Rustler War*.[230]

About the middle of April 1877 a Chisum trail outfit returned from the Eureka Springs Ranch in Arizona bearing news of the death of another Jinglebob foreman, James Wall Lockhart.[231] According to Walter L. Vail, a prominent rancher near Tucson who accompanied the drovers to purchase bulls along the Pecos, Lockhart had accidentally shot himself fatally while at a ranch some thirty five miles south of Fort Grant, Arizona. Local Justice of the Peace Miles Wood investigated the incident. Wood determined that the shooting had in fact been accidental, and involved no malice toward Lockhart or Chisum. Nonetheless, the incident served to further enrage an already disquieted John Chisum.[232]

A month after the Smith killing, on April 10, 1877, Nathan Underwood met James Dolan at Seven Rivers. Dolan had come to arrange for a quantity of cattle to be delivered to the army at Fort Stanton. Underwood claimed that while returning to his camp to meet Dolan he was intercepted by a group of six Chisum cowboys. Fearing an ambush they fired on the Chisum men before hastily returning to their camp.

Frustrated with the amount of cattle he was losing to the rustlers, Chisum sought help from the army at Fort Stanton. Captain George E. Purington, the post commander at the time, refused him aid claiming that cattle rustling was a civilian matter and he should seek the assistance of the local County Sheriff William G. Brady in Lincoln.[233] Sheriff Brady was clearly not inclined to help Chisum in any way since he had a close relationship with Murphy and Dolan. Brady hastened to explain that Seven Rivers was in Dona Ana County and was out of his jurisdiction.

Not surprisingly, John Chisum was infuriated by Brady and Purington's responses. He had endured about enough of the cattle rustling at this point, first by the Indians and now by local rustlers in league with Murphy and Dolan. On April 20, 1877 about thirty Chisum men surrounded the Hugh Beckwith house. They cut off the water supply and threatened to starve the occupants out, demanding that they surrender and be brought to justice for cattle rustling. Most believe that this group was led by Pitser, since John was down with smallpox at the time.[234] Instead of surrendering, the Beckwith clan decided to shoot it out with the Chisum outfit. A siege commenced, and sometime during the first night two men, Charles Woltz and Buck Powell, managed to sneak past the Chisum cowboys and head to the town of Mesilla. Woltz and Powell's plan was to obtain a warrant for the arrest of John Chisum, Robert Wylie[235] and James Highsaw for murdering Dick Smith. Although the ranchers of the Seven Rivers region had been a source of annoyance to Chisum, from time to time he needed temporary employees to manage his enormous cattle herds at the peak times of activity. During the winter of 1876–1877 several were known to have been on his payroll, and a number of them held out the claim that Chisum had not compensated them for their labor. This was a sore point with the Seven Rivers ranchers who were now being held at siege.

On the 21st Chisum's men sent in local ranchers Mr. and Mrs. Gray to try and convince Beckwith to send the women and children out of the house to safety. They refused to leave. On the 22nd Chisum's men began laying down a barrage of gunfire, but they did so from a distance of over 500 yards and were thus ineffective. The battle turned into a standoff. A stalemate had been reached. Next, some of the Chisum cowboys rebelled, claiming that they had been hired to herd cattle and not to fight rustlers. They protested that for the paltry sum of $30 a month they were being paid by Chisum they had not bargained on getting killed. Many decided to quit the fight. A Chisum representative was sent in under a flag of truce to the Beckwith ranch house to hold a parley with William A. Johnson who was Beckwith's son-in-law. Johnson claimed that he was unable to act as spokesman for the others. Many of those held as hostages were former Chisum employees who were due back wages. He added that until all debts were cleared any negotiation was out of the question. The matter was pressed no further.

In June the Grand Jury issued indictments charging John Chisum with unlawful assembly, riot, and larceny for waging what became known as the *Pecos War*. The rustling continued, as did the hard feelings between the warring factions. The already sharp divide was widened, and all that Chisum had accomplished was to make bitter enemies of a group of dangerous men.

On May 7, 1877 Buck Powell and Charlie Woltz returned from Mesilla with warrants to be served on John Chisum and Robert Wylie.[236] Andy Boyle, acting Deputy Sheriff at the time, assembled a posse consisting of Bob and John Beckwith, Wallace Olinger, William Johnson and Buck Powell. They went out to the Wylie camp and found John Chisum. He was gravely ill with smallpox. Next they rode to the Chisum ranch where they found Wylie. Apart from the warrants they had to serve, the group contended that Chisum owed them wages in arrears. Wylie promised that checks would be issued for all sums due.[237] They ultimately got their check and all of the men were paid.[238]

Chisum was among the ranchers who took direct action to protect his livestock. In the fall of 1877 he sent a band of armed cowboys to the Mescalero Indian Reservation to recover stolen horses. Chisum detractors recount this incident most harshly, claiming that his cowboys got the Indian agents drunk and took them out of commission while they murdered a large number of Indians within a few miles of the agency outpost.[239, 240] But some accounts of this incident may be less than accurate since Indian Agent Frederick C. Godfroy had, by some reports, fallen in league with the Murphy/Dolan faction. Historian and author Charles L. Sonnichsen alleges that Godfroy may also have been in partnership with another questionable personality at large at the time named Pat Coghlan, who was known locally as "The King of Tularosa". Godfroy was soon ousted from his position in 1879.

As a result of Chisum's activities in the spring of 1877 Seven Rivers ranchers filed warrants covering five replevin suits, larceny, and rioting against him. On June 20, 1877 an indictment was obtained in Mesilla against John Chisum, Robert Wylie, Thad Hendricks and James Highsaw for stealing cattle from Hugh Beckwith on May 5, 1877. By the time Powell returned much of the controversy had been settled however, and all charges against Chisum were either dropped or stricken from the docket. So by later in 1877 all of the pending suits by local ranchers against John Chisum were dropped and it seemed that the "Pecos War" may have ended.[241, 242]

By July 1877 Chisum cattle were once again on the move. R.D. Hunter had already sent for about 3,000 head, which were making their way to Kansas. The remainder were heading to Arizona. One herd was reported to have forded the Rio Grande near the site of Fort Craig, some one hundred miles north of Chisum's usual cattle crossing above Mesilla.[243] Chisum had changed his route to avoid the organized band of thieves that infested Dona Ana County.[244]

Sallie Chisum
Age 16 – Texas 1876.
Courtesy of The Historical
Center for Southeast New
Mexico at Roswell.

Later that year John's niece Sallie arrived, just in time for Christmas, reaching South Spring on December 24, 1877.[245] Leaving Denton County, Texas after the recent death of his wife, John's brother James had come to New Mexico with daughter Sallie and her two brothers Will and Walter. Sallie, like both of the boys, would be absorbed into the now expanded Chisum family at the South Spring Ranch. All were assigned their own respective chores and duties. Sallie would eventually manage the house for her Uncle John. John's first cousin Frances Johnson Towery had recently left that station and departed for California with her husband. Sallie filled many roles, including hostess.[246] A black woman named Mary Ann, who had come to New Mexico with John, was actually the housekeeper.[247] As an attractive young woman on the inhospitable frontier, nearly every cowboy in Lincoln County sought after young Sallie Chisum. Her arrival was, perhaps, the most pleasant thing that happened to John Chisum during 1877. Unfortunately 1878 would turn out to be an even more inhospitable year.

Walter, Will and Sallie Chisum.
Courtesy of The Historical Center for Southeast New Mexico at Roswell.

5

WAR IN LINCOLN COUNTY

Nothing is so contagious as an example.
We never do great good or evil without
bringing about more of the same on the
part of others.
—François, Duc de La Rochefoucauld

When I first began my study of the Lincoln County War I was quite certain that I had gained a comprehensive understanding of the matter, and that I had sorted out in my head all of the intricacies, causes, motivations, and of course most of all the pertinent facts. But in the end there are many conflicting facts, and just as many conflicting interpretations. As Joseph Priestly so wisely put it "In completing one discovery we never fail to get an imperfect knowledge of others of which we could have no idea before, so that we cannot solve one doubt without creating several new ones." I must have forgotten that learning is a continuous process and that "data is not information, information is not knowledge, knowledge is not understanding, and understanding is not wisdom."[248] So I am tempted to start again, at the point at which I first began, before I considered myself wise and when I first shouldered this conundrum called the Lincoln County War. Was it a classic struggle of good versus evil? And if so, who were the evil doers? How, as Frederick Nolan has put it, did poor, homesick John Tunstall come to such an end? And what of the enigmatic barrister Alexander McSween? Did he simply fall headlong and unawares into such a magnificent kettle of fish or was he the craftsman of his own, and John Tunstall's, doom? And what of the Cattle King of the Pecos? Trusted friend and ally of young John Tunstall and solicitor Alexander McSween or self-serving opportunist using his friends as tools to meet his own best end? Was James Dolan at fault, or was he simply a product of his own rough and violent upbringing … doing what all should have expected of him in the first place? Was William Bonney a fitting hero of this affray, or was he just an unknown saddle tramp and petty thief whose only claim to fame was that of killing a bully in a bar room fight in Arizona? Where did he come from? Was it Indiana, New York or Missouri? Will we ever know for certain? Moreover, how did Bonney emerge as the hero in the first place? And if Bonney truly was the consummate gunfighter that some have portrayed him to be then how is it that the only man he faced down and killed, in what appeared to be a fair fight at pistol range, is said by some to have had his revolver set by Bonney so that the hammer would fall on an empty chamber thereby insuring Bonney's victory? And what of poor Sheriff William Brady? Was he an evil man, fueled by spirits and carrying out the will of Lawrence Murphy and James Dolan without remorse, or was he just a simple lawman of average wit doing the best he could with the dim light that God gave him to see by? My sense of order and organization drives me to discover a villain and a hero in all of this mess. But for the life of me the longer I ponder the events, personalities and circumstances of the Lincoln County War, the more obsessed I become by it. I have no sage answer to offer the reader, simply more information from which one might deduce personal conclusions. One thing seems certain however. This was not a simple *good guy versus bad guy* affair.

By all accounts there was a growing plague of corruption

in Lincoln County, New Mexico during the mid 1870s. The humble community once known as Las Placitas del Rio Bonito had managed to survive the perils of Indian depredations, the coming of the Horrell brothers from Texas, and John Chisum's Pecos War. Now a group known as The Santa Fe Ring, primarily comprised of members of the Santa Fe Masonic Lodge,[249] held a tight grip on the local politics of New Mexico. Consisting in part of Samuel B. Axtell who was the U.S. District Attorney, Thomas B. Catron and William L. Rynerson the local district attorneys, and William Rosenthal who was a major cattle broker, the group controlled business affairs locally in Lincoln County through Lawrence G. Murphy, James J. Dolan, and John H. Riley.

Murphy had managed to secure an appointment as judge, giving him even more power and control locally. Catron had confronted John Chisum in court on various occasions, with Catron being the prosecuting attorney, as a rule. It is generally believed that Catron's personal aim was to cripple the cattleman's prestige and thereby compromise his range claim, so as to occupy parts of it to his own advantage.[250] And now Chisum was to be drawn into the Lincoln County War of 1878. This new conflict had been brought about by festering difficulties between the Murphy/Dolan group, called *The House,* arranged against Chisum's own attorney Alexander A. McSween and rancher John Henry Tunstall. McSween and Tunstall had openly defied Murphy and Dolan's economic stranglehold on the county, and acting with the support of Chisum had established a store and bank to compete directly with them.

Many have contended that although John Chisum played a part in the Lincoln County War, he was not as significantly responsible for it as has often been portrayed. To more clearly understand the part that Chisum played it is necessary to go back to the beginning, during the formative period where the groundwork was being laid down that would later become the basis of the conflict. The genesis of the events that would eventually lead up to the war actually dates to 1854, with the establishment of Fort Stanton. Although the fort was shut down for a time at the onset of the Civil War, it soon reopened. In 1866 the former post commander Emil Fritz formed a partnership with a military colleague named Lawrence G. Murphy in order to establish a post trading operation.[251] They were very successful over the years, with their business growing to include a thriving store and a brewery. The pair traded with local ranchers, purchasing grain, hay and cattle, which they sold to the army. In turn they sold requisite supplies such as bacon, beans, coffee and other provisions to the ranchers. Over time the men became arrogant and greedy. After an altercation in 1873 involving a young former soldier named James J. Dolan they were expelled from the fort. Soon they reestablished the trading business in the nearby town of Lincoln.[252] Founder Emil Fritz died in 1874.[253] Murphy took over the operations and filled Fritz's now vacant seat at the table with Dolan.

James Joseph Dolan, who some have perhaps correctly identified as "the most dangerous man in Lincoln County," was born on April 22, 1848 in Laughrea, County Galway, Ireland. We know from his military discharge papers that he was only five feet two inches tall and weighed a slight one hundred twenty pounds. Dolan had gone to work for Fritz and Murphy as a clerk after he was discharged from the United States Infantry in April 1869.[254, 255] Although scanty in stature, he was a decidedly powerful and fearless young man. Dolan was known to be dangerous when drinking, and it is said that he was practically always drinking. In May 1877 Dolan shot and killed Hiraldo Jaramillo. Dolan claimed self-defense, and was not charged. He said the young man attacked him with a knife, but did not say why. Lily Casey claimed Dolan's friend George Peppin was romancing Jaramillo's wife, and Dolan precipitated the conflict to take the heat off Peppin. George Peppin did later marry the young widow, and they had five kids. If this explanation is true, Peppin returned the favor by choosing Dolan's side during the Lincoln County War.

Soon another young man named John Henry Riley joined the business as a clerk. Also an Irishman, Riley was born on the island of Valencia off the southern coast of Ireland. In 1877, at the onset of the shooting part of the Lincoln County War, James Dolan and John Riley bought out the ailing Murphy and established J.J. Dolan & Co.. A scholar of the Lincoln County War must consider that Murphy and Dolan were both Irish immigrants, having fled the great potato famine of 1845 to 1852. Both had served in the army and were familiar with war, weapons and killing. Both had managed to succeed despite severe obstacles. Both were determined men who it seemed would stop at nothing. Dolan, in particular, was a fighter. Without question he subscribed to the code of the west, which simply put was "I'll die before I'll run." As John Wayne summed it up so well in the movie *The Shootist*.[256] "I won't be wronged. I won't be insulted. I won't be laid a hand on. I don't do these things to other people and I require the same from them." It is no wonder that the likes of James Dolan would soon collide with his adversaries Alexander McSween and John Tunstall in the Lincoln County War.

The young lawyer Alexander A. McSween and his new bride soon arrived in Lincoln. McSween was born on Prince Edward Island in Canada in 1843 and was educated as a Presbyterian minister.[257] Some believe that he may have been ordained. In 1871 McSween enrolled in the law department of Washington University in St. Louis. There he completed only half of the obligatory coursework, possibly due to his poor health resulting from his chronic asthma. McSween moved to Eureka, Kansas in 1872 where he taught school for a time. In spite of the fact that he had completed only a modicum of the legal training prescribed, he launched a law practice in Eureka on April 3, 1873. Not at all a robust man, he was a confirmed pacifist and turned to his bible in times of adversity. On August 23, 1873 McSween married Susanna E. Hummer in Atchison, Kansas. Sue McSween was something of a mysterious personality as well, with a sizeable unaccounted for gap in her early adult life. Her critics would later claim that she had spent it in a sporting house. One of the few statements attributed to her about her past was when she said she had been in a convent in Atchison, Kansas in 1871 and 1872. Since she was not a Catholic it seems unlikely that this "convent" was a regular religious establishment. In 1896 the respected Pinkerton agent John C. Fraser reported that "she (Susan McSween) is said to have handled her virtue in rather a reckless manner in former days, but of late she joined the church."[258] But attacking the virtue of Susan McSween by quoting gossip spawned by her detractors serves little purpose. The implications, however, do cast some doubt on her character and make it a matter worthy of note. She was a novelty around Lincoln, sporting a fine hairdo and adorned in luxurious attire. Although Susan McSween was an attraction, she was disliked by many. To her credit she later went on to become a highly successful rancher.

Having evidently failed at his law practice in Eureka, and in questionable financial circumstances, the McSween's departed Kansas and headed for New Mexico. They arrived in Lincoln on March 3, 1875. Alexander McSween soon accepted a clerical position with L.G. Murphy and Company. Fulton describes McSween as:

> ...an aggressive type and frankly ambitious to reap a fortune from his adopted section. He was a high priced lawyer, but usually gave value received by winning the cases. He had a knack of finding some strategy or technicality that would enable him to turn the tables on the opposing side.

He goes on to say that McSween... "was, however, of high professional ideals and did not hesitate to decline to take cases that he felt were not just." I feel compelled to disagree with Fulton's assessment of McSween's professional ethics however. His use of insider information about the Murphy/Dolan operation would soon bear out my dissension.

After his arrival in Lincoln, McSween first went to work for Lawrence Murphy and his enterprises, now referred to locally as *The House*. The House was a term that described Murphy's new store and base of operations, as it looked more like a grand house than it did a simple store. McSween was the only lawyer in Lincoln and Murphy/Dolan were for the most part the only significant businessmen. He also did some legal work for John Chisum, who was a close friend of lawyer Thomas Conway of Santa Fe.[259] As an insider, McSween soon learned the secrets of the Murphy and Dolan business. It would appear that he determined early on to emulate their strategy. Believing his to be the superior intellect, a fault shared widely by lawyers over the ages, he plotted to supplant their monopoly and craft his own. McSween's major obstacle was the funds necessary to launch his plan.

Lincoln County Courthouse. Author's Collection

McSween gradually distanced himself from Murphy and Dolan after having worked for them for about eighteen months. In lieu of cash, which Murphy was by now already running short of, McSween was deeded an old store building and forty acres of land on the north side of Lincoln's main street as full payment for services rendered. The former store building at the east end of the property would later become the site of the Tunstall store. At the west end of the property he constructed a dwelling house and law office. Ironically, local workman George Peppin was his contractor. The remodeled and reconstructed house was U-shaped, with a flat roof and a courtyard or plaza between the wings which ran north and south. It was about fifty feet in width. There were four rooms in the west wing and three in the east wing plus an alcove room in front of the west wing and a summer kitchen in the rear. Some records show that there were four doors in the front of the dwelling, although George Peppin's sketch only shows three.

Lincoln County Courthouse as it Looks Today. Author's Collection.

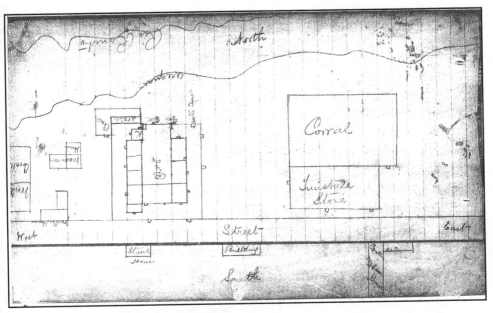

Andy Boyle's Sketch of the McSween House.
Courtesy of The Haley Memorial Library and History Center Midland, Texas.

The drawings show two doors on the east side, three on the west side and two in the rear—one of which was off the summer kitchen. Two gates through the front fence offered access to the small yard, and two on the east fence faced the location of the Tunstall store that was about thirty to forty yards distant.[260] The backyard was partially enclosed by an adobe wall on the west and north sides. Also located in the yard to the rear of the house was a privy, with the sink open to the north and located between the two rear gates. A poultry house and stable occupied the northwest corner of the backyard and extended east to a point near the gate in the back wall facing the Rio Bonito. The distance from the back door of the eastern kitchen to the rear gate was estimated by some to be about twenty four feet.[261] A plank fence enclosed the south, west and east sides of the complex. It would seem that all Alexander McSween lacked in order to implement his plan now was money. Two fortuitous events would soon provide that missing component. First was his administration of the estate of the late Emil Fritz, from which McSween would cleverly extract a handsome fee, although contention surrounding his work on the estate would ultimately play a significant part in his undoing. Second was the arrival of an ambitious young Englishman with a purse full of money.

John Henry Tunstall was only twenty-four when he arrived in Lincoln in 1877. Tunstall had worked briefly in Victoria, British Columbia at a business in which his father was part owner. His family had lived in a three story brick home on Queensbridge Road in the affluent section of Dalston, London. John's father, John Partridge Tunstall, had been listed on John Henry's birth certificate as a "professional traveler." It is apparent that he was a businessman employed at Copestake, Crampton & Co. Ltd. at the time of John Henry's birth. John Henry Tunstall was five feet eleven inches tall and weighed a scant one hundred thirty eight pounds when he left home in 1872. He had sandy hair, was clean-shaven, and was blind in his right eye from accident or illness, we do not know which. John Tunstall was clearly not the figure of a rough and rugged man of the American West. Having been raised in a far more genteel environment, it is clear from his actions that Tunstall subscribed to the English common law belief of self defense which held that when threatened a person had a "duty to retreat." In stark contrast was the prevailing belief at the time in the American West, which held that a man had "no duty to retreat." As C.L. Sonnichsen so aptly put it, "I'll die before I'll run." In other words, I will allow them to kill me in preference to consenting to giving up my principles.

A clash of doctrines was foreordained. But the young Englishman would eventually show evidence of his grit when he wrote to John Chisum complaining of Sheriff Brady's actions, and finishing his letter with the line "God damn him, he'll find I can't stand everything."[262]

For some time I have believed that if there was one single

factor that could be identified as the source of the conflict in Lincoln having escalated into an all out shooting war it was the broadly divergent cultural difference between the principals of the two factions. Had Dolan confronted a consortium of rivals of a similar makeup, their disagreements would have been settled quickly, in a flurry of fists or a flash of gunfire. The differences would not have smoldered and festered, until reaching a point of no return. Similarly, had Tunstall and McSween come up against adversaries of a similar makeup as their own, they would have launched into a battle of wits, a flood of lawsuits, and a struggle to outmaneuver each other on the battlefields of commerce and courtroom. Thus, the affray in Lincoln might not have come to such a deadly finish.

The role that John Chisum played in this affair seems less complex until one parses it. Chisum is claimed to have been a staunch supporter of John Tunstall. Although on its face this appears true, I believed that Chisum's association with the Englishman was neither straightforward nor purely honorable. It would seem that Chisum used Tunstall to advance his own purpose. Specifically, break the Murphy/Dolan cartel, secure the lucrative government beef contracts for himself, drive off the cattle rustlers who were allies of the Murphy/Dolan faction and increase his influence in Lincoln. The alignment of common purpose is startling. Although the monopoly of Murphy/Dolan had been successful in tying up commerce in Lincoln County, John Chisum and R.D. Hunter together controlled much of the national market for livestock from Chisum's operations on the Pecos and at the South Spring ranch. Cattle were shipped to the national markets in the Midwest which were controlled by Hunter, and Chisum drove herds to Arizona to supply the Indian reservations. Chisum's astuteness transcended the myopic vision of simply cornering the nearby commerce in Lincoln County and surrounding environs. Landing the local contracts for beef supply would simply be a plum for Chisum. The larger problem for the cattle king at the time was the ever increasing depletion of his herd, brought about by Murphy and Dolan's thirst for free cattle to fulfill contracts that they had entered into at shockingly low prices.

Chisum held his grip on the larger markets until some time after the arrival of railroad service at Las Vegas in 1879. The coming of the railroad, along with the gold mining activities at White Oaks, changed the economic landscape of Lincoln County by opening up a more expedient avenue for goods to come in and leave the region. It also provided a new, nonagricultural source of income for Lincolnites whose options had been somewhat limited to small scale ranching, farming, cattle rustling or somehow deriving an income by feeding off the Government by means of the nearby Indian reservations or Fort Stanton. It is important to reemphasize that the Murphy/Dolan operations were dependent upon the continued supply of stolen Chisum cattle, for which they invested nothing. The financial model for their scheme is clearly that of a failed enterprise. Murphy/Dolan could not continue indefinitely relying almost entirely on what seemed to be an endless flow of free livestock. Their business had been whipsawed into operating on a slim margin to begin with. From the $7.00 per hundredweight that Murphy had gleaned earlier in 1872 for his supply contract to the Indian reservations to the $4.49 per hundredweight that broker Van C. Smith had secured in his most recent agreement is a reduction of one third. In 1875 William Rosenthal of Santa Fe submitted an even lower bid of $1.63 per hundredweight.[263] Until this point Murphy had probably subcontracted the supply, but with the Rosenthal deal he became the Government supply agent.[264] The next annual contract also went to Rosenthal, at $3.78 per hundredweight. Over half a million pounds of beef were supplied between December 1876 and June 1877. By early 1878 delays and defaults by all suppliers were rampant, due to the violent conditions in Lincoln. The method of selling stolen cattle which Murphy and Dolan had devised worked well for a while. They sold the animals at $5.00 a head at a time when ranchers like Chisum could not afford to sell comparable cattle for $15.00 a head.[265]

But on balance, Tunstall and McSween's view that once the

monopoly held by their adversaries had been broken the market place would break wide open was an equally flawed assessment.[266] As cited earlier, for John Chisum using Tunstall and McSween to advance his own purpose of breaking the Murphy/Dolan cartel so he could secure the local government beef contracts for himself, and more importantly drive off the cattle rustlers who were depleting his herd, was the alignment of common purpose.

I remain convinced, however, that if one single factor could be identified as the source of the conflict in Lincoln having escalated into a shooting war it was the broadly divergent cultural difference between the principals of the two factions. I hasten to add that, as Dr. Hinton has often pointed out, one must *follow the money* to find underlying causes.

Another factor that played into the Lincoln County War was pointed out by Maurice Fulton, who is quoted as having said "Chisum did not stand by his friends. He was always missing when they were in danger. The picture of Chisum getting into his buggy and driving rapidly away after the Kid escaped confinement in Lincoln is that of a discreet, not courageous man."[267] As further evidence of this, John Chisum did not raise a hand to help protect James Highsaw when he was charged with the killing of Dick Smith. The indictment reflects that "when John Chisum failed to support his defense he (Highsaw) fled to Texas."[268] Further, one may infer from various chronicles of Chisum that he might have dissuaded Governor Wallace from reprieving Bonney. Bonney had demanded money from Chisum for services rendered…when Chisum refused to pay, Bonney balanced the ledger on his own by stealing Chisum's cattle.

Without question John Chisum had been at odds with Lawrence Murphy and James Dolan over the matter of continued cattle theft for some time before the arrival of Alexander McSween and John Tunstall. Sheriff Brady, a comrade of Dolan and Murphy, had refused Chisum help in dealing with the cattle theft incidents.[269]

It has been widely claimed that Chisum disliked Brady intensely. U.S. District Attorneys Thomas Catron and William

Rynerson of Santa Fe, who had a close alliance with Murphy and Dolan, worked against Chisum in the Pecos War. Murphy and Dolan enjoyed a monopoly on livestock trade, to the exclusion of John Chisum who was obliged to seek other markets. Chisum did not find the local ranchers to be amiable, perhaps since he had ridden roughshod over their earlier claims to the rich grazing land along the Pecos River. The entire concept of having a "cattle king" on the Pecos was a foreign one. Texas had cattle barons like George W. Littlefield, Charles Goodnight, Mifflin Kenedy, Richard King, Ike Pryor, Thomas Bugbee, Murdo Mackenzie, Robert Kleberg, Charles Schreiner and dozens more who had built huge ranching operations all the way from the Coastal Bend to the Panhandle and down to the Rio Grande to the Big Bend Country. Although Juan de Onate is credited with bringing the first cattle into New Mexico, John Chisum was the closest thing that the eastern portion of the territory had seen to a "cattle baron" in those days. Befitting a king, he built the frontier equivalent of a palace at South Spring, replete with gardens and exotic fowl. He constructed a cattle empire that was practically unrivaled at the time. Many of the large ranching operations of the day were run much like a benevolent dictatorship. It was not uncommon to have the local lawmen on your side, nor was it unusual to have a close relationship with the governor. Neighboring farmers often derived their livelihood from trade with the big ranchers, men who meted out contracts to those who were sympathetic to their particular causes. John Chisum was no exception as far as his baronial tendencies were concerned, and when the local Seven Rivers ranchers railed against him, it resulted in a deep seated and long lasting divide.

In all likelihood Chisum did welcome John Tunstall to New Mexico warmly and sincerely. Tunstall was by all reports an intelligent and likeable young man, placing him in stark contrast to the common ruffians who were rampant on the frontier at the time. Educated and refined, the Englishman no doubt brought an air of civility to their frequent meetings and a refreshing level of intellect to their business conversations. But Chisum's support of Tunstall was at best self serving and at worst manipulative. Chisum saw in Tunstall an avenue by which Dolan's operation in the county could be brought to its knees and the stranglehold that the Santa Fe Ring had on Lincoln weakened. As a lawyer, Alexander McSween could aid Chisum in combating the barrage of lawsuits and challenges he was receiving from his Seven Rivers enemies. With the line in the dirt already drawn between Chisum and Dolan, he had nothing to lose by supporting Tunstall. Possibly everything to gain.

This is a cynical view perhaps, but seldom in the history of the American West do we find powerful men like John Chisum doing charitable things for purely beneficent reasons. There is almost always an ox to be gored or a nest to be feathered. Pessimistic realism predisposes me to believe that Chisum's motives were not entirely without blemish. He had an empire to protect that he had labored long and hard to craft. Nonetheless, I am not aware of any solid evidence that John Chisum, any of his family or any of his cowboys (while at the time in his employ) ever fired a single shot during the Lincoln County War. Chisum could have fielded a sizeable army of cowhands; their sheer numbers would have clearly bested the Dolan crowd. Charles Goodnight commented some years later to the effect that "Chisum should have ridden up that hill and shot the son of a bitch (Dolan) and ended it all." But he chose not to become directly involved in the fray. Some have claimed that it was his brothers James and Pitser who turned down Tunstall's request for aid, since John was away at the time. Others maintain that John left specific instructions that he did not want to be involved in the shooting war, and John's brothers were just delivering the message. Based on the preponderance of evidence, I am most inclined to believe the latter.

While the local hostilities were building to a frenzy, there was comparatively little outlaw activity during the summer of 1877. Having committed to the plans that some believe were largely conceived by McSween, John Tunstall charged ahead with a perplexing medley of moneymaking schemes. In one of his frequent letters to his parents Tunstall wrote that he was going to get "the half of every dollar made in Lincoln County by "anyone."[270] He labored at setting up his store and issued grain notes to farmers in exchange for merchandise, to be redeemed against future harvests. This strategy subverted Dolan's operations by creating a grain supply monopoly.

As the year 1877 unfolded, John Chisum could be found spending more time in Lincoln with Alexander McSween and John Tunstall as they finalized their arrangements for the new store and bank. Ironically, the new Tunstall store was being built on a site that had previously been owned by Tunstall's adversary Lawrence Murphy. Murphy had used the original adobe building for storage of inventory while his displaced operations in Lincoln were limited to the small two room building across from the site of his new store during construction. Tunstall renovated the old structure, adding several rooms on the east end for a residence and incorporating steel lined window shutters for protection against gunfire. The hastily built additions and renovation took only about three months to complete.

The precise sources of the capital for each of the different projects that McSween and Tunstall undertook are still somewhat vague. What is quite clear, however, is that Alexander McSween had no money of his own. He had arrived in Lincoln essentially penniless. McSween had earned little in the way of hard currency while working for Murphy. He was using the $7,000 settlement he had taken as his fee from the work he performed on the Fritz estate, which at the time was still under contention in the courts by the Fritz family.[271] He used this money to build his home and a splendid law office. McSween also used some of the cash for the purchase of stock for the Tunstall store. He had received a draft from R.D. Hunter for $2,000 in March 1876 and a credit for $1,000 on October 30. Records of the deposit of the $1,000 credit make it look very much like a loan. Apart from a check for a paltry $42.83, which was deposited at about the same time, it appears as though lawyer McSween had no income.[272]

John Tunstall, on the other hand, had originally asked his father for the equivalent of roughly $30,500 to fund his various enterprises in Lincoln.[273] Tunstall's father sent about 3,000 Pounds

Sterling, the equivalent of around $15,200. Later, in 1879, Tunstall's father told the British Foreign Secretary that his son had invested 5,000 Pounds Sterling, the equivalent of about $25,000.[274] John Chisum and Col. R.D. Hunter fronted most of the capitol for the Bank of Lincoln County, which opened in August 1877 and was an enterprise hatched by Alexander McSween. With the help of John Chisum who was billed as the bank's president, and funding from Col. Hunter of St Louis, the venture was soon up and running.[275] In retrospect, Chisum's involvement with the bank and the associated enterprises of McSween and Tunstall would prove to have been unwise, as it drew the fire of men who had previously been indifferent to Chisum and his cattle business.[276] This polarization would transcend the Lincoln County War.

Chisum had been relying increasingly on his brother Pitser to look after dealings at the ranch. On one fateful trip to Lincoln, Chisum and George Hogg started out for the town on Saturday May 12, 1877.[277] George Hogg was now the Chisum foreman, having taken over for the ill fated and self exiled Jim Highsaw. Chisum left Hogg at the livery stable and headed to the McSween house. He told Hogg to meet him first thing Monday morning at the Tunstall store to load supplies. On this trip, like many others, Chisum stayed at the McSween house. Tunstall had already arrived there earlier that day, and the three of them discussed their business plan.

Tunstall indicated that he needed to go east to St. Louis to procure more supplies before he could open the store. He expressed his concern to the group about the recent plague of horse theft taking place in the Ruidoso and Bonito valleys. Both he and Chisum had been losing some of their horses. It had been reported that Jessie Evans and Jim McDaniel were behind the recent theft. All were quite certain that Sheriff Brady would not be inclined to do anything about the crimes. Tunstall told the men about his purchase of land that had previously belonged to Frank Freeman and Billy Mathews. The land had apparently been abandoned after Freeman, who had been accused of shooting a local man, had departed the county abruptly.

Tunstall had paid Mathews for the improvements on the land, but was concerned that if Freeman returned he might expect to receive his share of the money. If Matthews did not pay him his share it could result in Tunstall having to pay twice.

Freeman was known to be a contemptible and reckless character. As the men conversed Susan McSween brought a note to them that had been delivered by a boy on behalf of Jose Montano. The note said that Frank Freeman was in town and was with Charlie Bowdre.[278] The pair had forced Montano to open the bar and both men had been drinking heavily. Freeman had sworn revenge against Chisum some time earlier for an unknown transgression. With little delay Freeman and his men rode up to the McSween house and began to shoot out the windows, yelling and cursing at John Chisum. At that moment Gus Gildea,[279] one of Chisum's cowboys, showed up to report that long time Jinglebob cowboy Emory Peter was having trouble getting the herd through the mountains.[280] Dolan and Riley were said to have had a group of men out to intercept Peter and the herd of 2,350 cows before they could drive the cattle through the mountain pass and on to their market in Arizona.[281] It seems that Dolan had hired Jessie Evans and his Seven Rivers crowd to help with the dirty work, boldly claiming that if it took a hundred men to get the job done they intended to capture Peter and the Chisum herd. The *Mesilla Independent* wrote "The 'boys' have gone so far as to sell these beeves at $10 per head in advance."

Gildea, Tunstall and Chisum slipped out the back door and headed to Tunstall's store where they found George Hogg asleep on the floor. Alexander McSween remained in the house for the moment with his wife Susan McSween. Chisum sent Hogg to get Sheriff Brady. He then told Hogg to head back to the ranch and to send ten or twelve men southwest down the trail to Mescalero to help Emory Peter with the herd that was by now under siege. In due course the commotion subsided and the shooting in Lincoln ceased … at least for that night. Sheriff Brady, accompanied by an Army detachment, arrested Frank Freeman after a confrontation at the bar during which

Freeman struck Brady, and by some accounts during which Frank Freeman had shot and killed an army sergeant.[282] Freeman escaped during the melee, but his freedom was short lived. Several days later a combined military and civil force cornered and killed him at Charlie Bowdre's ranch.[283]

The following day Sheriff Brady captured Jessie Evans and three of his men; Tom Hill, George Davis and Frank Baker. The bunch had stolen Tunstall's horses and hid them at the Beckwith Ranch at Seven Rivers. Dick Brewer, Doc Scurlock and Charlie Bowdre had already been after the horse thieves with at least a dozen of their cowboys, so once Sheriff Brandy learned of this he had little choice but to make a move and arrest the Evans crowd. But Evans did not remain in jail long. Sheriff Brady, a notorious imbiber of spirits, was aggravated over Evans's escape and while on a exceptionally magnificent bender had threatened Tunstall in the presence of Chisum and McSween. Although the accounts of this meeting as McSween and Tunstall later separately relay them are strikingly, and humorously, different both are clear on the point that Brady threatened to kill Tunstall. He also accused Tunstall of having some complicity in Jessie Evans's escape. That was a foolish notion. True enough, John Tunstall had spoken with Evans while the latter was incarcerated, but the implication that Tunstall would have aided in Evans' escape seems to defy all logic.

On December 18, 1877 McSween and Chisum left Lincoln for Trinidad, Colorado where they planned on boarding the train for Saint Louis to celebrate Christmas in more tranquil surroundings.[284] Upon their arrival in Las Vegas they were met by the sheriff of San Miguel County and placed under arrest. There were two warrants, one from District Attorney Catron from Santa Fe and one from Rynerson from La Mesilla. These two attorneys were known members of the Santa Fe Ring, patrons of the Dolan/Riley firm, and connected with William Rosenthal, the notoriously conniving cattle buyer. All of the foregoing were strong adversaries of Chisum, Tunstall and McSween. McSween posted bond and was returned under guard to Lincoln to clear his name. Chisum was held, initially under trumped up charges of resisting arrest.[285] He remained in the Las Vegas jail for several weeks.

Lawyer Thomas Conway was brought in from San Miguel to represent Chisum. Early in January Chisum was served with an injunction that specified the particulars of eight unanswered court decrees. Previous attempts to attach his property had proven fruitless since Chisum had no goods, personal property, land or buildings in the county to place a levy.[286]

On examination of the charges against him it seemed that someone had signed Chisum's name to several forged notes in connection with the deal he had made some years earlier with Hunter, Evans and Company. His financial condition at the time was unclear, since he had essentially signed over all of his assets to Hunter, Evans and Company in 1875 as bond pending finalization of his agreement with them. This conclusion, as Hinton points out in *John Simpson Chisum,* was drawn from an investigation that culminated in a court decree, dated November 14, 1885. It declared that Hunter, Evans and Company had, in 1879, returned to Pitser Chisum certain property previously held by his older brother. This, it went on to say, had been done at John Chisum's request so as to ". . . defraud, hinder and delay . . ." settlement to his creditors, who, from that time until his death, were unable to collect as he had no apparent assets."[287]

Trouble was brewing back in Lincoln. John Tunstall sent a plea for help to John Chisum at the South Spring Ranch. But Chisum was still in jail in Las Vegas, and his brothers James and Pitser, acting independently or perhaps under John's specific direction, turned down Tunstall's petition.

On February 18, 1878 a large posse led by William Scott "Buck" Morton caught up with John Tunstall.[288] At the time Tunstall was trying to move some horses to Lincoln to comply with a court order, albeit an unjust and fraudulent one that had been levied against him in connection with Alexander McSween's legal problems with the Fritz estate.[289] At about 5:00 PM Tunstall, Dick Brewer and Robert Widenmann came upon a flock of wild turkeys. John Middleton and

William Bonney were about 500 yards in the rear. Dick Brewer and Robert Widenmann went off after the birds while Tunstall continued on with Bonney and Middleton riding behind. The approaching posse fired shots in the direction of Widenmann and Brewer, causing them to head for a tree covered hill, as they were in an open and rocky place where they believed they could not make a stand. The posse pursued them until they were close to the hill when suddenly they spotted Tunstall and their attentions were diverted. Fred Waite, who was driving the wagon for Tunstall, had split off from the rest of Tunstall's men about ten miles earlier. Tunstall and his men took the short cut through Pajarito Flats near Glencoe.[290] As accurately as the events of the day can be recounted from those who witnessed the proceedings, the posse caught up with Tunstall at around 5:30 PM at a point about eleven miles from Lincoln. As the men approached the Englishman "Buck" Morton and Tom Hill began firing at him with their rifles.[291]

A bullet struck Tunstall in the chest. He fell to the ground. One bullet also struck Tunstall's horse, mortally wounding the animal. Some have contended that Tom Hill dismounted, picked up Tunstall's own gun and fired a shot into the back of Tunstall's head, administering the fatal wound. Others claim that Hill or Morton had also struck Tunstall in the head with an earlier rifle shot, and that Hill fired two shots in the air from Tunstall's pistol to create the impression that the Englishman had fired at them first.[292]

The posse quickly gave up on pursuing the others and rode towards Tunstall. According to posse member George Kitt:

> Tunstall was some distance off and was coming towards them. Hill called to him to come up and that he would not be hurt. At the same time both Hill and Morton threw up their guns resting the stocks on their knees. Morton wished to shoot him and Hill said hold on till he comes nearer. After Tunstall came a little nearer Morton shot him in the chest and then Hill shot him in the head.

Not long after the shooting a neighboring rancher, John Newcomb, assembled a search party at his farm on the Ruidoso. The group consisted of Newcomb, Florencio Gonzales, Patricio Trujillo, Lazaro Gallegos, and Ramon Baragon. Baragon was an experienced tracker and it was he who found the body of John Tunstall. Tunstall's corpse had been concealed in the trees some distance away from where he had been killed. The body "was lying closely by the side of his horse," said Gonzales.[293]

Most citizens of Lincoln viewed the callous murder of John Tunstall as nothing short of an outrage. Disagreement had now escalated into open warfare. Alexander McSween feared for his safety. Together with his small band of allies he plotted legal action to seek justice and exact revenge. But John Chisum was still in jail in Las Vegas. Susan McSween had just returned from St. Louis. McSween's friends urged him to leave Lincoln at once for fear he should come to the same end as Tunstall. An English born doctor from Colorado named Montague Richard Leverson told the group of McSweenites how he had been in Santa Fe and learned some appalling things about their enemies there. Doctor Leverson would later write to the Secretary of the Interior Carl Schurz on April 1, 1878 charging that all of the United States law enforcement officers in Lincoln at the time were a "…gang of veritable thieves…." McSween was so alarmed that he immediately made out his will. Leverson, who proved to be a credible source of information as well as an astute interpreter of the ongoing events in Lincoln, went on to become a member of the bar and held a position on the Supreme Court of California and later on the Supreme Court of the United States.

District Attorney Rynerson had authorized Dolan and Riley to run attachments on everything McSween owned. Dolan was obviously trying to get at the store, since his business was floundering in the face of the competition. He thought he could do so on the grounds that Tunstall and McSween were partners. John Tunstall had given testimony concerning a partnership at an earlier hearing, but the agreement stipulated that McSween was not to become a partner until May of 1878. It was now just mid February and that agreement had not yet taken affect.

Alexander McSween did manage to gather himself somewhat, and began to take action. Believing that Sheriff Brady would probably not take any action against Tunstall's killers, at McSween's persuasion a group of Tunstall sympathizers was organized. Under the umbrella of their appointment on March 1, 1878 as constables by local Justice of the Peace John B. Wilson this band of men known as the Regulators was formed. Initially comprised of just a handful of men, the Regulators ranks would grow to roughly twenty strong over the coming months. Armed with arrest warrants issued by Wilson, the Regulators were tasked with bringing the individuals who had been involved in the Tunstall killing to justice. The group left Lincoln within days, and soon had run "Buck" Morton and Frank Baker to ground, eventually killing both men on the return trip to Lincoln while they reportedly *attempted an escape*. William McCloskey was also a victim of this incident. McCloskey claimed to be a supporter of the McSween faction, but was thought by some of its members to be a traitor. Ash Upson gives a chilling account of McClosky's killing.[294] He claimed that Frank McNab rode close to McClosky saying "so you're the son-of-a bitch that has to die before harm can come to these fellows" and shot him in the head. Francisco Trujillo, who was not present at the time, says that McClosky was shot behind the ear. McClosky's terrible fate seemed a lesson not to interfere with the justice being dispensed by the Regulators. John Chisum, who had posted $25,000 bond in March and had long since been released from jail and was noticeably absent from the planning, as well as the retaliation.

The capture and killing of Morton was by no means the end of the reckoning. An all out shooting war soon began as the warring factions numbering as many as fifty men at times and armed to the teeth, rode pell mell through the hills and valleys of the Sacramento Mountains seeking to exterminate each other. During the following weeks about forty combatants were killed. The death count was probably greater than one hundred, considering the poor record keeping of the time.

Although John Chisum managed to keep from becoming directly involved in any of the gunplay associated with the Lincoln County War, he did not remain neutral between the two warring factions. Chisum furnished McSween's boys with fresh horses to ride, food, and opened his house for the men to use while the officers of the law were pursuing them.[295] In an official report filed later that summer Sheriff Peppin also believed that the attorney's forces had been "fed, clothed and horses exchanged for fresh ones" by Chisum.[296]

Alexander McSween, who had been hiding out, rode into Lincoln on July 16 with over fifty heavily armed men. The group split into smaller parties and immediately barricaded themselves in various buildings around the town. By the next day, Sheriff Peppin's posses had surrounded their strongholds and declared his ultimatum that those for whom warrants were held surrender.[297] Peppin's demands were refused, and a sporadic exchange of gunfire between the factions commenced. By the third day of the siege a cavalry troop arrived from Stanton, but made no move to intervene as the civil authorities had the situation under control. As the situation escalated on the fifth day McSween's residence was set afire by late afternoon in an attempt to draw out the occupants. By nightfall the entire structure was ablaze. On July 19, 1878, just five short months after the murder of John Tunstall, an unarmed Alexander McSween was gunned down on the threshold of his own home as he tried to escape from the burning building where he had been held at siege. He had been defender and hostage simultaneously, as Sheriff George Warden "Old Dad" Peppin and his men surrounded the residence and for five days prevented the occupants from leaving as they huddled in fear for their lives.[298] McSween was buried beside Tunstall, wrapped in a dirty blanket, with no coffin. Also buried with Tunstall and McSween were two Regulators; Frank MacNab who was killed by the Seven Rivers Warriors in April 1878, and Harvey Morris, a noncombatant law student who was killed at the same time as McSween.

Ruins of the McSween House.
Courtesy of The Haley Memorial Library and History Center Midland, Texas.

The Regulators would continue their pursuit of the men responsible for Tunstall and McSween's deaths for some months to come as they made their way out of the country and north to Tascosa, Texas. But the remaining group disbanded by the end of the year and the leftover few, now under the leadership of William Bonney, turned to cattle and horse theft for their livelihood. For some, including William Bonney, the saga would not end until the middle of 1881.

Throughout the course of the Lincoln County War the Chisum ranch was a frequent hideout and resupply point for the Regulators and the McSween faction. But apart from providing occasional shelter, sustenance and resupply it seems clear that John Chisum and his clan were careful to maintain a safe distance from the McSween faction, thereby preserving a pretense of neutrality. There is an interesting legend that has managed to work its way into the text of otherwise historically accurate writings regarding Will Chisum and his involvement with Billy the Kid. As the story goes

Will Chisum, the fourteen year old nephew of John Chisum and son of his brother James, brought food to Billy while he was hiding out after the killing of Sheriff Brady. The story contends that young Will took the supplies to Billy at his hideout near the Bottomless Lakes, east of present day Roswell. Sheriff Brady was killed on April 1. Billy was at Blazer's Mill in Mescalero just three days later on April 4. It seems highly unlikely that the injured Billy would have ridden one hundred and twenty five miles, over broken ground, to take shelter at such a distant location. For that reason alone, not considering the fact that Billy was recovering from a gunshot wound at the time, the veracity of this legend is questioned.[299] But the whole of New Mexico and much of west Texas is loaded with such tales of Billy the Kid. He seems to have magically appeared practically everywhere west of the Pecos, and a few places east of the Pecos to boot! Everyone alive at the time, regardless of their age or gender, laid claim to having met, or had a relationship of some sort, with the young criminal. Adding to the confusion, after his death in 1881 more than twenty-five people claimed to have been Billy. On first examination some of their stories seemed quite convincing. But after closer scrutiny, most were little more than pathetic old men wishing to relive their squandered youth, having a longing to bask in the borrowed glory of the now legendary hero of the Lincoln County War. No one, to my knowledge, ever claimed to be John Simpson Chisum after his death. What a pitiful testimony to our twentieth century choice of heroes.

Shortly after the McSween siege, on August 17, 1878, William Bonney, Tom Folliard, Fred Waite, John Middleton, Henry Brown, and a group of former Regulators all arrive at South Spring Ranch.[300] They were headed away from Lincoln in the wake of the Five Day Siege. The group would ultimately make their way north, traveling through Fort Sumner and would eventually wind up at Tascosa, Texas where several of the former Regulators split off from the band.

The violence did not end in the backyard of the McSween home on July 19, 1878. En route to Lincoln, Peppin's party observed a lone horseman riding east and turned to investigate. The rider was

James Chisum, who, after a twelve mile chase managed to outdistance his pursuers. As he later related the incident at the ranch, there undoubtedly arose a feeling of apprehension for the personal safety of the Chisum household. In the weeks that followed, this concern became grave, particularly when a plot to disfigure Pitser Chisum was uncovered. In her book *Buckboard Days* author Sophie Poe recorded the story as she heard it in the fall of 1881 from John Chisum. She quotes him as saying:

> Some of the men who were against us planned to mutilate Pitser. They were going to capture him at Captain J. C. Lea's house, where he was visiting, and give his ears a jinglebob slit and put a Chisum Long Rail brand on him. Captain Lea got wind of it through an outsider. He sent his colored boy out to the corral to get Pitser's horse, and take it secretly to the back door. Luckily, it was a dark night, so he got away without much trouble. . .[301]

Charlie Bowdre brought news of the battle and the death of Alexander McSween when he reached the Chisum Ranch on July 20.[302] After a brief stay, the Regulators left the South Spring in late July 1878. The dogged Sheriff Peppin was still in pursuit of this small group now led by Bonney. The posse had scoured the countryside for the men, believing that they were holed up at the Chisum ranch. In fact they had been, but had long since departed. While Peppin's men roamed the broken plains around the South Spring ranch Bonney's crowd was miles to the west, in the mountains between Lincoln and South Fork. On August 5 the gang of nineteen former Regulators, now reinforced by around a dozen Mexican sympathizers, emerged briefly at the Mescalero Indian reservation where they are claimed to have gone to steal horses. Much controversy exists concerning the circumstances leading up to the killing of Bernstein, as well as the intended purpose of Bonney and his crew that day.

During a shooting affray that ensued Agent Morris Bernstein

was shot and killed.[303] Many would later blame Bonney for the killing, disregarding eyewitness reports to the contrary.

In spite of unsettled conditions in Lincoln, Chisum's ranch had maintained large-scale cattle activities throughout the spring of 1878. A succession of trail drives, with well armed cowboys, had left the Pecos and driven sizable herds to well removed markets. One of the groups elicited considerable comment however. Jesse Evans led this party of trail drivers, probably hired by Hunter, Evans and Company to facilitate deliveries during the perilous times on the Pecos. Evans would later become the general manager of the vast Comanche Pool cattle cooperative in Central Kansas. Comprised of roughly fifty men, several wagons and a large remuda of horses, the group had left Dodge City on April 5 bound for the Chisum range in Lincoln to move a herd of about twenty thousand head of cattle. Their arrival on the Pecos raised much interest. The *Mesilla News* on June 1, 1878 reported that "Chisum has hired 80 men to come down from Kansas to help him do his fighting and dirty work and swears he will run every small cattle owner or rancher off the Pecos River for a distance of 200 miles." Simultaneously, Chisum cowboys were rounding up cattle for delivery to Robert K. Wiley and Tom Coggin in Texas.[304] That herd was delayed until later summer, while the others that were gathering were shipped off to Hunter, Evans. Ultimately the Wiley/Coggin cattle were moved to the Pease River in the Texas Panhandle.

The disturbed state of civic affairs in Lincoln County that had attracted armed desperados and menaces, horse thieves and rustlers, would soon begin to draw to a close. But the development of the New Mexico Territory and its progression to statehood was impaired for years by the violent events and sequels thereto in Lincoln County.

6

THE FINAL YEARS

*Pale death knocks with impartial foot at
poor men's hovels and king's palaces.*
—Quintus Horatius Flaccus Horace

The summer of 1878 left Lincoln County in complete chaos. In the wake of the Five Day Siege in Lincoln, and the death of Alexander McSween, definite moves to close down the headquarters at South Spring were underway. James Chisum and his three children accompanied a herd of several thousand heifers north. The animals had been previously set aside as foundation stock for a proposed select beef herd. Pitser remained behind with a skeleton outfit to look after the ranch and the remaining stock. Based on the continued turmoil in the vicinity the Chisum caravan had no idea when they would return to the home ranch at South Spring.[305]

The group first made camp at the Bosque Grande on July 31. A fifteen-day layover was begun there. Two weeks later, under the direction of old time Chisum trail boss Charles Nebo, they moved north up the east bank of the Pecos.[306] Nebo was the wagon boss for the Chisum outfit at the time. Born in 1842 Charley Nebo lived a long and fascinating life, passing away at Portland, Oregon at the age of eighty-four. The tall, slender and light complected Irishman had a career as a cowboy that spanned more than forty years and is one of the little known and least chronicled characters of the era. John L. McCarty writes of Nebo in *Maverick Town, The Story of Old Tascosa* that "Charley Neebow, or Neibold, was Chisum's wagon boss in the Panhandle, and some of the men with him were Johnny Newell, Bill Hutch and Tom Pickett.... Billy the Kid, with the wages he had drawn as a gunman in the Lincoln County War cut off, gathered some of the other men in the same position about him and followed the Chisums to the Panhandle".[307] McCarty is citing an interview with Garrett H. Dobbs from 1942 during which Dobbs also said "All of the men from the Lincoln County War came out with Chisum".

And they did. Bonney's small crew of erstwhile Regulators trailed alongside the Chisum cattle drive as they retreated from the Pecos range and slowly plodded north towards the Canadian, intercepting the procession just north of Fort Sumner.

The Chisum party, including the former slave boy Frank Chisum who John had bought in Texas, helped in the drive. Frank had become an accomplished horse wrangler and he worked with the one hundred and fifty or so horses that trailed along nearby. It was a family migration of sorts, and John's niece Sallie drove one of the wagons.[308]

Three days out of Bosque Grande the drive halted for a brief rest a few miles southeast of Fort Sumner. According to entries in Sallie Chisum's journal this is the point where William Bonney and several other former Regulators joined the group. On September 11 the caravan once again began to move. They left the Pecos Valley and headed northeast, out onto the High Plains. John Chisum is believed to have joined the group at Fort Sumner. His nephew Will states that his uncle... "accompanied the outfit from the Pecos Valley to the Canadian."[309] Ten miles east of Fort Sumner near Red Lake, the Chisum procession turned north. They skirted the eastern edge of Taiban Mesa and after a week on the prairie they reached Fort

Bascom near Tucumcarie on September 17.[310] From there they pushed the herd into the southern drainage of the Canadian and headed due east along its banks to Ute Creek. Although the group probably made other brief stops, this was their last camping site in New Mexico. On Saturday September 28, they crossed the New Mexico Territory line into Texas. The group halted near the mouth of Trujillo Creek, about thirty miles west of Tascosa. Temporary shelters in the form of dugouts were constructed in shielded breaks, along with corrals for the livestock.[311] Not long after their arrival John Chisum left for Santa Fe.

Fred Nolan cites the founding of Tascosa as taking place around the spring of 1875, with the arrival of Jesus Trujillo and a party of immigrants from San Miguel County, New Mexico. When Dr. Henry Hoyt arrived at Tascosa from Colorado in 1877, by way of New Mexico, the town boasted two stores, a blacksmith shop and some Mexican houses on a plaza that was about one hundred yards across.[312] New Mexico and Arizona had been especially hard hit by a smallpox epidemic in 1877, which spilled over into the Texas Panhandle. Young Dr. Hoyt walked into the middle of it when he rode into Tascosa. Tascosa boasts a fascinating, wild and wooly history. It was located on the Canadian River at the site of an easy ford for cattle and freight. Having sprung from the desolate plains of the Texas Panhandle as a small settlement and supply point shortly after the 2nd Battle of Adobe Walls broke up that encampment it was the home to more than a few intriguing and eclectic characters with wonderful names like "Squirrel-Eye" Charlie Emory. The practically lawless village had a post office by 1878, and some limited law and order by the mid 1880s. Although it continued to grow, slowly, it was bypassed by the railroad in 1887, an event that signaled its eventual demise. By 1939 Tascosa was a ghost town.[313]

Early in October the newly appointed Territorial Governor Lew Wallace composed a rather lengthy report to President Hayes in which he outlined the lawless situation in New Mexico.[314] He asked the president to declare that a state of insurrection existed so that

Army troops could be ordered into the field. On November 13, 1878 the fledgling governor issued an amnesty for all parties involved in the Lincoln County War.[315]

Governor Wallace had found that the commander at Fort Stanton, Colonel Nathan Dudley, was implicated in the Lincoln County War and that he had favored the side of the Dolan Faction. Dudley's lack of action resulted in the murder of Alexander McSween. In order to keep peace in the yet divided and fragile county of Lincoln Wallace issued a pardon to all that had been involved in the war. In spite of William Bonney's cooperation, Wallace bowed to his powerful enemies, and did not grant Bonney a pardon. In March 1879 Wallace made a personal journey to Lincoln to investigate the situation, accompanied by the military commander for New Mexico, General Edward Hatch. Wallace twice requested Dudley's removal as commander, and Hatch finally suspended him on March 8.[316] Dudley was brought to trial for complicity in the murder of McSween but was acquitted.

On March 17, 1879 Governor Wallace had a face to face meeting with William Bonney.[317] Bonney, who was being called "The Kid" by some newspapers, was able to obtain the governor's agreement to pardon him if he would testify against James Dolan, Jessie Evans and Colonel Dudley in the recent shooting death of Huston Chapman.[318] His troubles not yet finished, Billy continued a hide and seek game with the law. The governor would eventually renege on the pardon agreement.

Life on the Pecos had not yet returned to normal. Tensions between the warring Lincoln County factions would carry over for years to come. In the spring of 1879, the Chisum party packed up and pulled out of Tascosa and returned to the Pecos. They found that many former partisans had also returned to their ranches. Stymied for years by the endless warring, immigration to the Roswell vicinity would soon be on the rise. John Chisum arrived in Mesilla, New Mexico, by stage from the west during the last week of February 1879. Hinton muses that he probably had spent the previous month in Arizona.[319] This is inferred from a statement in the *Arizona Silver Belt* on January 24. The newspaper mentioned that "the Chisum-Hunter interests had recently sued out a writ of attachment on a herd in that locale." When interviewed in Mesilla, Chisum made no comment on this affair, but did say that after a trip through Colorado, Utah, Nevada and California he had disposed of his Arizona holdings and returned to New Mexico. Several days later, he boarded the stage for Santa Fe.

Four detachments of cavalry were now on patrol in Lincoln, searching suspect ranches for stolen cattle and horses. Orders were to inspect known cow camps and corrals, and to impound and return any and all recognizably stolen animals to the county seat.[320] John Chisum obviously stood to benefit from these campaigns. For the most part, the cavalry were searching the lairs of Chisum's old adversaries. On March 26 Pitser Chisum wrote the new commanding officer at Fort Stanton, Captain Henry G. Carroll, and reported that peculiarly marked cattle were pastured in and around Bosque Grande. He added "Parties giving these brands never had a hoof of stock til recently."[321] In submitting this information, the rancher was hoping that the military would extend its reconnaissance north from Roswell into an area that was being overlooked. Three weeks later John Chisum wrote Governor Wallace outlining his plan to curb future depredations in the Pecos Valley. He penned… "If ten good men were stationed at a large spring twelve miles east of this place, it would prevent robbers from coming in off the plains onto the Pecos…. If twenty men were stationed at Pope's Crossing on the Pecos, it would prevent them from coming up the Pecos; having these two points guarded you have possession of the main keys to the settlement of the Pecos."[322] Although Captain Carroll did not specifically heed Chisum's advise, the patrols continued and the effects of them were soon felt.

Toward the end of the summer of 1879 Chisum cowboys completed preparations to move the now drastically reduced herd back from Texas to the home ranch at South Spring. John Chisum accompanied the stock on the trail drive home, arriving there by the first week of November 1879.[323]

During a stopover at Fort Sumner during the return trip to the South Spring ranch John Chisum had an unexpected meeting with William Bonney. Few, if any, facts concerning this encounter have survived. Once the myth has been separated from the surviving certainties it seems that Bonney approached Chisum and demanded payment for services previously performed while in Lincoln County. According to Chisum's nephew Will who witnessed the encounter, John replied, "You know just as well as I do that I never hired you to do anything for me." Bonney did not press the matter further.[324] In *John Simpson Chisum* Hinton comments that "Chisum's terse response reflected the general feelings of a region weary of erratic living conditions and too busy with the future to consider unsubstantiated debts to the past."[325] After a brief pause to contemplate, the former Regulator and now full time outlaw William Bonney replied "Aw, you aint worth killing." Bonney, who would soon be known to most as Billy the Kid, decided to drop the matter for the moment.[326] The enigmatic Bonney later decided to balance the books on his account with John Chisum by stealing more than his fair share of cattle to settle the debt. In the end, history would revere the life and misdeeds of Billy, who as Fred Nolan put it so well was "…little more to history than a candle in the wind."[327] John Chisum, on the other hand, would take his place at the back of the line with so many other historically significant giants whose lives and deeds remain largely unrecognized and widely misinterpreted.

The countryside was becoming far more peaceful now with the Lincoln County War behind them and his business running well. The final delivery of Chisum cattle to Hunter Evans from the deal that was made in 1875 had taken place in 1879, and at a sum reported to have been more than $300,000. Chisum owed the entire amount to others in accumulated debt however, so the finalization of this transaction benefited him little in terms of net proceeds. The herd now had new owners. Hunter, Evans and Company, temporarily holding title to the remaining stock, had transferred it to Pitser in the panhandle. In 1880 Pitser sold half interest in his cattle to his brother James Chisum.[328]

The ownership transfer made it necessary for Chisum to develop a new brand.[329] A lazy "U" burned high on the left shoulder was recorded in the brand books of San Miguel County in 1879.[330] Soon after they had resettled and began full scale ranching again Chisum experienced the worst plague of rustling along the Pecos to date. During the late fall of 1879 local herds were repeatedly struck by a band rustlers led by William Bonney. In January 1880 one Chisum outfit found about eighty head of "U" brand cows with brands and earmarks mutilated in Canyon Cueva, more than a hundred miles north of the South Spring ranch.

Bonney was finally shot and killed on July 14, 1881 by the recently appointed Lincoln County Sheriff Pat Garrett. Garrett and his posse caught up with the now famous outlaw at the home of Pete Maxwell in Fort Sumner, New Mexico.[331] Although some of the other former Regulators would live as long as the early 1940s, this chapter in the history of Lincoln County had finally ended. Or had it? Almost 130 years later historians and researchers continue to discover details that have been overlooked. Annually, several new authors are compelled to write yet another book about Billy the Kid and the Lincoln County War. The unlikely hero of the whole affair, Billy the Kid, has grown to become a cult figure of international popularity. European tourists still flock to Lincoln County simply to tread on the same ground and breathe the same air as their hero, Billy.

The early 1880s brought a cattle boom to the southwest, and John Chisum would benefit from it as much as anyone would. The organized rustlers that had been systematically depleting his herd were largely in check. Now deprived of their "free" Chisum livestock, their illicit cattle businesses began to wither and die.

It has been estimated that there were 500,000 head of cattle in the New Mexico Territory by 1881, yielding 90,000 marketable offspring annually. Of the half million head estimated, 300,000 were said to have been in Lincoln County. Young cows and calves were valued at $25.00, two year olds and yearling heifers at $12.00, yearling steers at $7.00 and bulls at $75.00. Simple "back of the envelope" arithmetic would place the value of the New Mexico cattle business at about $10 million.[332]

Chisum built a more comfortable ranch house at the South Spring as earlier described. He labored at improving his cattle breeding program. He became involved in local and territorial livestock associations. Some have claimed that Chisum was also active in the local Masonic Lodge in his later years, and was a Royal Arch Mason.[333] I can find no corroboration for this claim however, and mention it only in the interest of completeness.

Chisum bought good bulls in Kentucky and shipped them by rail to Kansas where they were driven to the Pecos to improve the genetics of his stock. He also bought all of the shorthorn stock he could from Tom Yearby, the rancher who had purchased the improved English herd from Pete Maxwell. Chisum continued his breeding program for the remainder of his life. In 1883, not long before he died, he bought one hundred and fifty Hereford bulls in Missouri and had them shipped to Pecos, Texas where they were trailed to his South Spring Ranch in New Mexico.[334] Although some report the quantity of bulls to have been somewhat less, and the breed to have been Durham Shorthorns and not Herefords, the fact remains that the cattle were "as fine a bunch of animals as ever held down hooves."[335]

Chisum's niece Sallie married William Robert at Anton Chico on January 26, 1880. That year, at the lavish Chisum Christmas party, a newly arrived rancher and fiddle player named Rufus Henry Dunnahoo entertained the large gathering. "Ruf" Dunnahoo would become the longest surviving pioneer of the Roswell area having arrived there in 1880 and living to the ripe old age of 89. He later chronicled events of the early days on the Pecos, and his transcribed oral histories provide us with a fascinating window into the past.

Lincoln County was slowly growing. Indian depredations, a succession of partisan wars as well as the lack of transportation infrastructure that made the region somewhat inaccessible had slowed the population growth. By 1880 the 20,000 square mile county had 2,513 inhabitants. More than a third of this new populace had been drawn to the area by a series of gold strikes, which began in the Jicarilla Mountains thirty miles northwest of Lincoln. Ranching along the verdant banks of the Pecos remained the major inducement for immigration, however, cattlemen like Chisum still monopolized the strategic water holes. But the days of the open range, and the *free grazer*, were quickly drawing to a close. Sheep ranchers and farmers, along with the growing populace that had been drawn to the new communities along the Pecos, began to break up the domain of the cattle kings. The town of Roswell, which had shown little growth, began to become more heavily settled by fresh immigrants. Many of them took up residence around Chisum's South Spring ranch. This new population provided seasonal help for roundups and cattle drives. Dozens of extra cowboys were needed to work the peak time at the ranch. But apart from a small nucleus of line riders for the winter, most of these men were laid off as soon as the need for them passed. Members of the Mexican population were often retained to clean irrigation ditches, work the garden and fields and perform household duties at the ranch headquarters. Chores such as herding the milk cows and running errands were the domain of Chisum's young nephews Walter and Will.[336]

Somewhat unique among the more permanent members of the Chisum ranch staff was Frank "Chisum." After the end of the Civil War, and emancipation, Frank had elected to remain with his former master John Chisum. He had come to New Mexico with his younger brother, who had also been bought by Chisum, on the early cattle drives of the mid 1860s. Frank, now an accepted and trusted family member of the Chisum clan had developed into an all around cowboy and an excellent horse wrangler. A chronic stutterer, it is said that he was frequently the butt of a joke. Frank eventually accumulated a small herd of his own and became one of the most successful black ranchers in the region.

Benjamin Franklin "Frank" Chisum. Courtesy of The Historical Center for Southeast New Mexico at Roswell.

Often overlooked is the fact that Chisum did a great deal to advertise the potentialities of the Pecos Valley, and to induce immigration into that region. As early as 1877 he recognized the agricultural possibilities of the Hondo-Pecos area. He had constructed a large canal capable of irrigating a thousand acres. The ditch ran parallel to the south bank of the artesian stream and east into a sown field onto land owned by Felix McKittrick. McKittrrick experimented with various varieties of wheat, buckwheat and rye. Mormon settlers in the area were also experiencing good results from their agricultural efforts.

Frank Chisum on Chuck Wagon.
Courtesy of The Historical Center for Southeast New Mexico at Roswell.

John Chisum was now approaching sixty years of age. A chronic malignant disease of the throat was causing him great pain. His father and grandfather had died from what is believed to have been similar afflictions. On April 23, 1884 ten plaintiffs filed suit in the District Court of Lincoln County after numerous attempts on their parts individually to settle claims with Chisum. The suit against John, James, Pitser and John's son-in-law William Robert totaled $57,030.86.[337] Chisum, already a dying man when judgment was rendered against him, was further insulted that the Santa Fe law firm of Thomas B. Catron, leader of The Santa Fe Ring, represented the claimants.

In 1884 Chisum's herd of cattle totaled about 30,000 head. This is probably a low estimate, since in 1883 his cowboys branded 6,000 calves alone. He knew the value of quality livestock, and bulls valued at as much as $1,000 roamed his range, serviced his cows, and improved the genetics of the herd.

John Chisum decided to go to Kansas City for treatment of the ever-increasing growth on his neck. On July 24 surgeons removed the tumor. He was told the operation was a success, so after a brief recovery he began his journey home. In the midst of the return trip Chisum fell ill in Las Vegas, New Mexico. He was advised to go to Eureka Springs in Arkansas for further treatment and care. Unfortunately his tumor returned, this time even larger than before. It became so large it was difficult for him to hold his head erect, and towards the end he was practically unable to speak. On December 22, 1884 John Simpson Chisum died in Eureka Springs with his family at his side. He was buried on Christmas Day at the old Chisum family plot in Paris, Texas, alongside his father and mother. He left his estate to his brothers James and Pitser.

Some report the inheritance to have been valued at over half a million dollars. Although Chisum had owned thousands of acres in his lifetime, his total land holdings at the time of his death was 11,221 acres. Most of that land was in Lamar County, Texas and was valued at just $27,724. In a few short years the Chisum ranch was facing tough financial challenges. It had not been well run by Sallie's husband William Robert and John's brothers James and Pitser. In 1888 they filed papers to incorporate, setting the capital stock value at $300,000. That maneuver only forestalled inevitable bankruptcy, the declaration of which took place on December 10, 1890. James and Pitser were never known to have been astute businessmen, but niece Sallie was not alone in placing most of the blame for the loss of the ranch squarely on the shoulders of William Robert, whom she soon divorced.[338]

The last vestiges of the old Chisum home in Paris, Texas have long since disappeared. The home was located just west of the Frisco-Santa Fe round house and the old family burying ground where John Chisum's remains now rest. Sadly, the site of the old Chisum place, and cemetery, may soon be threatened by recent industrial infrastructure development plans in Paris. Texas State Historical Marker # 6960 identifies where John Chisum's house in Bolivar once stood. The actual text on the marker reads: "Here stood the home from 1856 to 1862 of John Simpson Chisum, cattle king. Born, August 16, 1824; Died, September 22, 1884 at Paris, Texas. (3 mi. N of Bolivar, Denton County)." The marker is, unfortunately, quite incorrect. John Simpson Chisum died on December 22, 1884 ... not September 22. He died at Eureka Springs, Arkansas ... not Paris, Texas. Hopefully someday the State of Texas will find it in their budget to replace marker # 6960 with a corrected one, and leave a more accurate legacy of one of the State's most prominent but least celebrated heroes.

John Chisum's ranch headquarters on Home Creek near present day Trickham is long gone. Most of the operation was housed in simple dugouts. The store, which was about a mile below the old army post at Camp Colorado, was sold to L. L. Shield and today there is nothing more than the outline of a foundation remaining to mark where it once stood.

The route John Chisum blazed for his cattle drives west began near Bolivar, Texas and continued through the new camp on Home Creek. From there the trail struck out to the west, across the largely uncharted country which lay in the southern part of the Texas Panhandle. Curving southwest to meet the Pecos River at Horsehead Crossing the trail then turned north, through the present day towns of Carlsbad, Artesia, Seven Rivers, and Roswell on the way to Ft. Sumner and Bosque Redondo. Sometimes called the Loving-Goodnight Trail, this route was originally traveled by John Chisum and his cowboys as early as 1864. The casual tourist or traveler can easily speed past the relatively few historical markers that designate the points where the trail crossed the improved automobile highways that now crisscross Texas. But, almost a century and a half later, an astute observer can still detect the telltale evidence of the passing of the great herds on the parched and barren plains of West Texas. Now mere ghosts of a bygone era, the long lonely columns of Texas Longhorn cattle that once stretched out for miles across the dry land of the Permian Basin have vanished. They are little more than memories of our ancestors. Like the Cattle Kings and the legions of cowboys, they are gone forever.

John Chisum's South Spring Ranch, once called The Long House, is still in operation. It is located on Old Dexter Highway, three miles south of Roswell, New Mexico. James John Hagerman purchased it in 1892 after Chisum's heirs filed bankruptcy. Hagerman built most of the buildings that are standing on the ranch today around the turn of the last century. The operation is now called the Jinglebob Land & Livestock Company. John Chisum would hardly recognize the place, squeezed by a crush of civilization and urban development. The once freely flowing streams and rivers have now been reduced to a trickle from the demands of an exploding population. Helicopters and all terrain vehicles have largely displaced mounted cowboys. The majestic Texas Longhorn, apart from small aggregations of principally ornamental livestock that adorn the pastures of the wealthy "new money" ranchers have all but vanished. Fallen victim to genetic engineering, the tough, stringy and water wise bovines no longer grace the plains.

The Old Chisum Cemetery has only three graves. It lies within the city limits of Paris, on West Washington Street between two railroad tracks in Block 203 of the city of Paris. Buried there are John Simpson Chisum (August 16, 1824 – December 22, 1884), his father Claiborne C. Chisum (June 22, 1802 – October 21, 1852), and his mother Lucinda Armstrong Chisum (October 21, 1804 – October 31, 1837). A large marble monument poignantly marks the spot where John, his father and mother now rest. Although the stone memorial has been vandalized over the years, as thieves have removed the two urns that once bracketed the edifice, it still remains along with the three individual headstones.

To quote the famous and epigrammatic opening line from Walter Noble Burns's seminal book on the Lincoln County War, *The Saga of Billy the Kid*—*"John Chisum knew cows."* But perhaps more accurately, John Chisum knew the cattle business.

Chisum Cemetery
at Paris, Texas.
Courtesy of James Owens,
Hobbs, New Mexico.

John Simpson Chisum's
Grave at Paris, Texas.
Courtesy of James Owens,
Hobbs, New Mexico.

Although not the consummate American cowboy one might wish to envision, Chisum was a larger than life cattle king, leading an adventurous, exhilarating and decidedly unconventional life. Accounts of his exploits and experiences are, to this day, a whirlwind of fact and myth. Among his more admirable traits, Chisum was known to be a generous man, well liked by his cowboys. He definitely was a man who placed a high value on family. On the less admirable side of the ledger it has been said that Chisum was arrogant in his dealings, and focused largely on personal gain. He had a propensity to abandon his friends and colleagues when they were in the greatest need if coming to their aid interfered with his goals. The log book of his business dealings is pock marked with questionable practice.

Regardless, John Simpson Chisum left an unforgettable mark on the history of the American West. His legend will survive, and he will be long remembered.

EPILOGUE

*Our greatest glory is not in never falling, but
in rising every time we fall.*

—Confucius

Philosopher, poet, and literary critic George Santayana may have had it right when he penned, "History is a pack of lies about events that never happened told by people who weren't there." Many began believing that Cow John Chisum, Cattle King of the Pecos, was the consummate Texas cowboy and Indian fighter. He became known as the Pioneer of the Chisholm Trail, a brave gunfighter who nearly single-handedly held the dangerous Murphy/Dolan camp at bay during the Lincoln County War. He was the man who whipped the notorious Jessie Evans and the Seven Rivers gang of cattle rustlers. He was also the dynamic Texas cattle baron who fathered two children by a mulatto slave woman named Jensie. Many believed he owned a ranch in New Mexico that covered an expanse practically as large as the state of Rhode Island. His legend was that of a towering figure, respected by all decent citizens and feared by outlaws and evildoers.

Once the myth has been separated from the facts, we end up with a far different John Simpson

Chisum. An ordinary looking but decidedly extraordinary individual who cannot be credited with much of what his legend claimed. On the other hand, Chisum deserves credit for numerous accomplishments that historians have largely remained silent about. The valued patriarch and friend to many left a lasting legacy and mark upon the land. An almost forgotten figure, cast adrift on the dark and silent sea of unwritten history.

When John Chisum pushed the first herd of gaunt and weary, wild eyed Texas Longhorn cattle up the Pecos River to Bosque Grande there were only a handful of beef cows in the entire territory. The largely barren region had been home to the Apache and Comanche Indians for generations. Although Spanish explorers had come through the Pecos Valley more than a century before, few Mexicans and even fewer Anglo settlers had made their way to the vicinity by Chisum's time. By 1873 John Chisum alone controlled sixteen hundred sections of land…more than a million acres.

Today, thanks to irrigation and modern ranching techniques, about 87% of the State of New Mexico is pastureland and farmland. John Chisum's South Spring Ranch, which once stood alone on the open prairie below the present day town of Roswell, is surrounded by new development. Roswell boasts a population of over 60,000 people, ranking fifth in the state in residents. By comparison, when Chisum pushed west from Lamar County in the 1850s, the entire territory of New Mexico contained a population of just 3,900 inhabitants, of which more than a fourth were slaves.

The old Cattle King would be pleased to finally have his story told accurately. If you try hard enough, you can practically hear him laughing, loudly and deeply, at the parts that are finally written down right. There would be the slightest hint of a grin on his lips when he saw the parts of his story that we do not know yet about. Chisum would no doubt revel in the fact that he had covered his tracks well.

Farewell old friend. Keep a place for us around the campfire and save enough good bourbon to go around. We shall be along to join you in due course.

Monument to John Chisum, Roswell, New Mexico. Author's Collection.

APPENDIX I

THE CHISUM FAMILY ORIGINS & GENEALOGY

There is no king who has not had a slave among his ancestors, and no slave who has not had a king among his.

—Hellen Keller

No legitimate attempt at a biographical study would be complete without some reference to family origin and genealogy. The family of John Simpson Chisum has its roots firmly planted alongside the very earliest immigrants to the New World, with ties to the American Revolution and the early formation of the United States. The blood of our ancestors, be it good and bad, courses through our veins and contributes to the people we become. But it is through our actions that we define ourselves, not through our breeding. As Lord Chesterfield put it so well "The scholar without good breeding is a nitpicker; the philosopher a cynic; the soldier a brute and everyone else disagreeable."

John's father, Claiborne was an early Texas pioneer, arriving just one year after Texas declared its independence from Mexico. Historians place the population of Texas at about 50,000 in 1836, which includes only about 30,000 persons of Anglo American ancestry and 14,200 Indians.[339] Individual contributions were more significant then in this sparsely populated land, thus Claiborne Chisum and his extended family played an important role in the development of Lamar County, Texas. His son John Simpson Chisum would become a pioneer Texas cattle baron, and in the company of men like Charles Goodnight, Oliver Loving and James Patterson would open up the frontier of West Texas to free grazing and spearhead the first cattle drives to the Pecos River region of New Mexico.

The origins of the Chisum family name extend back in time for several millennia, well beyond the founding of this fledgling nation. The surname of Chisum is said to be an old Border name from the barony of Chisholm in the parish of Roberton, Roxburghshire.[340] Spelling variations include Chisholm, Chissolm, Chisholme, Chism, Chisolm, Chisolt, Chissum, and other less prominent derivations.

The name moved north through Scotland during the 14th Century. The Highland Chisholms being distinguished from the Lowland Chisholms as the Chisholms of Strathglass.[341] Early records mention John de Chesehelme, Roxburghshire 1254. John de Chesolm, was recorded in Berwickshire in 1296. Robert de Chesholme was sheriff of Inverness in 1359. John de Sheshelm was the burgess of Aberdeen in the year 1439, and three members of the family of Chisolm of Cromlix held the bishopric of Dunblane in the 16th century. Surnames as we recognize them today were probably introduced by the Normans after the Invasion of 1066.[342] The first mention of such names appears in the Domesday Book, and they were later adopted between the 11th and 15th centuries.[343]

The family name had originally been spelled "Chisholm," and remained that way until about 1815 when it was changed to "Chisum." Although some speculation for the rationale exists, the specific reason for the surname change has been lost to time. Owing to the fact that the family had its roots in England, where reasonably accurate records have survived, genealogists have traced the lineage further back in time to Richard Chisholm of London, England who was born in 1613.[344] Any attempt to identify Richard Chisholm's reasons for leaving London would be purely speculative, but in the context of history one must keep in mind that England was beset with various plagues during the 1600s. In 1609 and 1610 the country witnessed several grim outbreaks of the bubonic plague. In 1625, when Richard was twelve years old, another great flare-up occurred. The year 1645 brought one of the most severe plague epidemics on record, and 1665 marked the onset of the *The Great Plague*, or Black Plague, which significantly impacted residents of London in particular.[345]

So far as Chisum genealogy is concerned, I begin with John Simpson Chisum's great-great-great grandfather John Chisholm.[346] John Chisholm was born at Lancaster County, Virginia in 1681. He married Elizabeth Bradley at Richmond County, Virginia in 1707. John died in 1734. The couple had two sons. John, who was born at Caroline County, Virginia in 1704 and William whose place and date of birth are unknown but who later married Deborah Cook. Skipper Steely indicates that this William Chisholm may be the progenitor of the Jesse Chisholm line.[347] Some family genealogists have not picked up William as a son of John and Elizabeth. Others have claimed the possibility of additional children, although none have identified those offspring by name.

John lived an unusually long life for the day, reaching the age of eighty eight before he passed at Richmond County, Virginia on October 9, 1792. John and his wife Ellender Guillinton, sometimes spelled in the more conventional manner as Eleanor Gillington, had a prodigious array of children. They were:

- Isham: Born About 1738 to1740, Amelia County, Virginia. Died Christian County, Kentucky. Married Russell.
- Chloe: Born Amelia County, Virginia. Married John May 1777.
- Anna: Born Amelia County, Virginia. Married Ambrose.
- Priscilla: Born Amelia County, Virginia. Died Logan County, Kentucky. Married John H. Hill.

- Sarah: Born Amelia County, Virginia. Died Logan County, Kentucky. Married William Pattillo.
- John (Captain): Born About 1732, Virginia. Died 1806, Sparta, White County, Tennessee.
- James: Born About 1734, Caroline County, Virginia. Died 1786, Virginia. Married Barbary Estes.
- Elizabeth: Born 1736, Caroline County, Virginia. Died before 1796, Logan County, Kentucky.
- Absolom: Born about 1740, Orange County, Virginia. Died Logan County, Kentucky
- Adam: Born about 1742, Orange County, Virginia. Died Spartanburg, Spartanburg County, South Carolina.
- Elijah (Captain): Born About 1744, Amelia County, Virginia. Died 1818. Married Lucy Claiborne about 1772.
- Obadiah: Born about 1767, Amelia County, Virginia. Died January 18, 1837, Springfield, Tennessee. Buried Chisum Cemetery, Franklin County, Tennessee. Married Maryann Cardwell 1789.

John Simpson Chisum descended from the line of the aforementioned Captain Elijah Chisholm. By 1787 Elijah was operating a ferry over the Holston River. Elijah was a Captain in the Revolutionary Army and was active in Tennessee politics. He was at the North Carolina Constitutional Convention of 1789 that was called to ratify the new United States Constitution.[348] Elijah married Lucy Claiborne of Amelia County, Virginia in 1773. By 1806 he had been elected County Clerk of White County, Tennessee.[349] Elijah and Lucy Claiborne had five children. They are as follows:

- Thomas: Birth and death dates are unknown.
- James Stewart: Born November 26, 1774, Halifax County, Virginia. Died before November 1834 in Bolivar, Hardeman County, Tennessee. Married Betsy Gibbons in 1794.
- John: Born about 1776 in Henry County, Virginia. Died 1833 in Hardeman County, Tennessee. Married Mary Armstrong 1798.
- William: Born 1778 at Henry County, Tennessee. Died about 1831-1835. Married Nancy Armstrong.

- Malinda: Born Hawkins County, Tennessee. Died (day uncertain) Lamar County, Texas. Married Thomas Gibbons Jr. 1801.

John Simpson Chisum's father Claiborne descended from James Stewart Chisholm. James Stewart, who had been born in Virginia in 1774, married Betsy Gibbons, daughter of Thomas and Mary Epps Gibbons Sr. There were ten children from this union:

- Mary: Born March 26, 1795 in Hawkins County, Tennessee. Died March 23, 1853. Married John Johnson.
- Claiborne C.: Born June 22, 1797 in Granger County, Tennessee. Died October 24, 1857 Paris, Lamar County, Texas. Married twice (perhaps three times). Details cited below.
- Lucinda: Born January 16, 1800 in Grainger County, Tennessee. Died about 1834. Married William Hill.
- Rebecca: Born January 31, 1802 in Claiborne County, Tennessee. Died January 21, 1880 at Hardeman County, Tennessee. Married Walter Robinson.[350]
- Nancy Epps: Born February 21, 1804 in Claiborne County, Tennessee. Died October 5, 1844 at Hardeman County, Tennessee. Married Robert Hicks Vernon in 1823.
- Thomas Gibbons: Born March 20, 1806 in Claiborne County, Tennessee. Died February 27, 1855 at Rusk County, Texas. Married Malinda Chisum about 1829.[351]
- Lavinia: Born February 10, 1808 in Claiborne County, Tennessee. Died after 1874 in Tennessee. Married Andrew Turner.[352]
- James Simpson: Born January 24, 1810 in White County, Tennessee. Died about 1836 at Hardeman County, Tennessee. Never married.
- Elizabeth: Born August 27, 1812 in White County, Tennessee. Died about 1893. Married Jonas Robinson.
- John Gibbons: Born December 4, 1818 in White County, Tennessee. Died after 1856. Married Elizabeth Pirtle in 1839.

There is some evidence that Claiborne Chisum, eldest son of James and Betsy Chisholm, was married three times. His first marriage is believed to have been to a woman named Nancy. His second marriage was to John Simpson Chisum's mother Lucinda Armstrong. They wed in 1822.[353] Although such gaps in age were not uncommon on the frontier, Lucinda was only sixteen at the time and Claiborne was already thirty-three. Claiborne's third marriage was to Cynthia Ann Henderson Latimer (widow of Daniel Fitch Latimer) of Clarksville, Texas.[354]

Claiborne Chisum and his second wife Lucinda Armstrong had seven children:

- Nancy Epps: Born January 22, 1822. Died January 6, 1869. Married Benjamin Franklin Bourland on April 16, 1839.
- John Simpson: Born August 16, 1824. Died December 23, 1884.[355]
- James Thomas: Born September 25, 1827. Died March 12, 1908. Married Ara Josephine Wright 1853.
- Thomas Jefferson "Jeff": Born About 1830. Died 1866.
- Alexander: Born about 1833. Died Unknown.
- Pitser Miller: Born February 28, 1834. Died January 2, 1910. Married Angie Isa Wells.
- David: Born 1836. Died 1860.[356]

All were born in Hardeman County, Tennessee, in the years before the Chisum family immigrated to Texas. Claiborne's third marriage to Cynthia Ann Henderson Latimer produced five additional Chisum siblings:

- Robert "Bob": Born 1842. Died 1856.[357]
- William Claiborne "Tony": Born October 30, 1849. Died June 5, 1931. Married Sarah (Sallie) Wilhite 1871. 2nd Marriage Amanda Wilhite 1876.[358]
- Laura: Born 1843. Died Unknown.
- Mary Susan: Born 1844. Died 1859.
- Robert Claiborne "Bob": Born May 10, 1858. Died November 15, 1933.[359] Married Emily (Emma) B. Johnson (Born June 30, 1862. Died October 25, 1911).

Along with raising their own sizeable medley of offspring, Claiborne and Cynthia Ann reared two of Claiborne's cousin Robert Bell's children Mary Ann and Malinda Bell.

In about 1837 news of the good fortune of the families that had already made the journey from Tennessee to Texas began to filter back to the Chisum clan. The Moor and Jarman groups had preceded the Chisums to the Red River Valley of Texas. James Chisum, Claiborne Chisum's father, had recently passed away. The family was growing larger and straining at the bounds of their territory. In 1810 Claiborne's sister Polly had married John (sometimes cited as Johnny) Johnson. They lived upstream from Claiborne and his family. By 1837 the Johnson's had eleven children. Thomas Gibbons Chisum, a brother of Claiborne, married Malinda Chisum who was a daughter of their Uncle John.

Claiborne's sister Lavina had married Major Andrew Turner. Another sister, Elizabeth, married Jonas Robinson. John Gibbons Chisum later married Eliza Pirtle and they had ten children. By now one develops the understanding that for the Chisum clan westward expansion was an economic necessity. The family land holdings, although sizeable by any interpretation, were simply not sufficient to support the ever-increasing offspring.[360]

Skipper Steely, in his manuscript *Forty Seven Years,* says he believes that word of Asa Jarman's willingness to sell one of his several land grants in Texas to Claiborne reached the Chisum patriarch in Tennessee. This, Steely believes, is what prompted Claiborne, Thomas Gibbons and John Johnson to make their move west. Steely goes on to say that it is also possible that Abner Kuykendall's success in Texas may have further influenced the Chisum move. But Steely hastens to add that citing one singular factor that caused the move to coalesce would be difficult.

In the years to come the influence that the Chisum family, and the small group of Tennessee immigrants that accompanied them, would have on the Red River Valley and the emergence of Lamar

County would be incalculable. Perhaps secondary, however, to the impact that John Simpson Chisum would have on the New Mexico cattle trade and the development of the Pecos River Valley.

APPENDIX II

THE PERSISTENT MYTH
JENSIE JOHNSON CHISUM AND HER CHILDREN

The great tragedy of Science—the slaying of
a beautiful hypothesis by an ugly fact.
—Thomas Henry Huxley

There is a longstanding fable that John Chisum fathered two children by an attractive young mulatto slave girl named Jensie. No account of John Chisum's life story would be complete without some mention of this legend. The majority of what is known about Jensie has been so tainted by myth and legend, and further fouled by family genealogy gone amok that one fears her roots are forever lost to history. At the risk of being too harsh, erroneous accounts of her sale to John Chisum as well as dubious speculation that Chisum himself fathered two of her children (Almeady and Harriet) has resulted in a generation of historians and genealogists perpetuating this fable.[361]

Most family oral history passed down over the generations suffers from some degree of interpretation error, or intentional aggrandizement. Many of the interviews with the pioneers of the late 1800s done during the 1920s and 1930s suffer from lapses in historical accuracy as a result. Both types of mistakes are certainly understandable, and forgivable, since they are the result of the fading memories of individuals who are generally in their advanced years. They are the products of interviews transcribed by eager journalists ready to absorb the information without question. But historians are expected to take what we discover from the past and seek to learn new truths through analysis, interpretation, and further research. In our research we rely on data from the past, as well as newly uncovered information from current sources and interviews.

Jensie Johnson Chisum was, in all likelihood, born in Tennessee, between about 1837 and 1842. She first appears on the 1850 census records in that state.[362] Her death occurred at Denton, Fannin or Lamar County, Texas around the turn of the last century. It is claimed, although unproven, that Jensie is buried in an unmarked grave in Bonham, Fannin County, Texas.

Earlier writers have penned that Jensie was a particularly attractive mulatto woman who appeared to be about sixteen when Chisum purchased her in 1858.[363] Based on census records she was actually about twenty at the time. The reoccurring myth made popular in earlier published writings alleges that John Chisum bought Jensie from a wagon master named Joseph Baines at Boliver, Texas. Baines is said to have been from Arkansas, and at the time of Jensie's sale was traveling through Texas as a member of a larger group that were headed to California. It is further claimed, as cited previously, that John Chisum paid Baines somewhere between $1,400 and $2,000 for Jensie.[364] However, we known for certain that John Chisum purchased Jensie in 1858, at Gainesville, Texas, from his first cousin Frances Johnson Towery and her husband Tom V. Towery. At the time of her purchase by Chisum Jensie already had three children; Phillip (born 1852), Harriet (born 1855) and Almeady (born April 13, 1857). Jensie had belonged to John Johnson,[365] Frances Johnson's father, and was mentioned in his will.[366] When Johnson died on September 27, 1852,

Jensie was willed to Mary Ann Johnson Stell.[367] Mary Stell transferred ownership of Jensie and Phillip to her sister Frances and her husband Tom. They later used Jensie and the children as collateral for a note of $814. Some have speculated, with perhaps a reasonable basis for doing so, that Jensie was fathered by John Johnson. She appears on the 1850 U.S. Federal Census Slave Schedule as being thirteen years old at that time, and owned by the Johnsons.

Sometime in 1862, while John Chisum was away on a cattle drive, Jensie is said to have taken Almeady, her sister Harriet and brother Phillip to Gainesville.[368] A severe drought had struck the area around Bolivar and Denton County that year, and Indians had repeatedly raided and attacked the ranch, laying waste to the land. But Chisum actually left Jensie and the children in Bonham in about 1863.[369] Explaining that life would be too difficult on the frontier without the protection of his armed cowboys, Chisum moved Jensie and the children into a boarding house in Bonham. Folklore has it that John Chisum always provided for Jensie and the children, and he is said to have looked in on them during his infrequent trips back to Paris, Texas.[370] An account of John Chisum's travels would indicate otherwise, giving rise to the speculation that the foregoing is simply another aspect of the protracted family lore. Nonetheless, Jensie remained silent about her relationship with John Chisum all of her life. But so did John Chisum for that matter. What does seem certain is that John Chisum was evidently very fond of Jensie. The extent of that fondness is open to speculation and will no doubt remain as another undiscovered aspect of the Cattle King's life.

both real and personal having been allotted to Mrs Lavina Thomas, and she having before & since the death of her farther John Johnson recd from his estate the sum of $346.00 and by agrement among all of the Heirs to said estate, she is chargable for Negro hire for the present year to the amount of $74.94, Which Sums added to the estimated value of the real & personal property makes the sum of $3852.96. her rich part of her farthers estate, Mrs Thomas is to pay to Jane Johnson's Heir the sum of $38.50, amount Over drawn in the above Lot

Mrs Stell.

Lot 7th Consist, of what is Known by the Heirs to this estate, as The property attach to the Richey House, in the town of Paris valued at $815.00, also what is Caled the Upshaw Block in Paris valued at $450, also One Negro Girl named Iency and her child named Philep valued $900.00, William $300 Allen $300, and Marshall valued at $250, also 2 Mules worth $110.00, This Lot having been Allotted to Mrs Mary Stell and she being chargable with the sum of $418.50 the amount of property recvd by her from her Farthers estate, before and since his death, and by agrement among all of the Heirs, she is also chargable for Negro hire for the present year to the amount of $116.11. which when added makes the sum of $3859.61, and the sum of $6.65 Over her proportional part of the estate of her Farthir, & she is instructed to pay the said $6.65 to Mrs Thomas

Mrs Taylor

Lot No 8 Consist. of One tract of land Known as the Johnson & Chisum tract, containing 575 acres & 100 poles, for a full description of said lands, your Commisions herwith file the plot & Certificate of Jno T Harman Surveyor for said Known as No 1 in said division and valued at $1157.00 by, Marked E One Half of lots 1 & 2 in Block 3 in the Town of Paris valued at $250.00, also One Negro man named David $1000. Amy and child Sintha $625, Polk $300, One Glass Cash 75 cts

Will of John Johnson. Author's Collection.

Jensie chose the surname "Chisum" in lieu of the family name of her original owner John Johnson. In describing the complexity of researching the background of African Americans of the period Natalie D. Cottrill, genealogical researcher, writes:

> The first time enslaved blacks were required to have last names was in 1867. Research experience has shown that some slaves adopted last names earlier than 1867. The notion that many slaves took the name of the family who owned [they] is a myth. Freed slaves sometimes took their owners' surnames, but they were free to take whatever names they wanted to, including famous people they admired. Sometimes they wouldn't settle on a permanent first and given name combination for awhile, and they'd change their names a few more times. Even then, many individuals preferred nicknames. This is one of many challenges that compounds the research of pre-1880 African American families.

Jensie's youngest daughter Almeady, known as *Meady*, was born April 13, 1857. Given the timing, and the location of her mother's owner at the time, she is thought to have been born in Denton County, Texas. That is where her owners, Tom and Frances Towery, lived at the time. She was sold with her mother, brother and sister to Chisum in 1858. Almeady's daughter would later claim that her mother said that she had been born where the courthouse now stands in Gainesville. That would seem logical considering that Chisum bought the family at Gainsville one year after Almeady was born. We do not know who Almeady's father was. It may have been Tom Towery, who was the owner at the time. That, however, is purely supposition. First hand interviewers of descendents of Almeady Chisum have noted that there appeared to be a wide difference in visible racial features among the group, giving rise to the speculation that Aleamdy's father was an African American.

The life story of Almeady Johnson Chisum is a wonderful

tale, regardless of her father's identity. She was raised in Bonham, Texas. A young man by the name of John Dalford "Bob" Jones who was traveling from Medlin to Bonham caught Almeady's eye at a dance.[371] This attraction led to an exchange of letters. In 1874 Bob traveled to Bonham once again and returned to Medlin with Almeady as his bride. John Dalford "Bob" Jones was born June 26, 1850 and was brought to Texas by his slave master, Leazur Alvis Jones[372] from Fort Smith, Arkansas in 1862. Traveling with Jones was his slave wife Elizabeth[373] and their children Ellen, Josie, George Anne and Jim. Leazur had left his first wife Mary Brown (who was white) in Fort Smith with children Alice Jane, Blake T., Martha Luellen, Richard C., Roxie Geneva and Captain Jinks (for whom Jinks Jones was named). Elizabeth was buried in Medlin Cemetery along with children Josie and George Anne.

Bob Jones was freed in Texas near the Medlin community where he stayed for the remainder of his life.[374] He obtained fifty acres of land on which he began a farming and livestock business. As with most families in the last part of the 19th century, Bob and Almeady managed to support themselves by raising a vegetable garden and an orchard to augment the chickens, hogs, milk cows, sheep, cotton, and corn for the livestock. Bob supplemented his income by raising horses. Bob increased his holdings to 2,000 acres by the time of his death on December 26, 1936. The ranch was located east of Roanoke on highway 114, then north toward Grapevine Lake to Bob Jones Road. The land located there had been in the Bob Jones family since 1868 and remained so until the construction of a dam to form Grapevine Lake in 1948. Located on Denton Creek, a tributary of the Elm Fork of the Trinity River, the dam later facilitated the construction of Dallas Fort Worth Airport.

Bob and Almeady Jones had ten children, Eugie,[375] Jinks, Alice, Emma, Jim, Virgie, Artie, Harriett, June and Emory. Daughter Eugie Jones-Thomas would later comment during an interview on May 19, 1976 with Yvonne A. Jenkins that her father was an exceptional person, bringing to his family and community a heritage of work, education, family pride, self improvement and a love of the land. Her mother also expressed the same feelings. Prior to her death on April 10, 1949 she told Eugie, "don't ever sell the home place…we must have a place for the children to come back to." Eugie recalls that she felt no hostility or discrimination other than the fact that she could not go to school. That did not stop Bob and Almeady Jones. After the school term was over in Dallas Bob hired a private teacher to come and live on his farm and teach his children spelling, history, English, arithmetic and geography. At one point he bought a home and lot in Denton and each spring, Almeady and the children moved to Denton so that the children could attend school. Later Bob built a one room schoolhouse next to his home so that there could be school year round.

Daughter Eugie married McKinley Thomas on July 11, 1926. Thomas ran a truck farming operation on the thirty seven acres left of the original home place. Bob Jones divided his land among his children and Eugie swapped acreage with her brother Emory so that she retained the home place. In 1948 the family home burned, destroying most of the family records.

The middle child of Jensie Johnson Chisum was Harriet. Harriet Johnson Chisum was born sometime in 1855, and the exact date and place of her death is unknown, but believed to have been between 1935 and 1940. Less is known about Harriet than is known about Jensie. We know Harriet was born in 1855, presumably in Gainsville or Paris while she was still the property of Mary Ann Johnson Stell. We know that she was sold, along with her mother, sister and brother to John Chisum in 1858. The last date on which there is any information about her is in 1860 when she was listed as part of the Thomas Davis Sunday School of white Methodists from Lamar and Fannin. Oddly, this information differs from other well documented accounts in that she is believed to have been at the settlement of Bolivar in Denton County until 1862 when her mother Jensie took her and her siblings to Gainsville, in Cook County. Harriet is said to have married a man named Cloud, moved away from the area and had at least one daughter named Margaret who married Clarence Benningfield. There are no records that confirm any of the foregoing, however. Conversely, the records of a Margaret Benningfield, born 1890 and the wife of Clarence Benningfield, indicate that she was born in Georgia or Arkansas. That account lists her as a white woman and not a mulatto or black.[376, 377] Clarence was the son of Janie Benningfield, listed as a widow in the 1900 census. She had come to Texas from Tennessee and was, presumably, married there. There are no reliable records of any kind for Harriett, under the name of Chisum, Johnson or Cloud.[378]

Similarly, little is known about Phillip Johnson Chisum, the eldest child of Jensie.[379] We know that he was born in about 1851 or 1852. Most historians have presumed that he was born in Gainsville or Paris, Texas. However on closer examination it is clear that he was born in Tennessee prior to his owner John Johnson coming to Texas. We believe that Phillip moved back to Gainsville in 1862 with his family. Census records document that by 1870 Phillip was living in Denton County, Texas and was married to a woman named Charity Chaney from Lamar County. Charity was the daughter of Pasthena Chaney, living with four other children at census time in 1870 but with no husband.[380] From earlier census records it seems that Pasthena and Charity had been born in Louisiana. They were owned by the McKnight family there, and appear on the 1860 census.[381] By 1880 Phillip and Charity were still living in Denton County, where he was listed as a "stock keeper" on the census. Subsequent to 1880 the trail goes cold. After diligent search using all alternate spellings there seem to be no further records of either Phillip or Charity.

Interestingly, Phillip Chisum actually listed his place of birth as Tennessee on the 1880 census, making it even more curious that historians have missed this important detail until recently. As cited earlier, a search of the Tennessee slave census reveals that both Jensie and Phillip were born in Tennessee and were the property of John Johnson.[382] John Johnson was born August 30, 1790 at Nashville, Davidson County. His wife is listed as Mary, and although the record does not indicate her maiden name as "Chisum" there is no other John Johnson who wed a "Mary" within any reasonable timeframe.[383] The slave schedule matches up so far as names and ages are concerned with respect to Jensie and Phillip. We know from other reliable records that Mary Chisum did wed John Johnson, and that their daughter Frances Johnson Towery and her husband Tom V. Towery owned Jensie and the children before they were sold to John in 1858.

No doubt the speculation about Jensie and her family will continue. Some genealogists and respected historians remain convinced that Almeady, and possibly Harriet, were fathered by John Chisum prior to his purchase of Jensie from the Towry's (or from whomever they cite as her owner). I defer to the records, which prove otherwise. But detractors will claim that the possibility of John Chisum having fathered Almeady does exists, since a day by day account of John Chisum's travels between 1855 and 1857 simply does not exist. Holding out that speculation seems far fetched. But given that there are hundreds of descendents of Jensie and her children who claim to be blood relatives of John Simpson Chisum I am certain that the previously cited documents which prove otherwise may be challenged or ignored. The fact remains, as Thomas Henry Huxley put it, it is ... *the slaying of a beautiful hypothesis by an ugly fact.*

APPENDIX III

SALLIE LUCY CHISUM
MAY 26, 1858 – SEPTEMBER 12, 1934
THE FIRST LADY OF ARTESIA

The person who has lived the most
is not the one with the most years
but the one with the richest experiences.
—Jean Jacques Rousseau

Sallie Chisum lived a long, exhilarating and productive life. She passing away in 1934 at the age of seventy-six. Sallie was blessed to have lived to see the land along the Pecos River in New Mexico become a civilized and thriving place. She made her home along the Pecos, arriving there in 1877 at the age of nineteen. She never left. From rugged beginnings, starting with an Indian raid at her Uncle John's ranch at South Spring on the very day she arrived, Sallie saw the surrounding countryside develop into productive ranch land. Punctuated by thriving communities and irrigated ranch land, eastern New Mexico would soon benefit from the oil discovery and the first successful drilling operations in the 1920s. Sallie would live through it all. Active and aware to the end, she became a living historian of Eddy and Lincoln Counties and contributed mightily to the recording the events of those early years for posterity.

James Chisum and Daughter Sallie in 1905.
Courtesy of The Artesia Historical Museum and Art Center.

Sallie Lucy Chisum was born May 26, 1858. Her father was James Thomas Chisum born September 25, 1827 in Hardeman County, Tennessee.[384] Her mother was Ara Josephine Wright, born September 25, 1827. Ara Wright and James Chisum were married in Denton, Texas on December 21, 1853. Ara died on March 2, 1875 in Sanger, Denton County, Texas and is buried in the Knox Cemetery in the Johnson Plot.

Sallie had two brothers and one sister:

- Walter: Born September 25, 1861. Died on October 3, 1919 in Rock Springs, Wyoming.[385]
- Mary Lady: Born 1863. Died about 1875.
- William C.: Born 1865. Death unknown.

After her mother died Sallie came to New Mexico to manage the household for her Uncle John Simpson Chisum, arriving there on Christmas Eve of 1877. The South Spring Ranch was about three miles below the site of present day Roswell. Sallie looked after the large and bustling household operations. The ranch, and particularly its dining hall, was known to be open to all and fed anyone who showed up. James Mullens wrote, "The Chisum ranch was a free hotel, to all who liked, they came, stayed as long as they wished, and were never allowed to pay a cent." [386]

Among the enormous number of guests, dignitaries, military officers, businessmen, ranchers, cowboys and common drifters she met while running the household at the South Spring Ranch was William Bonney who would later be widely known as Billy the Kid. Bonney, who may have been a casual employee of her Uncle John's at one time, was working for John Henry Tunstall. [387, 388] Some have disputed the claim that Chisum employed Bonney prior to working for Tunstall. Among the dissenters is James Mullens, who wrote "Billy never at any time worked for John Chisum or the Jingelbobs." [389] But recalling the Kid's statement concerning his arrival on the Pecos, John P. Meadows would later say that Bonney "…joined Mr. Chisum's outfit in some way, but he was with Chisum [only] a while and then drifted off up the Hondo. . . ." Probably Florencio Chavez made the simplest, yet the best observation regarding the Chisum-Bonney relationship when he said, "I know that he (Bonney) was often with John Chisum, but was only riding around with him." Fred Nolan holds out the possibility that Bonney had worked for Chisum at his Eureka Springs, Arizona ranch. [390] Upon leaving Arizona Bonney headed east into the Ruidoso country, south of Lincoln. Meadows continues, "He told me about living with Dick Brewer and Frank and George Coe. He stayed quite a while with them and then went over and went to work for Mr. Tunstall, who had cattle on the Feliz." [391]

William Bonney was the name that this mysterious young man first chose to identify himself by when he arrived in Pecos

River country. Calling himself William Bonney, Kid Antrim or simply The Kid, he arrived from Arizona in the fall of 1877. Conventional wisdom is that Bonney, who would later be given the enduring nickname of Billy the Kid, was actually Henry McCarty. But in spite of more than 130 years of diligent research by scores of historians the true identity of Billy the Kid, and his genealogical origins, remain something of a mystery. "He was nothing but a kid and a bum when I knowed him back there" as Add Casey described him some years later. But apart from his few detractors the Kid was well liked by most. As historian and author Robertus Love put it in his February 27, 1926 article in the St. Louis Post-Dispatch "Long before Sheriff Pat Garrett of Lincoln County, N.M. ended the career of this amazing outlaw with a bullet, the Kid virtually had forgotten his own family name".

Legend has it that Sallie and William Bonney became instant friends. Many of the local cowboys seemed to have fallen for this attractive, nineteen year old flaxen haired girl.[392, 393] As is the case with most things involving Billy the Kid, the veracity of this story comes under question. Practically everyone in New Mexico, and half of Texas, born in 1881 or earlier claims to have met or had a relationship with Billy the Kid. Psychoanalyzing Billy the Kid 130 years after his death, or musing about how he enjoyed horseback rides in the company of a young woman, strains at the bounds of historical research. Suffice it to say that there is ample documentation from sources including Sallie herself confirming that the two were at least acquainted.[394] The totality of their relationship, if one can call it that, remains a question. In Sallie's own diary she penned "... two candi hearts from William Bonney on the 22 of August (1878)." Lily Klasner claimed that Billy did write, what he perhaps thought would be his final letter, to Sallie from his confinement at the McSween house on July 18, 1878. Some have rushed to conclusions about their relationship on the basis of that letter. I am less eager to do so. Sallie later wrote "the happiest I ever was on the 29 of Oct. 1879, Tuesday night bid my friend R___ goodbye on the 6 of

Nov. 1879."[395] Clearly the mysterious "R__" was not Billy the Kid. It seems unlikely that Sallie, who came from a reasonable well to do background, would have seriously considered choosing a common criminal and cowboy such as Billy for a mate and "marrying down."

Sallie Chisum married George William Robert on January 26, 1880. Robert was born in June 1854 in the town of Preetz, Schleswig-Holstein that at the time belonged to Denmark. It would be annexed to the German Empire making William a German citizen by the time he came to America in his youth. He was an only son, and his father's family was prominent in banking. John E. Robert, William's father, was cashier of a bank for forty-five years. William's mother was Agnes Henningsell. Agnes's father was a farmer and her grandfather was Bishop Hansen, head of the Lutheran Church in the Schleswig diocese. In 1873 William came to America, passing through New York on his way to join an uncle in St. Louis. From St. Louis he went to Las Animas, Colorado where he worked as clerk for Bartel Brothers & Kilberg. In 1877 he moved to New Mexico where he opened a store of his own at Anton Chico. Along with selling merchandise he traded in cattle and sheep. Robert came to the Roswell, New Mexico area in 1879. There he met Sallie Chisum.

Following a brief courtship the couple were married in Anton Chico, New Mexico. After the marriage they remained at the South Spring Ranch where William worked as John Chisum's bookkeeper. When John Chisum died in 1884, Robert remained active in the ranch business until 1890 when he took some of his cattle from the South Spring Ranch to the Cimarron River and became identified with what is now the X-I ranch. His motto was *Be good, do good, think good, speak good and make good. Then you have not lived in vain.*

The couple's first child, John Reinhart, died at birth and is buried at Anton Chico, New Mexico. They had two more children:

- John Ernest: Born December 24, 1881. Believed to have died in Arizona in April 1966.[396]
- Fred Theodore: Born June 30, 1884. Died in April of 1968 in Oklahoma.

Both boys eventually settled with their father in Kansas and were educated in the public schools of Hutchinson, Kansas, also taking a classical course of study at Lubeck, Germany. Following their return from Germany the boys maintained very little contact with Sallie. John E. went into the cattle ranching business in Meade County, Kansas and married the daughter of his father's partner at the X-I, Bessie Adams. The couple had three children, Agnes Bessie, John E. Jr., and Horace. The other son, Fred T. started his own cattle ranch near Valiant in McCurtain County, Oklahoma. He married Eva Marie "Effie" Shearman of Roswell, New Mexico on June 17, 1914. They had one son, William Lee.

Sallie and William Robert separated in 1890 and subsequently divorced in 1895. William Robert moved to Meade County, Kansas and went into partnership with H. G. Adams on the X-I ranch. Sallie, her father James, and her two sons, moved to Eagle Draw about forty miles south of South Spring Ranch. There they built a house that was later destroyed by flood. After the flood they rebuilt, and soon a community called "Blake" began to come together on that site.[397] Sallie married Baldwin G. Stegman on September 1, 1895. The town of Stegman, New Mexico, which had earlier been called Blake, was named after him. Sallie became the town's first postmistress in 1899. She eventually divorced Stegman. The town was renamed Artesia in 1903 after the first artesian well that was drilled on Sallie's land. The town was incorporated in 1905 and soon after the Artesia Homesite Company was founded. Sallie became a successful cattle-woman, much like Susan McSween, and was often called *The First Lady of Artesia*. She died in 1934 and is buried in Roswell.

Here Sallie speaks about the Comanche Indians on the Chisum Cattle Trail:[398]

In 1867 John S. Chisum brought his first herd of Jinglebob cattle across the plains and through the buffalo hunting territory of the hostile nomadic Comanche Indians. Scout riders were sent ahead by the trail blazers to protect the herd from the Indians who were numerous in the lower Pecos Valley until after the extermination of the buffalo during the years 1877 and 1878. The Jinglebobs were brought over safely and placed on grazing lands around the headquarters established at Bosque Grande, thirty-five miles northeast of Roswell, on the Pecos River. A younger brother, Pitser M. Chisum, was placed in charge. In 1932 the writer of this article was one of the Old Timers who rode in the Old Timers parade in Roswell. I rode side-saddle and wore a long old fashioned riding habit. Sallie again told the story everyone loved to hear of her experiences on the journey and after arrival in the Pecos Valley, and about her first night spent on the Chisum Ranch. It was fifty-five years ago, this next December 24th. 1932, since I arrived in the Pecos Valley, said Mrs. Robert. We went to Uncle John's ranch five miles south of here. Uncle John was known as the Cattle King of the west but that had no effect on our equilibrium. My Uncle John never married. My father, James Chisum, my two brothers Walter and William and I all left home in Texas and traveled through the open country expecting Indians attacks at any time. We had three wagons, a hack and our saddle horses. We spent one month on the road. We had packed all the fruit trees, flowers and shrubbery we could in the wagons, and they were the beginning of the first Pecos Valley orchards and flowers. Some of the plants from those old fashioned roses brought over the plains by Sallie Chisum still flourish and bloom on the Redfield place in Roswell. Our last night on the trail we spent at the R. M. Gilbert ranch on the Ponasco River (Rio Penasco), said Mrs. Robert. Six cowboys had been sent by Uncle John to meet us at Horsehead Crossing to act as bodyguards and protect our stock from Indian attack at night. The first night we spent at the Chisum ranch, we were all tired out. We put our stock in the fenced in lot, locked the gate and all hands went to bed and slept soundly. The next morning we were amazed to find the stock all gone, and the gate still locked. The Indians, Comanche's, had lifted the gate from it's iron pivots removed all our stock replaced the gate very carefully and had completely disappeared leaving only their tracks to tell the tale. We could not tell how many Indians were in the raid. They got twenty-five horses and mules. I was heartsick for we had left our home at Denton Texas to get away from Indians. Cheer up Sallie, the worst is yet to come, said my father. I knew he was right when I first saw Roswell. There was only one residence called a hotel and one store, which contained the Post Office. These two buildings had been built in 1869 by Van C. Smith and Aaron O. Wilburn on the block west of where the Court House stands at the present time. In the post office was stationed here with Van Smith appointed as postmaster. He named the town Roswell for his father Roswell Smith of Omaha, Nebraska. There were six little trees trying to grow on the west side of the main road. On the east side there were a few houses some made of adobe and some of just mud, sticks, and gunnysacks. It was a cheerless looking place, and I said to Brother Walter I want to go back home. The request of his sister to return to her home in Denton Texas was repeated in the writer in 1905 by Walter Chisum as we walked through his beautiful orchard near the old Chisum Ranch at South Spring.

The account of Sallie Chisum is that of a strong pioneer woman who played an important role in opening up and developing Artesia. She had a long and full life, leaving behind a large collection of diaries, fifty items in all, chronicling her times and the stirring events that took place along the Pecos between 1870 and 1929.[399] Although more genealogical information is available on Sallie and her descendents I elect not to share it in respect for those family members who are yet living and whose privacy should be respected.

Sallie Lucy Chisum Robert Stegman died on September 12, 1934 in Roswell, New Mexico at the age of 76. She is buried there in the South Park Cemetery.

APPENDIX IV

OTHER CHISUM FAMILY MEMBERS

In consideration for the privacy of the descendents of Claiborne and Lucinda Armstrong Chisum, as well as those of Claiborne and Cynthia Ann Henderson Latimer Chisum, I have not included family members who are still living. The following summary is by no means complete. In some cases I have had to rely on family genealogy for source information. To the extent that some genealogical research used in the following summaries was not sourced by the researchers, and as such may not be entirely reliable, I have made every effort to verify and cross check the data wherever possible.

Pitser Miller Chisum
Born February 28, 1834. Died January 2, 1910

Like John and James, Pitser was born in Hardeman County, Tennessee. He served during the Civil War as a Quartermaster Sergeant in the 19th Regiment of Texas Infantry and saw action in the operations against

Union General Nathaniel Banks during the Red River Campaign.[400]

Pitser made the first cattle drive to New Mexico with John. He remained in New Mexico and aided John in establishing the South Spring ranch. Always a diligent and reliable ranch manager and trail boss, Pitser and his brother James were the driving force behind the actual ranching part of the Chisum operations. Brother John focused on finding markets and making the deals. Pitser was a sergeant in the 9th Texas Artillery during the Civil War. He knew how to manage and lead men.

After John's financial difficulties during the 1880s, title to much of the ranch and livestock went to Pitser and James. As the malignant growth on John Chisum's neck became increasingly more painful he left the running of the ranch to James, Pitser and Sallie's husband William Robert. Pitser and John are said to have had periodic difficulties working together.[401] After John's death in 1884 Chisum's cattle empire literally crumbled. James, Pitser and William Robert managed the operations until ultimately losing it in bankruptcy on December 10, 1890.

Pitser had returned to Paris in 1884, supposedly with $50,000 cash in his pocket and possibly a bank note for a similar sum as well.[402] On February 18, 1884 the timid Pitser Chisum married Angie Isa Wells, daughter of Isaiah Wells, in Lamar County, Texas.[403] Angie had been born on October 4, 1856. Pitser and Angie remained in Paris.[404] The couple had one child, Mi Alma born February 18, 1891. She died on May 5, 1941. Mi Alma remained in Paris, Lamar County and married Robert Phillip Young I (born August 15, 1878). The couple was wed on January 18, 1916. Robert and Mi Alma had one child, Robert Phillip II, who was born on March 17, 1920 and died the following day.

Grave of Pitser Chisum at Paris, Texas.
Courtesy of James Owens, Hobbs, New Mexico.

Pitser Chisum died on January 2, 1910 and Angie died on December 1, 1926. Both are at the Evergreen Cemetery, in Paris, Texas.

James Thomas Chisum
Born September 25, 1827. Died March 12, 1908

Like John and Pitser, he too had been born in Hardeman County, Tennessee. James served during the Civil War in Company "K" of Chisum's Regiment, Texas Dismounted Cavalry, 2nd Texas Partisan Rangers. John's younger brother James eventually followed him to New Mexico in 1877, coming shortly after his wife and oldest daughter died. James was not as strong a leader as Pitser. Nonetheless he was a good cowman and handled much of the ranch and farm work. He married Ara Josephine Wright (born September 25, 1827) in Denton, Texas on December 21, 1853. They had four children:

- Sallie Lucy: Born May 26, 1858. Died September 12, 1934 (see Appendix II).
- William James (Willie): Born August 7, 1864 (see separate heading).[405] Died June 12, 1956 at Los Angeles, California.
- Walter P.: Born September 25, 1861. Died October 3, 1919 (see separate heading).
- Mary Branch: Born September 1, 1855. Died November 21, 1873.

James's wife Ara died on March 2, 1875 in Sanger, Denton County, Texas and is buried in the Knox Cemetery in the Johnson Plot. Daughter Mary Branch had died two years earlier. The remaining three children accompanied James on the move to New Mexico. James was the range boss for John, a job that required him to be with the cattle nine to ten months of the year. During the few months that he was at the ranch he made it his special chore to set out trees along the irrigation ditch and to plant and develop the fruit orchard. After the ranch was sold, James went into the sheep business for a time with his son Walter.

At the age of eighty, while tending a small herd of goats he had acquired, he was robbed by outlaws who tied him to the tongue of his wagon and left him to die. James managed to escape by gnawing through the ropes that tethered him to the wagon. Thereafter, not feeling safe, he remained with his herd of goats for three entire years making his bed in the open and on the ground and never sleeping in a house the entire time.[406]

James died near Artesia, New Mexico and is buried in that town at the Woodbine Cemetery. On his deathbed he is claimed to have said that he had never killed a man his entire life. Although he had fought Indians, and repelled outlaws, he believed his record was clean. He had never robbed anyone, stolen anything or cheated anyone that he could recall. He demonstrated the finest qualities of the early pioneers.

Thomas Jefferson "Jeff" Chisum
Born 1829. Died 1866

Jeff Chisum was usually a quiet man, and was afflicted with epilepsy. Jeff served during the Civil War for a time as a Corporal in Maxey's Company, Texas Light Infantry and Riflemen which was part of the home guard and also known as the Lamar Rifles.[407] He was soon excused from duty as a result of his epilepsy.[408]

In 1863 Jeff Chisum was involved in a rather heated altercation with a man named Turner Edmundson over a boundary line or some shrubs or trees on Jeff's place which was located about two miles west of town.[409] Edmundson, the former mayor of Paris, was a big rough character who provoked Jeff Chisum's fury. Edmundson beat the frail Jeff Chisum profoundly. When Jeff finally recovered after two weeks in bed he went to town with his shotgun and waited for Edmundson outside Stamper's tailor shop. When Edmundson appeared Jeff stepped inside and shot the man. Although he was acquitted of the murder charge, Jeff soon left Paris and followed John and Pitser to New Mexico on one of the cattle drives of the mid 1860s.[410] Jeff died in New Mexico at Puerto De Luna in 1866.[411]

Walter Pitser Chisum
Born September 25, 1861. Died October 3, 1919

Walter Pitser, son of James Thomas and Ara Josephine Wright, was born September 25, 1861. He married Inez V. Simpson, who had been born in 1862. Their marriage took place on November 15, 1887 in Chaves County, New Mexico. Inez died on March 17, 1936 in Oregon. Their children included:

- James W.: Born February 1899 (possibly 1898). Died December 17, 1960.

- Ara V.: Born June 9, 1892.[412] Died August 1974 at Baker, Baker County, Oregon.
- Oscar William: Born June 9, 1892. Died August 21, 1953.

Walter Chisum
Courtesy of The Historical Center for Southeast New Mexico at Roswell.

Walter Pitser died on October 3, 1919 at Rock Springs, Wyoming. His body was returned to New Mexico for burial at South Park Cemetery, Roswell, New Mexico. His wife Inez moved to Santa Ana, Orange County, California with James W. and Oscar W., sometime before 1920. By 1930 she was living in Troutdale, Multnomah County, Oregon with son James W..

Oscar's World War I draft registration card shows his permanent address as 2058 N. Bush, Santa Ana, Orange County, California. The document shows his birth date as June 9, 1892.[413] The file goes on to say that he held the commission of 2nd Lieutenant in the New Mexico National Guard and had graduated from the New Mexico Military Institute. By 1930 he had married a woman named Hellen and he lived in Pasadena, Los Angeles County, California. Oscar died on August 21, 1953 at San Diego, California.

Ara married Wayne E. Phillips on January 12, 1920 at Medford,

Oregon. Wayne had been born on March 1, 1898 at Mabton, Yakima County, Washington. He died on June 4, 1968 at Baker, Baker County, Oregon.[414] The couple had at least two children:

- Frederick A.: Born October 21, 1921. Died April 1976.[415]
- Wayne E.: Born February 12, 1924. Died December 15, 2005.

Ara died in Baker, Oregon in 1974.[416] Her son Wayne E. died in 2005 in Klamath Falls, Oregon.[417]

James W. married Effie Madeline Doss. Effie was born on June 6, 1892 at Decatur, Alabama. They were married on June 16, 1920 at Salt Lake City, Utah. She died on March 23, 1994 at Gresham, Multnomah County, Oregon. The couple had at least three children:

- James Bailey: Born February 6, 1923. Died August 28, 1998 Columbia County, Oregon.[418]
- Richard S.: Born 1925 (last lived at San Carlos, California in 1993).
- Catherine I.: Born July 1928.

William James Chisum
Born August 7, 1864. Died June 12, 1956

William "Willie" or "Will" was born August 7, 1864 and died June 12, 1956 at Los Angeles, California. He married Perlina Price "Lina" Tucker (born about 1863) on July 3, 1887 at Dodge City, Kansas. The couple's only child was:

- Josephine Branch: Born July 25, 1889. Died March 23, 1942 at Los Angeles, California

Josephine Branch married Frank J. Howitt, who was seven years her senior, some time around 1918.[419] On the 1920 census they were shown as living in Los Angeles with her parents. By the 1930 census

Josephine was still using her married name, Howitt, but husband Frank was no longer living with the family and any further record of his whereabouts has eluded research thus far. The couple had one daughter:

- June E. Howitt:[420] Born July 2, 1920.[421]

It has been said that Walter and William James, known as "Will," did not get along. Will is claimed to have said that his brother "was too high living for him, and a Mason." Both left New Mexico about 1913, Will for Los Angeles and Walter for Medford, Oregon. Will thought that Walter would soon come down to San Diego. As teenage boys during much of the events leading up to, during, and after the Lincoln County War their lives and experiences would be fascinating reading for youngsters. Among Will Chisum's many recollections of his teenage years at the South Spring Ranch was an impromptu fishing adventure with Billy the Kid. The Kid had stopped at the ranch on March 8, 1878. As Will later recalled in an interview in 1952 with Allen A. Erwin the two of them "hauled them in" that day.

Mary Ann Chisum Johnson
Born March 3, 1795. Died March 23, 1853

Mary Ann Chisum was the aunt of John Simpson Chisum, daughter of Elizabeth Gibbons and James Chisum. She is buried in the Old City area of Paris, Texas in an unmarked grave. Mary Ann was the wife of John Johnson, the owner of Jensie and Phillip.

Mary Ann married John Johnson on October 22, 1810 in Overton County, Tennessee. They came to Lamar County, Texas in 1838. Her husband John obtained a land grant near downtown Paris and was the owner of the Paris Inn. She was the mother of ten daughters and one son: James M. Johnson, Sarah A. Johnson McDonald, Elizabeth

Johnson Turner, Lucinda Johnson, Nancy Chisum Johnson Wright, Rebecca Johnson Dodd, Lavina Johnson Thomas, Mary Ann Johnson Stell, Martha Ann Johnson Taylor, Margaret Johnson McCuistion, Frances Johnson Towery.

John Johnson
Born August 30, 1790. Died September 27, 1852

John Johnson was an early pioneer from Tennessee who accompanied the Chisum family to the Red River Valley of Texas. The families were close, with several links by marriage. A complete history of John Johnson and his family can be found in Skipper Steely's manuscript *Forty Seven Years*, which is on file at the Texas A&M University Gee Library at Commerce, Texas. John Johnson is buried in an unmarked grave although he may be buried in a stone crypt near his daughter, Sarah Johnson McDonald. Married Mary Ann Chisum.

Nancy Epps Chisum
Born January 22, 1822. Died October 5, 1868[422]

Nancy Epps married Benjamin Franklin Bourland on April 16, 1839. She was just seventeen years old. Benjamin had been born at Hopkins, Kentucky on March 14, 1818. He died on August 17, 1900 at Wolf City, Hunt County, Texas. The couple had eleven children:

- Lucinda M.: Born April 4, 1840. Died January 12, 1927 at Enid, Garfield County, Oklahoma.
- Nancy Matilda: Born January 14, 1842. Died September 27, 1923 at Fannin County, Texas
- Martha Isabell: Born May 1844. Died October 7, 1934 at Alameda, California.
- Cynthia Adelaide: Born July 28, 1846. Died December 18, 1885 at Blue Ridge, Texas.

- Benjamin Claiborne: Born April 1850. Died 1920 at Greenville, Texas.
- James Patrick: Born January 22, 1853. Died April 19, 1935 at Bristow, Oklahoma.
- Mary Ellen: Born May 1855. Died 1935 Bentonville, Arkansas.
- William Hampton: Born May 23, 1858. Died February 27, 1888 at Indian, Maine.
- Sarah: Born 1859. Died (Unknown)
- Laura Josephine: Born July 1860. Died September 19, 1907 at Shasta, California.
- Camilia Elliot: Born 1866. Died September 11, 1951 at Oklahoma City, Oklahoma.

Lucinda married Jonathan S. Whatley on October 31, 1958 at Fannin County, Texas. They had one son:

- James P. Whatley: Born (Unknown). Died August 11, 1924 at Oklahoma City, Oklahoma.

Martha Isabell married twice. Her first marriage was to William C. Hicks on September 4, 1860. William Hicks died in 1863. Her second marriage was to Francis Marion Thomas August 27, 1865. Martha and William Hicks had one son:

- Frank C.: Born September 4, 1861. Died 1933 at Tarrant County, Texas.

Her marriage to Francis Marion Thomas produced nine children:

- Albert Richard: Born February 8, 1867. Died 1940 Mills County, Texas.
- Oliver Claiborne: Born February 19, 1869. Died 1951 at Throckmorton County, Texas.
- Mary E.: Born August 4, 1871 . Died June 22, 1903 at Roger Mills, Oklahoma.
- Mattie Matilda: Born August 4, 1874. Died 1900 Dewey, Oklahoma.

- Thomas Marion: December 25, 1876. Died April 24, 1954 at Sacramento, California.
- Lou Ellen: Born May 9, 1878. Died November 18, 1931 at Redding, California.
- Sadie Myrtle: Born July 20, 1880. Died 1900 Roger Mills, Oklahoma.
- Stella Laura: Born June 6, 1882. Died 1920 Shasta County, California.
- Lillie Elliot: Born May 10, 1886. Died 1916 Shasta County, California.

William Claiborne "Tony" Chisum
Born October 30, 1849. Died June 5, 1931

John's half brother Tony Chisum married Sarah E. Wilhite in 1871.[423] Sarah had been born in Alabama in about 1848. The marriage produced one son:

- Ernest Claiborne: Born 1872. Died 1933. Married Annie E. Wilson. Son William Dowell born January 7, 1898 and died May 6, 1929. William Dowell married Rosa Lee Williams.

Tony's second marriage was to Amanda H. Wilhite in 1876. Amanda had also been born in Alabama, in about 1856, and was the sister of Sarah E. Wilhite. Both were the children of Claiborne L. and Sarah W. Wilhite of Morgan County, Alabama. The couple had three children:[424]

- Myrtle: Born about 1874.
- Effie: Born January 28, 1879.
- William Claiborne: Born May 2, 1883.

Robert Claiborne "Bob" Chisum
Born May 10, 1858. Died November 15, 1933

Robert Claiborne "Bob" married Emma B. Johnson on December

14, 1882 at Lamar, Texas. Emma had been born on June 30, 1862 and died October 25, 1911 at Mineral Wells, Texas. The couple had four children:

- William Claiborne "Tony": Born May 2, 1883. Died November 13, 1920 at Galveston, Texas.
- Cynthia: Born October 1883. Died (Unknown). Married a Wilkins in about 1903.
- Robbie L.: Born August 1888. Died (Unknown). Married a W.A. Thomas in about 1912.
- Bessie L.: Born May 1891. Died October 27, 1913.

Benjamin Franklin "Frank" Chisum
Born March 25, 1857. Died March 6, 1929

Like so many subjects related to John Chisum the contradictory data regarding Frank Chisum's background is perplexing. One commonly held account is that John Chisum bought Frank while on a cattle drive to Vicksburg where Chisum had driven stock to supply the Confederate forces.[425] In this fable Chisum is claimed to have traded a horse for the young boy who was four years old at the time. In *The Illustrated Life and Times of Billy the Kid* author Bob Boze Bell alleges that Chisum bought Frank from a man named Benjamin Franklin Daley at Boliver, Texas and that the cattle king paid $400 for the four year old boy. But most historians have relied on Dr. Hinton's findings, which claim that John Chisum bought Frank in about 1862 from Dr. Hiram Daily of Denton County, Texas, a boy crippled from birth who had been born into slavery.[426] Without question Dr. Hiram Daily and family owned a number of slaves. There were sixty-seven to be precise, ranging in age from infancy to one hundred years of age.[427] However, since the given names of the slaves were not listed on the census it is difficult to be certain as to which one is Frank. There are at least a half dozen entries that could be Frank.

It has also been claimed that Chisum paid $700 for Frank, and that he bought him when he was about ten years old.[428] Through the course of time Frank's year of birth has vacillated between 1853 and 1858, depending upon which document or census report one believes. Some have claimed that Chisum bought Frank as early as 1861, and that the boy was just four years old at the time.[429] Perhaps this confusion was brought about in part by the fact that when one examines the few documents that are available it seems, on first analysis, that there may have been two black men named Frank Chisum who lived at precisely the same time. The "other" Frank Chisum was born in 1858, which would have made him about four years old when Chisum purchased the authentic Frank from Dr. Daily. But after more digging the trail of both men seems to merge, but once again diverge. Given that census records of the day were notoriously inaccurate I have proceeded with the proposition that there was but one authentic Benjamin Franklin "Frank" Chisum and that he was probably born at Nashville, Tennessee on March 25, 1857 as he himself claimed on his marriage license in 1909.[430] As for the confusion concerning his year of birth, Frank himself has claimed literally every year beginning with 1853 through 1858 on one document or the other during the course of his lifetime. Frank was said to have been an intelligent man, therefore some of the inconsistencies with regard to his birth year are seemingly the result of transcription errors.

By the 1870 census Frank appears in Coleman County, Texas living with a fairly large group of Chisum cowboys.[431] On that census he is listed as being fifteen years old, which would have made his birth year 1855.

While most black men who were attached to a cattle operation at the time were either cooks or common laborers Frank was generally assigned chores similar to those that a family member would be given. Anecdotal stories allege that John Chisum had the youthful Frank sleep at the foot of his bed to keep the Cattle King's feet warm on cold nights. Frank later became John Chisum's horse wrangler. During the

Lincoln County War Frank feared for his life. Some have professed that Frank was Chisum's bodyguard, although the veracity of this claim comes under a great deal of scrutiny when one considers that John Chisum had a camp of armed cowboys surrounding him much of the time. The assertion that a Chisum relied on a crippled black man to escort him seems somewhat inconceivable.

Taking his total savings Frank bought two hundred yearling cattle and drove them to Texas in 1878 when the entire Chisum clan, who along with Samuel R. Coggin left the Pecos and took a larger herd north to the Canadian thereby escaping the wake of the hostilities of the Lincoln County War.[432] Frank turned his cattle loose on the Coggin and Wylie range in the panhandle and remained there until Coggin and Wylie sold out to the Matador outfit in 1881.[433] There seems to be no record of Frank on the census of 1880. Given that he was in the wide-open country of the Texas Panhandle at the time the absence of this record is not particularly perplexing.

Frank's virtues as a horse wrangler have been widely extolled. John Chisum's nephew Will referred to Frank as "...an all-around cowboy." Later in life he took up preaching, but as a consequence of his speech impediment Frank was not especially good at this new vocation. Some have claimed that Frank's stuttering became more pronounced when he was being questioned or interviewed and was pressed for information.[434] Frank remained extremely close to John Chisum until the cattle king's passing in 1884, seldom leaving his side. During Chisum's bout with smallpox in 1877 Frank remained at the cattle king's side until he had recovered. It is claimed that Chisum did the same for Frank when he eventually contracted the same illness.

Frank returned to the Pecos after Chisum's death and located at Roswell. He kept his livestock separate from that of James and Pitser Chisum, which proved to be a wise decision when considering the fate of John Chisum's ranch empire after his passing. Frank was one of the wealthiest African American cattle ranchers in the territory. He married the widow Jane Allen on March 10, 1909.[435]

Although the clerk who transcribed the records seemed to have a problem understanding what information went on which particular line of the requisite form when one notes that Jane's information is where Franks's should be, the record of this marriage seems to show that Frank's date of birth was March 25, 1857, as previously cited.[436] Jane brought three children to the marriage: Kelly Foster, Joel Foster and Nettie Nesby. The couple purchased property at 312 N. Michigan in Roswell. Although the marriage did not last Jane lived at that address until her death on October 8, 1945.[437]

Frank's second wife was Jennie Brown, who had also been previously married. They wed on August 12, 1920 and soon took up residence at 206 S. Kansas in Roswell.[438] Jennie died of the flu on January 10, 1923 and is buried at the South Park Cemetery in an unmarked grave.

Frank may have been married before he wed Jane Allen in 1909 however, giving him a total of three marriages in all. There is a record of a black man named Frank Chisum who married a black woman named Harriet Berry on January 17, 1884 at Falls, Texas. Harriet was the widow of Jiles Berry. All of the information seems to match up with our Frank Chisum in terms of location, time frame and associated detail. Frank had returned to Texas to be at the side of John Chisum close to the time of the cattle king's death. I have discussed this possible third marriage of Frank with other historians whom, although they find it intriguing, can offer no corroboration. In the interest of completeness I am offering the foregoing information, but can not fully attest to its accuracy.

Although Bob Boze Bell claimed in his book *The Illustrated Life and Times of Billy the Kid* that Frank sold his herd of cattle and moved to Los Angeles the document trail seems quite clear so far as proving that Frank remained in New Mexico for some time after the death of Jennie, then moved to Wichita Falls, Texas in 1928.[439] It has been claimed that Frank went to Texas to be near his brother Tom.

There does not seem to be a census record for Frank's brother Tom Chisum for 1910, 1920 or 1930. The last record shows him living at Decatur, Wise County, Texas during the 1900 census.[440] By then Tom had a wife and family.

Frank died at Wichita Falls on March 6, 1929 and was buried on March 8 at the Lakeview Cemetery.[441]

Frank Chisum, much like Addison Jones (born 1845 and died March 24, 1926) was but one of a large number of exceptional black cowboys of the era who are too often neglected in the annals of Old West history. Addison Jones's birthplace is uncertain, but he was probably born in Gonzales or Hays County, Texas. His cowboy skills led to him being recognized throughout west Texas and eastern New Mexico as "the most noted Negro cowboy that ever 'topped off' a horse".

Addison was often mentioned in memoirs and accounts of prominent cattlemen and cowboys who worked with him on the Littlefield Ranch (LFD). His skills at roping and breaking horses distinguished him among cowboys who usually led lives of anonymity. Add rose to the distinguished rank of range boss for the LFD outfit, and was known as one of the best cowhands on the Pecos.[442]

Tom Chisum
Born About 1855. Died After 1920

Tom Chisum was the younger brother of Frank, although depending upon which birth year one believes for Frank, Tom may have been his older brother. He was also bought by John Chisum in about 1862 from Dr. Hiram Daily of Denton County, Texas. There seems to be little in the way of reliable information about Tom. Records of his birth appear to confirm that he was born in Texas some time around 1855.[443] Some former slaves selected the surnames of their former owners while others did not. Some later changed their last names, making accurate research all the more challenging. Thus, after Chisum purchased Tom in 1862 there is virtually no record of the man until he appears on the 1900 census.[444] By that time Tom was married and had seven children. Due to the scarcity of reliable information about Tom Chisum I hesitate to speculate further with regard to his family or legacy.

Giles Chisum
Born About 1842. Died About 1920

Giles Chisum was born in Texas in about 1842. He made the cattle drive to Vicksburg with John Chisum and soon after accompanied him to New Mexico on the drive of August 1866. He may have also been with the earlier drives of 1864 through 1866 but no record has been discovered as yet to confirm this.

Giles returned to Texas, and by 1870 he was living in Denton County where he had married a woman named Almyra Hembry from Missouri.[445] They had one son named Jimmy.[446] By 1880 the family had increased to include four more children; Mary, Thomas, Jennie and Ella. There is no further record of Jimmy.[447] Based on the fact that he was one year old in 1870 and gone by 1880, the presumption is that he died during one of the epidemics that were so rampant in Texas at the time.

NOTES

1. Hinton, Harwood P. Jr.. "John Simpson Chisum: 1877–1884." New Mexico Historical Review Volume XXXI. July 1956. Number 3.
2. John Chisum's cattle trail was not actually named. Although established earlier than Goodnight's route, it generally followed the same path as the Goodnight-Loving Trail that was used from about 1866 on.
3. Trickham is the oldest community in Coleman County and is located on Mukewater Creek and Ranch Road 1176 in the southeastern part of the county, twelve miles southeast of Santa Anna. There were earlier settlers in the region, like Charlie McCain, Dave Upton, and Jake Dofflemyer who were all killed by Indians in the 1860s and 1870s. Trickham was not established until 1879, when the settlement acquired its first post office. By 1884 Trickham had grown to boast a population of seventy five and had several stores, a hotel, two cotton gins, two churches, a blacksmith shop, steam planing mills, and a school. Bruce, Leona Banister. 1966. *Trickham, Texas: A Neighborly Chronicle.* Salado, Texas: Anson Jones Press.
4. Chronologically speaking, reference to William Bonney by his nickname "Billy the Kid" in an incident that occurred in the spring of 1880 may stretch at the bounds of historical accuracy. Frederick Nolan asserts that it was not until the end of his last full year of life that the byname "Billy the Kid" was used. Nolan, Frederick. 2007. *Tascosa.* Lubbock: Texas Tech University Press. p 46
5. Jesse Chisholm was an Indian trader, guide, and interpreter. He was born in the Hiwassee region of Tennessee around 1805 or 1806. His father, Ignatious Chisholm, was of Scottish ancestry, son of John D. Chisholm of the early Watauga Settlement in eastern Tennessee, and had worked as a merchant and slave trader in the Knoxville area in the 1790s. It is believed that Jesse is related to John Chisum (see Appendix I). During the late 1820s Jesse Chisholm moved to the Cherokee Nation and settled near Fort Gibson in what is now eastern Oklahoma. Chisholm became a trader and in 1836 married Eliza Edwards, daughter of James Edwards, who ran a trading post in what is now Hughes County, Oklahoma. He was active in Texas for nearly twenty years. In 1865, Chisholm and James R. Mead established a trading post at Council Grove on the North Canadian near the site of present Oklahoma City. The route later became the Chisholm Trail, which for

the most part was not in Texas. The trail connected Texas ranches with markets on the railroad in Kansas. Chisholm died of food poisoning at Left Hand Spring, near the site of present Geary, Oklahoma, on 4 April 1868.

6. McCoy, Joseph G.. 1940. *Historic Sketches of the Cattle Trade of the West and Southwest.* Glendale California. pp 339–340

7. Burns, Walter Noble. 1953. *The Saga of Billy the Kid.* New York: Konecky & Konecky. p 12

8. Steely also describes Chisum as being five feet eight inches in height.
Steely, Skipper. *Forty Seven Years.* Unpublished Manuscript. Texas A & M University Gee Library. Commerce Texas. p 672

9. William J. Chisum to Harwood P. Hinton (cited hereafter WC to HPH), February 1, 1954. Tape Numbers 8 and 9. From recordings of interviews between William Chisum and Allen A. Erwin during the summer of 1952 in the Arizona Pioneers' Historical Society, Tucson (cited hereafter as Tape).

10. Hinton. *John Simpson Chisum.* p 183
It is claimed that Chisum did carry a Winchester carbine in his saddle scabbard and a Colt revolver in a holster on his saddle horn.

11. WC to HPH. Tape. March 22, 1954

12. Ward, C.F.. "John S. Chisum, Pioneer Cattleman of the Valley." *Roswell New Mexico Daily Record.* October 7, 1937

13. Hinton. *John Simpson Chisum.* p 180

14. Harwood P. Hinton to Clifford R. Caldwell (cited hereafter as HPH to CRC) September 23, 2009

15. Klasner, Lily 1972. *My Girlhood Among Outlaws.* Tucson: University of Arizona. p 71

16. Mary V. Daniel to HPH, March 27, 1954. Miss Daniel's father, Captain J. M. Daniel, was a close friend of the Chisum brothers.

17. Klasner. *My Girlhood Among Outlaws.* p 71

18. *Kansas City Livestock Indicator.* March 7, 1889

19. Dobie, J. Frank. 1964. *Cow People.* Boston: Little Brown & Company. pp 261–262

20. The statement of Mr. J. Smith Lea in regard to John Chisum was in the possession of Mrs. J. E. Balmer, Wahiawa, Oahu, Hawaii at the time of Hinton's manuscript in the New Mexico Historical Review Volume XXXI. July 1956. Number 3. It is referenced therein by Hinton as Number 3.

21. Cox, James. 1895. *Historical and Biographical Record of the Cattle Industry.* New York: Antiquarian Press, Ltd.

22. Traditional usage of the term equates the "free-range" with "unfenced," and with the implication that there were no herdsman or cowboys keeping the livestock together or managing the animals in any organized or routine way.

23. The "home ranch" stands in contrast to an outlying camp, cow camp or line camp, which are all temporary shelters from which cowboys tended stock. The term "home ranch" lends an air of stability to the otherwise speculative business of free ranging cattle.

24. In 1867, two inventors tried adding points to smooth wire in an effort to make a

more effective deterrent for containing livestock. One example was not practical to manufacture, the other experienced financial problems. In 1868, Michael Kelly invented a practical wire with points that was used in quantity until 1874. Joseph F. Glidden of Dekalb, Illinois invented and patented a successful barbed wire in the form we recognize today. Glidden fashioned barbs and placed them at intervals along a slick wire, then twisted another wire around the first to hold the barbs in place. The U.S. Patent Office granted nine patents for improvements to wire fencing to American inventors, beginning with Michael Kelly in November 1868 and ending with Joseph Glidden in November 1874.

25. The term "live water" refers to an active flowing stream, creek, spring or river. It is in contrast to water held in some form of a man made stock tank or a naturally formed catch basin.

26. Nolan, Frederick. 1998. *The West of Billy the Kid.* Norman: University of Oklahoma. p 75

27. Steely. *Forty Seven Years.* p 376

28. U.S. Census Year 1830. Census Place Hardeman, Tennessee. Roll 176, p 374.

29. As an example, James McIver of North Carolina signed over 1,280 acres north west of Bolivar on the branch of the Hatchie River called Clover Creek.

30. Steely. *Forty Seven Years.* p 379

31. Ibid

32. Steely. *Forty Seven Years.* pp 373–374

33. Prater, Stephen B.. 2009. *Prater/Walker Family Tree.* Unpublished Manuscript. p 41

34. Ibid. pp 374–380

35. Clark, Pat B.. 1937. *The History of Clarksville and Old Red River County.* Dallas: Mathis Van Nort & Co.. p 1
Red River County is perhaps the "mother county of Texas," or so it has been claimed. The first Anglo-Saxon settlement in Texas, begun in 1814, was in Red River County on what is now the west border of Bowie and the east border of Red River County. The Stephen F. Austin settlement began in 1824, ten years later than Red River County. Red River County at one time included what are now Bowie, Cass, Titus and Franklin counties, and a portion of Hopkins and Marion Counties, plus all of Delta, Lamar and Fannin. Also see Timmons, Bascom N.. 1948. *Garner of Texas, A Personal History.* Harper & Brothers. p 2

36. Steely. *Forty Seven Years.* p 374. Lamar County would later be formed from a portion of Red River County.

37. Adams, Clarence S. and Brown, Tom E..1972. *Three Ranches West.* New York: Carlton Press

38. Steely. *Forty Seven Years.* p 374. Also Steely Collection. *Ruth Milligan Papers Notebook.* p 57. Steely also references Hinton. *Chisum.* p 84

39. In *Forty Seven Years* Steely notes that there is a story claiming that the Chisums spent some time living near Bois d' Arc Creek in present day Fannin County before finally settling at Paris.

40. Lamar County Texas Deed Book 106. p 246

41. Taylor, Thomas Ulvan.1936. *The Chisholm Trail and Other Routes*. San Antonio: Printed for Frontier Times. p 510

42. Steely. *Forty Seven Years*. p 380

43. Wilbarger, J.W.. 1889. *Indian Depredations in Texas*. Austin: Hutchings Printing House. p 391, p 404

44. Steely. *Lamar Papers*. IV. Pt. 1. p 276

45. Strickland, Rex W.. *Anglo-American Activities in Northeastern Texas, 1803–1845*. (Ph.D. dissertation, University of Texas, 1937) p 327

46. Steely. *Forty Seven Years*. p 418

47. There is some dissension concerning "Pinhook" (sometimes spelled Pin Hook) being the original name of the town of Paris. In Steely. *Forty Seven Years*, p 385 Steely makes reference to "Pinhook" as being the site of the town of Faulkner. In the end notes section of *The Last Indian Massacre* chapter on p 448, note 33, Steely mentions that Nancy Wright has referred to Paris as "Pinhook." Other sources, including regional historians, frequently refer to the town of Paris as having formerly been named Pinhook. The name "Pin Hook" was applied in the late 1830s to the area where Paris was platted. The name may have been borrowed by the present Pin Hook community after Paris became the Lamar county seat in 1844.

48. Mrs. C. L. Taylor, a descendant of the Chisums, states that John was born ". . . about ___miles west of Cloverport," which is north of Bolivar, Tennessee. Mrs. C. L. Taylor to HPH, February 16, 1954. Mrs. J. M. Pipkin, a second cousin to John Chisum, wrote of his early boyhood, the nickname, his visits to Tennessee, and in general had collected quite a bit of Chisum genealogy prior to her death. Mrs. J. M. Pipkin to Roy W. Black, October 17, 1939, in personal files of Roy W. Black, Bolivar, Tennessee.

49. Klasner. *My Girlhood Among Outlaws*. p 231

50. Lamar County has had six courthouses. The first in 1841. The second through sixth were built in Paris in 1844, 1847, 1873, 1897 and finally 1917.

51. *The Paris Press*. September 16, 1878

52. U.S. Census Year 1850. Census Place Precinct 6, Lamar, Texas. Roll M432_912. p 289. Image 156. John R. Craddock was an early pioneer of the Red River Valley and was born in South Carolina in 1808. He married Louisa E. who was born about 1823 in Tennessee.

53. John S. Chisum to James Vernon, September 29, 1851. In the personal files of Roy W. Black, Bolivar, Tennessee.

54. Steely. *Forty Seven Years*. p 484

55. Klasner. *My Girlhood Among Outlaws*. pp 238–240

56. Hinton. *John Simpson Chisum*.

57. Steely. *Forty Seven Years*. p 485. Steely implies that John Chisum's assistant Jacob Long actually did most of the work.

58. Ibid. Jacob Long was elected next, after Chisum, and served until 1862.

59. Ibid. Steely. p 485

60. Klasner. *My Girlhood Among Outlaws.* p 238

61. Ibid

62. Steely. *Neville Papers.* p 144

63. Adams/Brown. *Three Ranches West.* pp 37–52

64. Klasner. *My Girlhood Among Outlaws.* p 238

65. Adams/Brown. *Three Ranches West*

66. Ibid. p 239

67. Klasner. *My Girlhood Among Outlaws.* pp 5–6

68. Mary V. Daniel to Harwood P. Hinton, March 27, 1954. Miss Daniel's father, Captain J. M. Daniel, was a close friend of the Chisum brothers.

69. Klasner. *My Girlhood Among Outlaws.* p 232

70. Lily Klasner was born on the Texas frontier in 1862. She journeyed on foot to New Mexico with her father after the Civil War. After her father was murdered when she was just a young girl Lily strapped on a six gun. Klasner was a friend of John Chisum as well as many of the legendary outlaws and lawmen of the era. She died in 1946 and left behind a wonderful collection of manuscripts about her life.

71. Turner Edmundson is mentioned in the "First Church of Paris," where Edmundson and his wife are noted as having made a donation of land for the Shady Grove Camp Ground to a Methodist congregation.

72. Steely. *Forty Seven Years.* p 381. Steely mentions Jeff's place of death as Puerto de Lugo. Note correction to Puerto de Luna.

73. *Paris News.* December 31, 1936. "Backward Glances." Neville. It has been claimed that John Chisum resigned his post as clerk in 1854. Neville's research shows that Chisum did not resign as has been stated by others. Chisum may have spent much time in Denton County in 1854.

74. Some accounts claim that Chisum's partner was Oliver Keep, but most agree on Fowler as his partner.

75. Steely. *Forty Seven Years.* p 485

76. U.S. Census Year 1850. Census Place Representative District 3, Orleans, Louisiana. Roll M432_234. p 225. Image 298

77. Information regarding the partnership between Chisum and Fowler can be found in the following reference: Bates, Edward F.. 1918. *History and Reminiscences of Denton County.* Denton, Texas: McNitzky Printing Company. p 305. Bates came to Denton County in 1851. Also see Cox. *Historical and Biographical Record.* p 300 and *The Standard,* May 5, 1855. The Chisum patent, which states that he settled in Denton County in February 1855, is recorded in the General Land Office at Austin, Texas. See Abstract No. 278, Preemption Certificate No. 156, 3-16-59, Patent No. 39, Vol. 24, Fannin 3rd Class, File No. 2396.

78. Klasner. *My Girlhood Among Outlaws.* p 234

79. Wallis, George W.. 1964. *Cattle King of the Staked Plains.* Denver: Adams. p 53

80. Taylor, Taylor U.. *Trailing John Chisum to New Mexico,* Frontier Times, Volume 13 Number 8, June 1936. p 422. Taylor claims that Chisum took some form of a claim on land in Denton County in 1853 but did not move his herd there until 1854.

81. On June 6, 1849 a camp on the bank of the Trinity River was established and named Camp Worth in honor of General William Jenkins Worth (born March 1, 1794 and died May 7, 1849). In August 1849 the camp was moved to the north-facing bluff which overlooked the mouth of the Clear Fork. The camp was officially named Fort Worth on November 14, 1849 after the recently deceased General Worth. Although Indians were still a threat in the area a new line of forts was built further west, the army evacuated Fort Worth on 17 September 1853.

82. The site of Fort Belknap is about three miles south of Newcastle, Young County. Fort Belknap was the northern anchor of a chain of forts founded to protect the Texas frontier from the Red River to the Rio Grande. It was a post without defensive works. From it troops pursued raiding bands of Indians. The fort was named for Civil War hero Captain Augustus Belknap (born March 19, 1841 and died June 22, 1889). After the war Belknap was a successful businessman and prominent local figure in San Antonio, Texas.

83. The Old Chisholm Trail, most of which is not in Texas, ran through Indian Territory into Kansas and was founded by Jesse Chisholm. Jesse Chisholm was the son of Ignatius Chisholm and a Cherokee woman (Rogers), and who may be related to John Simpson Chisum through their common great-great-great grandfather. Historian Donald E. Worchester writes of the Chisholm Trail…"The Scot-Cherokee Jesse Chisholm began hauling trade goods to Indian camps about 220 miles south of his post near modern Wichita in 1864. At first the route was simply referred to as the Trail, the Kansas Trail, the Abilene Trail, or McCoy's Trail. Though it was originally applied only to the trail north of the Red River, Texas cowmen soon gave Chisholm's name to the entire trail from the Rio Grande to central Kansas. The earliest known references to the Chisholm Trail in print were in the *Kansas Daily Commonwealth* of May 27 and October 11, 1870. On April 28, 1874, the Denison, Texas, *Daily News* mentioned cattle going up *the famous Chisholm Trail*."

84. Probate Records of Lamar County, Texas. *Will of John Johnson*. filed December 19, 1853. Approved December 27, 1853. This document reflects the spelling of the name of the slave girl called Jensie as "Jency". Steely. Chisum. Denton Collection. *Dragon Notebook*. 14 - 4 - 116

85. Adams / Brown. *Three Ranches West*. p 83

86. Ibid. Spelled Philip in the original probate records of John Johnson.

87. Ibid

88. Ibid. Steely. Chisum. Denton Collection. *Dragon Notebook*. 14 - 4 - 116. Cooke County. Deed Book 4. p 70, p 105.

89. Mary Ann Johnson Stell was born December 14, 1827 and died June 1873. She married James W. Stell about 1847 in Tennessee.

90. HPH to CRC. September 23, 2009

91. The party from Texas was believed to be in search of gold. By the mid 1850s the California Gold Rush had all but ended. In March 1858 some Californians discovered placer dust and nuggets in paying quantities on the Fraser River near

Fort Hope in British Columbia. Hill's Bar, a mile and a half south of Fort Yale, was soon named after the first man who found gold there and it became the longest worked bar on the lower Fraser.

92. Abraham Rhine was born in Germany in 1825. The precise identity of Abraham's brother Henry Rhine is unclear. It is believed that he made the trip to California and died before 1870. U.S. Census Year 1850. Census Place Precinct 6, Lamar, Texas. Roll M432_912. p 291. Image 160

93. Steely Collection. Joggles Wright Collection. *Milligan Notebook*. 30. Also see Steely. *Neville Papers*. p 535

94. *Fort Worth Press*. October 6, 1963

95. Anderson, George B.. 1907. *History of New Mexico: Its Resources and People*, Volume 2. Los Angeles New York Chicago: Pacific Publishing Company. p 1025

96. Lamar County, Texas, *Record of Marks and Brands of Animals Volume I - 1848–1894*, 1852. There it states *swallow fork and under bit in left and upper half cross (crop) in right*.

97. This Dick Fiveash, whose family had come to Texas from Louisiana, was born in 1862, and therefore was not a first hand witness to any of Chisum's operations at Boliver. He was not related to E.H. Fiveash of Cherokee who was born in Georgia in 1820 and had come to Texas in 1846.

98. Even before the elimination of the Apache threat, white ranchers were moving into the Guadalupe Mountains. Felix McKittrick acquired land at the mouth of the canyon that now bears his name. The canyon is located near the Texas state line

99. J. Evetts Haley Library. Robert N. Mullin Collection. RNM 763

100. The Coggins brothers, Moses J. (Mody) Coggin and Samuel Richardson Coggin were born in North Carolina. The family moved to Tennessee in 1836 and to Mississippi in 1837. In 1851 Moses and Samuel moved to the vicinity of Rusk, Texas, where they established a business hauling freight to Bell County. In 1854 they purchased their first cattle herd and moved to Bell County. After losing about half the herd, they moved to Brown County in 1857. The brothers acquired large landholdings in Brown and Coleman counties and increased their herd. They moved cattle to Home Creek in Coleman County in 1860. After the war the Coggins continued to be plagued by Indians and white cattle thieves. When the trailing industry began on a large scale in 1866, the two cattlemen planned to market their own herds at Kansas railroads. By 1870 the firm had also contracted neighbors cattle for delivery to the railheads. The Coggins sometimes developed and sold an entire herd to one buyer, thus avoiding the long drive. W. Clay Parks, a Coleman County rancher, formed a partnership with the Coggins in 1868. Their combined herds numbered over 25,000 head-a total ranking them among the largest operators in the state. In 1871 the three partners lost 7,000 cattle to Indian depredations, a loss of $175,000. Continued losses in Concho County compelled the Coggins to move back to Brown County to reestablish their herd. During the 1870s they engaged in money making cattle arrangements with John S. Chisum and Charles Goodnight who were two of the state's most reputable cattlemen.

In 1878 Coggin cattle also ranged near the Tongue River in southwestern Motley County and later in Dickens, Runnels, and Mitchell counties. They found themselves involved in the fence cutting wars of the 1880s in Brown and Coleman counties. Though cattlemen first, the Coggin brothers found farming profitable and raised wheat on their acreage along Clear Creek in west central Brown County. In 1888 they moved their Three Diamond Ranch to Terlingua Creek in Brewster County. Although the venture was profitable, the Coggins left the Big Bend country in 1895 and leased land in Collingsworth, Wheeler, Donley, Gray, and King counties. In the early 1890s they pastured cattle in Indian Territory. Sam and Mody Coggin never retired from the ranching business. They had ranched over much of Texas and what is now New Mexico and Oklahoma. Coggin cattle had grazed the Cross Timbers, the Concho country, the Panhandle, the Big Bend, and Indian Territory, as well as parts of Kansas, Colorado, and Montana. After 1903 the brothers largely confined their ranching to Brown County. They operated their home ranch in the southwestern part of that county and by 1899 had added the 4,400-acre Wright Ranch to their holdings. By 1902 their Grape Creek Ranch along the Colorado River in Runnels, Concho, and Coleman counties had expanded to nearly 20,000 acres. On March 31, 1881, the Coggin brothers established the banking firm of Coggin Brothers and Company. They became partners in a successful mercantile business in 1882.

EXCERPTS FROM HANDBOOK OF TEXAS BIBLIOGRAPHY: Frank Collinson. 1963. *Life in the Saddle.* Mary Whatley Clarke . Norman: University of Oklahoma Press. James Cox. 1894. *Historical and Biographical Record of the Cattle Industry* 2 volumes. St. Louis: Woodward and Tiernan Printing. Havins, Thomas Robert. 1958. *Something about Brown: A History of Brown County, Texas.* Brownwood, Texas: Banner Printing. Paddock, Buckley B.. 1911. *History of Central and Western Texas* 2 volumes. Chicago: Lewis.

101. In 1855 Camp Colorado was temporarily established at a site near that is now Ebony, in Mills County. In August 1856 Troops A and F and United States Cavalry under Major Van Dorn moved the camp to Mukewater Creek about six miles north of the Colorado River. The post was later moved in July 1857 to a site about twenty-two miles north to Jim Ned Creek.

102. William "Bill" Franks was born Oklahoma Territory December 15, 1849 and died October 15, 1896 at Oakwood, Leon County, Texas.

103. Emory Peter had a crippled hand and required the assistance of Bill Franks to manage the strenuous duties of the store. Some have mistakenly reported Emory Peter as having been John Chisum's brother-in-law. This error appears, for example, in *The History of Coleman County and Its People,* 2 volumes, San Angelo: Anchor 1985 as well as Adams/Brown. *Three Ranches West.*

104. George Washington Teague was born February 22, 1855 and died February 20, 1944. U.S. Census Year 1880. Census Place Precinct 6, Fayette, Texas. Roll T9_1303. Family History Film 1255303. p 211.3000. Enumeration District 61.

105. Gay, Beatrice Grady. 1936. *Into the Setting Sun .* San Antonio. p 83

106. Such gruesome use of human skin is not without precedent. Human skin was often used for bookbinding until about the 18th century. Scalps were taken in wars between the Visigoths, the Franks and the Anglo-Saxons as early as the 9th century according to the writings of Abbott Emmanuel H. D. Domenech.

107. Lamar County. *Probate Box 53.* File 160

108. Steely Collection. *Neville Papers.* 173. Mary Daniel Papers. 413. From Steely. *Forty Seven Years.* p 486

109. Volume D, p 516 of the probate records of Lamar County, Texas showed the estate to contain 640 acres in Lamar Co., 640 acres in Hunt County 1,280 acres in the Prairie Farm tract of Lamar County and 10 acres on Aud's Creek in Lamar County as well as a number of slaves valued at $15,000.

110. Ibid. *Mary Daniel Papers.* p 417. Mary left notes saying she understood that one evening James Chisum poked a pistol through Cynthia's window and shot her in the shoulder.

111. U.S. Census Year 1860. Census Place Denton County, Texas. Microfilm Copy in State Archives, Austin, Texas. Hinton. *John Simpson Chisum.* p 186

112. Steely Collection. *Neville Papers.* p 168. Steely writes that Ed Gibbons contracted cancer in 1879, and while still mayor of Paris committed suicide by shooting himself at his home in the fall of 1880.

113. This, of course, in spite of the obvious difference. The hired help were free to go, while the slaves were not.

114. Elisha M. Pease was elected to the first two of his three terms as governor in 1853 and 1855. He became provisional governor in 1867. Pease was the first governor to inhabit the present Texas governor's mansion.

115. James M. Norris (born 1819 and died 1874) assumed command of a new ranger battalion on January 29, 1862. The forty two-year-old former lawyer soon learned that he could not solve discipline problems by court-martialing all of his troops. His patrol routine proved disastrous. Historian William Curry Holden writes of Norris that on January 29, 1862, he was appointed by Governor Lubbock as colonel of the Frontier Regiment but resigned the command in 1863. Norris's tenure as commander of the regiment was not memorable. He lacked experience in Indian fighting and had serious discipline problems with the troops and junior officers. The harshest criticism leveled against Norris concerned his failure to take an aggressive stand in frontier defense. He later practiced law in Burleson, Coryell, and McLennan counties.

116. Adams/Brown. *Three Ranches West.* p 143

117. Borland, Margaret papers. 1858–1879. University of Texas at Austin. Dolph Briscoe Collection

118. Texas State Archives. Austin, Texas: *Texas State Troops,* Call Number 401-33. Caldwell Files. *Chisum*

119. U.S. Census Year 1870. Census Place Precinct 1, Denton, Texas. Roll M593_1582. p 128. Image 256. Giles Chisum was born in Texas about 1850. He is listed on the 1880 Census for Denton, Denton County, Texas as black. His wife is listed as

Almyra, or "Mira". Her maiden name is believed to have been Henry or Hembry. At the time of the 1880 census the household contained several children including Mary, Thomas, Ella and Jennie.

120. Almira Peter McKittrick was born January 18, 1834 and died on November 3, 1860. She is buried at the IOOF Cemetery in Denton, Texas.

121. Hunter, John M.. 1925. *The Trail Drivers of Texas*. Nashville: Cokesbury Press. p 952

122. Texas State Archives. Austin: *Texas State Troops*. Call Number 401-33. Also see Caldwell Files. *Chisum*

123. Steely. *Forty Seven Years*. p 671

124. Adams/Brown. *Three Ranches West*. pp 158–159

125. Often incorrectly identified as Benjamin Franklin "Frank" Chisum. See Bell, Bob Boze. 1996. *The Illustrated Life and Times of Billy the Kid*. Phoenix: TriStarBoze Publications.

126. Giles Chisum was born in Texas in about 1842. By 1870 he was living in Denton County, Texas and had married a woman named Almyra Hembry. The couple had one son named Jimmy. U.S. Census Year 1870. Census Place Precinct 1, Denton, Texas. Roll M593_1582. p 128. Image 256.
By 1880 the family had increased to include Mary, Thomas, Jennie and Ella. There is no further record of Jimmy. U.S. CensusYear 1880. Census Place Denton, Denton, Texas. Roll T9_1300. Family History Film 1255300. p 31.2000. Enumeration District 102.

127. Steely. *Forty Seven Years*. p 671

128. James M. and Martha (Bridges) Waide came to Bolivar in 1861 and were farmers and horse raisers. They occupied land that was once a part of the Chisum range in Lamar County.

129. John S. Chisum to James Waide, March 7, 1862. In the personal files of Joe D. Waide, Denton, Texas.

130. Evidence and frequent reference shows that Chisum left Jensie and the children in Bonham about 1863. Clarke, Mary W.. 1984. *John Simpson Chisum*. Austin. p 117.

131. Petersen, Paul R.. 2007. *Quantrill in Texas: The Forgotten Campaign*. Nashville: Cumberland House Publishing. p 131

132. Felix McKittrick military service records. National Park Service. U.S. Civil War Soldiers, 1861–1865. Civil War Soldiers and Sailors System.

133. Bent's Fort was a trading post for mountain trappers and Indians dealing in furs and buffalo robes. It became a point of supply, a social center, a place of refuge and safety, a rest and relaxation point for every white man and many Indians. Fur traders William and Charles Bent built the Fort in 1833 and it boomed until 1848. In 1859, William sold the fort to the U.S. Army.

134. Probably William B. "Jim" Spoon who was born 1847 in Texas and had come from Dallas County.

135. Smith, Sidney W.. 1927. *From the Cow Camp to the Pulpit*. Cincinnati: The Christian Lead Corporation. p 89. Included as a separate chapter in this book are the

personal recollections of Matt C. Smith, Sr., a forebear of the author. They concern his period of association with John Chisum, who was a relative, during the 1860s.

136. Bates, Edward F..1918. *History and Reminiscences of Denton County.* Denton: McNitzky Printing Company. p 305. Note that Chisum's agreement with Fowler was of a ten year duration, and had been formed in 1854. It now being 1864 the agreement had run it course, thus the use of the term "expired" in lieu of "severed" might have been a better choice of wording.

137. Haley, J. Evetts.1936. *Charles Goodnight, Cowman and Plainsman.* Norman: University of Oklahoma. p 232

138. Ibid. Note that Chisum and Folwer were investors in the packing house business and not partners per se. As cited previously, John Chisum was a party to many business arrangements through the remainder of his lifetime but he never again formed a partnership with anyone that was structured along the lines of his 1854 arrangement with Fowler.

139. Keleher, William A.. 2008. *The Fabulous Frontier.* Santa Fe: Sunstone Press. p 58. Keleher, records the date at 1865, but goes on to say that Chisum had brought 10,000 head of cattle by then. The initial, smaller drives began as early as 1864.

140. After Jeff Chisum killed Turner Edmundson in 1863 it is believed that he immediately left Paris, Lamar County and removed to Denton. From Denton he traveled to New Mexico with his brothers. It is unclear if he participated in their first drive.

141. HPH to CRC. September 23, 2009

142. Klasner. *My Girlhood Among Outlaws.* p 72

143. Cramer, Dudley T..1996. *The Pecos Ranchers in the Lincoln County War.* Oakland, California: Branding Iron Press. p 42. Tom and James Patterson had established themselves as government agents at Bosque Grande as early as perhaps 1864.

144. Haley. *Charles Goodnight.* pp 198–199

145. Klasner. *My Girlhood Among Outlaws.* p 235

146. James Patterson was born in Ohio in 1833. Little is known of his early life. Patterson first came to New Mexico about 1860. He may have been in the U.S. Army prior to the Civil War. Patterson became a cattle rancher, driver and merchant in both Texas and New Mexico. He later moved on to Colorado, but returned to New Mexico where he was killed on August 2, 1892 by an employee of his mine, the Western Belle.

147. Klasner. *My Girlhood Among Outlaws.* p 235. Also see Steely. *Forty Seven Years.* p 672

148. Nelson, Morgan. "First among the first." *Wild West History Journal.* Volume II Number 5. October 2009. pp 3–5. Also, for information on Robert Kelsey Wylie see note 217.

149. Ibid

150. Translates from Spanish to "round wood"

151. Redfield, George B.. "Chisum Makes a Trail." *The New Mexico Sentinel.* December 8, 1939

152. U.S. Census Year 1860. Census Place Denton, Texas. Roll M653_1292. p 451. Image 378. John Chisum named the boy "Frank Chisum." After the slaves were emancipated near the end of the Civil War Frank elected to remain with Chisum and became a capable and trusted hand and frequent companion.

153. Frank Chisum was crippled from birth and walked with his right shoulder hunched forward. His handicap did not seem to impair his effectiveness as a cowboy however. His full name was Benjamin Franklin Chisum. Frank was born in about 1858 while still under the ownership of the Daily Family.

154. Frank's younger brother is believed to have been Thomas Jefferson Chisum. Some accounts have Dr. Daily's surname spelled incorrectly as Daley. See Bell. *Illustrated Life*

155. Adams/Brown. *Three Ranches West.* pp 279–288

156. Castle Gap is located about 12 miles north-northeast from Horsehead Crossing. The mile-long break in the ridge of the Castle Mountains requires that the two peaks be given separate names. King Mountain is on the southern end, while Castle Mountain is the northern peak. Cabasa de Vaca passed through the gap in 1500. The Comanche Trail to Mexico passed through the gap, as did the Butterfield Stage route and the Goodnight-Loving Trail (also called the Western Cattle Trail).

157. Adams/Brown. *Three Ranches West.* pp 279–288

158. Horsehead Crossing is twelve miles northwest of Girvin in northeastern Pecos County. It was one of the few fordable points on the Pecos River in the 1800s. Steep, muddy banks, unpredictable currents, and quicksand were natural barriers to travel. After long treks across the surrounding desert, thirsty animals were often poisoned by the briny river water or became hopelessly mired in the quicksand at the crossing.

159. HPH to CRC. September 23, 2009

160. Located along the banks of the Pecos River, Carlsbad, New Mexico was originally christened the town of Eddy on September 15, 1888 and organized as a municipal corporation in 1893.

161. Taylor, Thomas U. "Trailing John Chisum to New Mexico." *Frontier Times.* Volume 13 Number 8 June 1936. p 426

162. Steely. *Forty Seven Years.* p 672

163. Ibid. p 671

164. Cramer. *The Pecos Ranchers in the Lincoln County War.* pp 50–51

165. Ibid. p 52

166. Mehren, Lawrence L.. "Scouting for Mescaleros: The Price Campaign of 1873." *Journal of the Southwest.* 1968. Mehren claims that Loving's attackers were Apache Indians.
Utley, Robert M.. 2002. *Lone Star Justice: The First Century of the Texas Rangers.* Oxford: Oxford University Press. p 149. Utley claims that the attackers were Comanche Indians.

167. Translates from Spanish to "large forest" it is located about thirty five miles north

of Roswell on the Pecos River.

168. Anderson. *History of New Mexico: its resources and people, Volume 2.* p 1023

169. Although there are several versions of how unbranded cattle came to be known as "mavericks," nearly all of them involve Samuel A. Maverick. Maverick was a native of South Carolina who moved to Texas in 1835 and moved his family to the Gulf Coast in Matagorda County between 1844 and 1847. Maverick had apparently accepted a herd of 400 cattle instead of being repaid a $1,200 loan. When the family returned to San Antonio, he left the animals in the care of a black family. The cattle were neglected, and many of the calves were not branded. Residents soon began to refer to any unbranded cow as "one of Maverick's." Soon any unbranded cattle were claimed as "Maverick's" and branded. By 1857 people around San Antonio were referring to unbranded cattle over one year in age as "mavericks." Unbranded calves under that age and still suckling were considered to be the property of whoever owned the mother. Dary, David. 1981. *Cowboy Culture: A Saga of Five Centuries.* New York: Knopf

170. Haley. *Charles Goodnight, Cowman and Plainsman.* p 233

171. Nelson, Morgan. "First among the first." *Wild West History Association.* Journal Volume II Number 5. October 2009. p 3

172. Haley. *Charles Goodnight, Cowman and Plainsman*

173. Haley Memorial Library & History Center. From the *Dallas Herald* . Appeared on May 16, 1868, May 23, 1868, May 30, 1868, June 6, 1868 and June 13, 1868.

174. U.S. Census Year 1870. Census Place Precinct 3, Lincoln, New Mexico Territory. Roll M593_894. p 289. Image 30. Collier was spelled incorrectly on the census of 1870 as "Colyer." He later married Dora B. Horn of Texas in 1873. They moved to Trinidad, Colorado and by 1900 had moved to Los Angeles, California. Collier died some time after 1910.

175. U.S. Census Year 1870. Census Place Precinct 1, Guadalupe, Texas. Roll M593_1589. p 359. Image 14. Frank Rhodes is believed to have been a nineteen year old cowboy from Guadalupe, Texas.

176. Haley Memorial Library & History Center. JEH–II–B. The man identified as "Sloan" was in all likelihood a young man from Indiana named William Sloan who was born in 1847. William Sloan remained in New Mexico until after 1880. U.S. Census Year 1880. Census Place La Plata, Rio Arriba, New Mexico. Roll T9_803. Family History Film 1254803. p 223.4000. Enumeration District 29.

177. Keleher. *The Fabulous Frontier.* p 58

178. Ibid

179. Deed executed by James Patterson to John Chisum, December 15, 1874. It was later published in the *Roswell Record* on October 7, 1937.

180. The town of Roswell, New Mexico began as a crossroads where several springs provided cattle herds with water. In 1869 Roswell began to take shape with the arrival of Van C. Smith, a professional gambler who filed his claim in the spring of 1871, and changed the settlements name to honor his father, Roswell Smith. Historians hasten to note that James Patterson actually occupied the site at the

spring and built the first house there which Van C. Smith later took over.

181. Deed executed by James Patterson to John Chisum, December 15, 1874. It was later published in the *Roswell Record* on October 7, 1937.

182. Nelson. "First among the first"

183. Burns, Walter Noble. 1999. *The Saga of Billy the Kid.* Albuquerque: University of New Mexico Press. p 322

184. James Chisum is reported by many to have been responsible for the importation of the vast assortment of flora planted at the South Spring Ranch.

185. After Chisum's financial difficulties on the 1880s, title to most of the ranch and livestock went to Pitser and James, who together with Sallie's husband William Robert ran the operations until they ultimately lost it in bankruptcy on December 10, 1890.

186. Keleher. *The Fabulous Frontier.* p 58. There are two Apache reservations in New Mexico: 1) The Jicarilla, which is near Dulce in the northern part of the state and, 2) The Mescalero, which is located in Mescalero near Ruidoso.

187. The Honorable Erwin C. Watkins was born in Genesee County, New York on January 15, 1839. In his early days he read and practiced law under his father, who was then a Justice of the Peace. Watkins later took a regular course of law in Grand Rapids. He distinguished himself during the war. After the war he practiced law for a few months, then purchased mill property in Rockford, Michigan removing from Grand Rapids to Rockford in the fall of 1865. Watkins was elected to the Michigan Legislature in 1871, and reelected in 1873. In 1875 Watkins was appointed General Inspector of Indian Affairs, but resigned in 1879. This is the same Indian Inspector Erwin C. Watkins who on November 9, 1875 submitted a report to Washington, District of Columbia, stating that hundreds of Sioux and Cheyenne Indians associated with Sitting Bull and Crazy Horse were hostile to the United States. In so doing, Watkins set into motion a series of events that led to the Battle of the Little Big Horn in Montana the following year. See Caldwell, Clifford R.. 2008. *Dead Right, The Lincoln County War.* Lulu. p 244

188. The spelling of Jessie Evans given name remains a topic of often heated controversy. In the footnote reference below (Haley. RNM-II-D) Evans signed his given name "Jessie." At the time he signed with his left hand, since his right wrist had been wounded during a recent exchange of gunfire on March 9, 1878. However, when he entered Huntsville Penitentiary in Texas to serve his sentence for the killing of Texas Ranger Bingham his file indicates that his given name was spelled "Jesse". This record can be found in the Texas State Archives as #9078. Both spellings abound. I have chosen to use the "Jessie" spelling for consistency, and to aid in differentiation between Jesse Evans of the Comanche Pool cattle cooperative.

189. Haley Memorial Library & History Center. RNM–II - D
Jessie Evans statement June 14, 1878 . Number 1291 Jessie Evans Affidavit Number 3. County of Lincoln, Territory of NM

190. See page 51 for a complete explanation of the Comanche Pool.

191. Chrisman, Harry E.. 1990. Lost Trails of the Cimarron. Athens: Swallow Press. pp 180–185

192. Haley Memorial Library & History Center. RNM–II - D
Jessie Evans statement June 14, 1878 . #1291. Jessie Evans Affidavit #3. County of Lincoln, Territory of New Mexico. In this affidavit Evans is referred to as "Jessie J. Evans." He signed the document "Jessie" in his own hand.

193. Census Year 1860. Census Place English River, Washington, Iowa. Roll M653_344. p 88. Image 89.
Jessie Evans, claimed to have been born in Morgan County, Alabama in 1853. He came to New Mexico from Texas (although in 1878 Evans himself said Texas was his place of birth). Others believe that Jessie Evans was born in 1850, in Kalona, Washington County, Iowa.

194. John Hittson was born at Nashville, Tennessee on October 11, 1831. The Hittson family moved to Rusk County, Texas, in 1847. Four years later John married Selena Frances Brown, by whom he had ten children. In 1856 John moved to Palo Pinto County where he ranched and served as the first county sheriff until 1861. Hittson moved westward to settle at old Camp Cooper, an abandoned federal camp. By branding ownerless cattle and marketing them in Mexico, John Hittson became the wealthiest man in the region by 1865. The next year he moved his ranch headquarters to Callahan County and allowed his cattle to range over an eight-county area.

195. The Comancheros were natives of northern and central New Mexico who conducted trade with the nomadic plains tribes along the Llano Estacado. They cut trails followed by traders, and later ranchers and settlers. They were so named because they resided in the lands occupied by the Comanche Indians who were considered their best customers. The term was popularized during the 1840s by Josiah Gregg and subsequently used by United States Army officers who were familiar with Gregg's accounts. Initially their lucrative practices were considered legitimate. Increased demand for cattle in New Mexico, however, led to them become "rustlers by proxy" who traded stolen cattle to the Indians. The resulting hostility between Indians and settlers led to army intervention in 1874 and the eventual demise of the Comancheros. Between 1850 and 1870 thousands of animals stolen by Indians were traded by them to merchants in New Mexico and Arizona who had, in turn, contacts with government beef contractors. The addition of firearms, ammunition, and whiskey to the list of trade items from New Mexico added to their worsening reputation.
Haley, J. Evetts. "The Comanchero Trade." *Southwestern Historical Quarterly*

196. Haley. *Charles Goodnight, Cowman and Plainsman.* p 195

197. Kenner, Charles L.. 1969. *The Comanchero Frontier: A History of New Mexican-Plains Indian Relations.* Norman: University of Oklahoma Press. p 197.
Additional source: Johnson, M. L.. 1935. *Trail Blazing: A True Story of the Struggles with Hostile Indians on the Frontier of Texas.* Dallas: Mathis Publishing Company

198. U.S. Census Year: 1870. Census Place Fernando de Taos, Taos, New Mexico

Territory. Roll M593_896. p 632. Image 646.

Believed to have been thirty four year old Smith H. Simpson from New York whose home was at the Red Willow Indian Reservation of Taos Juan Santisteben, Taos, New Mexico Territory.

199. Haley. *Charles Goodnight, Cowman and Plainsman.* pp 233–234

200. Roswell. *New Mexico Daily Record.* October 7, 1937

201. Atherton, Lewis. 1967. *The Cattle Kings.* Indiana University Press. p 135

202. His real name was Frank Baker and he was believed to have been born in Syracuse, New York. He also used the name "Hart," or "Little Hart" as an alias. According to what few records are available his first name may have been Edward (this according to Maurice Fulton). Baker first came to New Mexico in the spring of 1873 with the Horrell Party. He was a noted Mexican hater. Baker was a member of the Horrell group who stole two horses from Aaron O. Wilburn. He returned to Texas with the Horrells in 1874, but soon returned to Lincoln County where he was a cowboy in the employ of John Chisum, working with Augustus Montaigne (A.M.) "Gus" Gildea on a cattle drive in November 1877. Baker joined Jessie Evans and his group in 1876 and fought on the side of the Dolan faction during the Lincoln County War. He was related to Harry Baker who had a ranch at Seven Rivers in 1877.

203. Haley Memorial Library & History Center. JEH–II–B

204. Estimate is noted in Santa Fe New Mexican, November 23, 1875. *Mesilla News.* Mesilla, New Mexico

205. Hunter, J. Marvin. 2003. *The Trail Drivers of Texas.* Austin: University of Texas Press. pp 976–986

206. Keleher. *The Fabulous Frontier.* p 60

207. *Colorado Chieftain* (Pueblo). December 3, 1875

208. Keleher. *The Fabulous Frontier.* p 60

John P. Risque was killed by Indians in April 1883 at Grant, New Mexico. He had come to Pinos Altos, New Mexico from St. Louis where he was a lawyer, having earned his degree at Washington's Georgetown University.

John B. Patron was murdered by Mitchell Manley at Puerto de Luna on April 1, 1884.

209. Hinton. *John Simpson Chisum.* p 190. January 16, 1878. John S. Simpson interview, Las Vegas, NM. Reported as having said the he "sold cattle to R.D. Hunter in 1875"

210. The entrepreneur Robert Dickie Hunter, known as Colonel Hunter, was born on April 5, 1833, in Ayrshire, Scotland. Robert was the son of Adam and Janet (Dickie) Hunter. As a youth he emigrated with his parents from Scotland to a farming community near Mount Olive, Illinois. He married Janet Webster of Bunker Hill on April 8, 1858. Hunter organized the Texas and Pacific Coal Company in 1888 at Thurber, Texas, which for over thirty years was one of the most productive bituminous coal mining communities in the state. Hunter speculated in the mining industry in Colorado, and later entered the cattle

business where he quickly won a reputation across the Southwest as a raiser, trader, commissioner and broker. In 1873 Hunter joined Captain Albert G. Evans to form Hunter, Evans, and Company, which became one of the leading cattle commission firms in the country. In the late 1880s, Hunter sold his interest in the company to Evans and invested in the Johnson Coal Mining Company of Strawn, Texas, located seventy five miles west of Fort Worth on the route of the Texas and Pacific Railway. In late September 1888 Hunter purchased a controlling interest in the Johnson coal mine and founded the Texas and Pacific Coal Company. The purchase comprised 23,014 acres in Erath, Palo Pinto, and Eastland counties.

Hunter served as president of the company and general manager of the company owned town of Thurber, Texas until he retired in 1899. By 1900 more than 2,500 Texas & Pacific employees and their families resided in Thurber, described as Hunter's own fiefdom. He died on November 7, 1902 at his home in Fort Worth and was survived by his wife and two daughters. He was buried in Bellefontaine Cemetery in St. Louis, Missouri. By the time of his passing Hunter had built an estimated $1 million fortune as a cattle broker and mining entrepreneur.

211. Author Unknown. *The Diamond Jubilee Historical Souvenir Program.* Coldwater, Kansas. August 30 through September 2, 1959

212. Burns. *The Saga of Billy the Kid.* p 10

213. Thrapp, Dan L.. 1988. *Encyclopedia of Frontier Biography.* Glendale, California: A.H. Clark. p 85

214. Nolan lists the Beckwith's date of marriage as December 22, 1849 at Santa Fe, New Mexico. Nolan. *The Lincoln County War.* p 445

215. Hinton. *John Simpson Chisum.* p 192

216. Peter had managed Chisum's store at Trickham, in Cooke County, Texas and accompanied him to New Mexico.

217. Robert Kelsey Wylie, trail driver and rancher, was the son of Samuel Kelsey and Maria (McNeil) Wylie. He was born in Tishomingo County, Mississippi, on June 6, 1836. Wylie moved to Texas with his parents about 1850 from Mississippi and settled on a farm in Anderson County. As a youth he learned to build brick chimneys. He accepted cattle as payment and in 1852 moved to Erath County, where he and three brothers engaged in ranching. In 1862 Wylie joined several families in establishing a settlement called Picketville (later Ballinger) in an area that became Runnels County. Soon afterwards he located the Flat Top Ranch on Elm Creek to the southeast in Coleman County and remained there during the Civil War. In June 1865 Wylie and four others drove a herd south for sale in Mexico, and in the late summer he entered the employ of James Patterson, a beef contractor at Fort Sumner, New Mexico. In the fall of 1865 Wylie piloted his first herd over a well charted cattle trail (later followed by Charles Goodnight) up the Pecos to Fort Sumner. Wylie delivered cattle to Patterson and others on the Pecos for nearly ten years. In 1873 Wylie sold a herd to John Chisum on credit, settled at Ballinger, and built up a stock herd under his Cross brand with imported Durham

bulls. In 1878 Wylie and the Coggin brothers reclaimed 8,000 cattle from Chisum and sent them to the head of the Pease River in Motley County, where they were sold to form part of the foundation herd for the Matador Ranch. In 1879, with other ranchers contesting his range in Runnels and neighboring counties, Wylie moved a herd to Horsehead Crossing on the Pecos and established the first ranch there. He also purchased and fenced land to preserve his claims in Runnels County (organized in 1880). By 1885 he had started a sheep ranch in the Van Horn area. His flock soon increased to 60,000. The Wylie Mountains, with Bob and Mollie peaks, are named for him and his wife.

218. Erwin, Allen A.. 1965. *The Southwest of John Horton Slaughter.* Glendale, California: Arthur H. Clark Co.. pp 112–127

John Horton Slaughter went on to have a long and distinguished career in law enforcement. He became Marshal of Cochise County, Arizona and died at Douglas, Arizona on February 16, 1922.

219. U.S. Census Year 1870. Census Place District 11, Hardeman, Tennessee. Roll M593_1533. p 251. Image 505

220. Keleher. *The Fabulous Frontier.* p 61

221. Haley Memorial Library & History Center. JEH–II–B

222. DeArment, Robert K.. 2007. *Deadly Dozen: Twelve Forgotten Gunfighters of the Old West, Volume 1.* Norman: University of Oklahoma Press. p 116. In *Deadly Dozen* DeArment records that this incident occurred on March 10, 1877. All other sources seem to be in agreement that it occurred on March 28, 1877.

223. Mesilla Valley Independent. June 23, 1877. Also Coe. *Frontier Fighter.* pp 138–141

224. James Highsaw Indictment. March 10, 1877. County of Dona Ana. Signed by Rynerson. On file at the Haley Memorial Library & History Center.

225. Grand Jury Record #451 . Mesilla, New Mexico at the county seat at Dona Ana County . Signed by District Attorney William Rynerson.

226. Oden, Bill. 1965. *Early Days on the Texas New Mexico Plains.* Canyon, Texas: Palo Duro Press. pp 1–69

227. In 1879 the Sixteenth Texas Legislature appropriated three million acres of land to finance a new state capitol building. The destruction of the old capitol building by fire on November 9, 1881, made construction of the new building urgent. The land was used as partial payment, and was valued at $3,224,593.45 based on its share of the relative cost of the new capitol building. Since it was in the unsettled panhandle area, the syndicate established the XIT Ranch to utilize the land until it could be sold. The syndicate attracted wealthy British investors like the Earl of Aberdeen and Henry Seton-Karr, a member of Parliament, Farwell returned with the equivalent of roughly $5 million in American currency. From the first, the Capitol Syndicate had intended to run cattle only until the land could be utilized for agriculture; long-range goals were to promote settlement, eventually subdivide the acreage, and gradually sell it off piecemeal. In the spring of 1885 the first pasture fence was completed and on July 1, 1885, the first herd of 2,500 head of longhorn cattle arrived at the ranch.

Within the next year 781 miles of XIT range was fenced, and by November 1886 some 110,721 cattle valued at $1,322,587 had been purchased.

In 1887 the XIT reached its peak with 150 cowboys who rode 1,000 horses and branded 35,000 calves in one year. In addition to its vast panhandle acreage, the XIT maintained maturing grounds for its cattle in the northern plains, first in South Dakota and later, in 1889, on a range north of Miles City, Montana. For eleven consecutive years, 12,500 cattle were driven annually to these northern pastures and fattened for the Chicago markets. By the turn of the century 325 windmills and 100 dams had been erected on the XIT ranges, all at a cost of around $500,000. Cross fences divided the ranch into ninety-four pastures, and 1,500 miles of fencing had been completed.

228. Probably George W. Hysaw who was born about 1865 and who married Lelia Graham at Frio County, Texas October 12, 1844.

229. RNM 580 Haley Memorial Library & History Center Library

230. Cramer, T. Dudley. 1996. *The Pecos Ranchers in the Lincoln County War*. Oakland, California: Branding Iron Press. p 57

231. James Wall Lockhart was born in Georgia in 1847. He was shot and killed near the Chisum Ranch at Fort Grant, Arizona on March 23, 1877. Lockhart worked for cattleman John Chisum.
He was originally buried in the fort's graveyard. Years later, after the fort was closed, all graves were transferred to the National Cemetery in Santa Fe, New Mexico.

232. Nolan, Frederick. 1998. *The West of Billy the Kid*. Norman: University of Oklahoma Press. p 51. Miles Leslie Wood was born in Newbury, Ontario, Canada on March 27, 1848. He arrived in Tucson, Arizona in 1869 and went to work for Henry Hooker. In the fall of 1869 he drove a herd of cattle to Fort Bowie where he remained until about 1876 when he moved to Fort Grant. There he became a notary public and Justice of the Peace and later worked as a government contractor for hay. He also ran the Hotel deLuna. Wood died in Arizona on December 11, 1930.

233. George Augustus Purington was born at Athens, Ohio on July 21, 1837. He attended Western Reserve College and while a sophomore there he enlisted in the Nineteenth Ohio Volunteer Infantry at the outset of the Civil War. Purington soon reached the rank of captain in the Second Ohio and had a distinguished military record, logging participation in sixty battles during the war. By July 1866 he was a member of the 9th Cavalry, under the command of Colonel Edward Hatch. By the summer of 1877 Captain Purington, then in charge of Company "H" of the 9th Cavalry Buffalo Soldiers, had arrived at Fort Stanton, New Mexico. In March 1883 Purington was promoted to major and transferred to 3rd Cavalry. He died at Metropolis, Illinois on May 31, 1896.

234. HPH to CRC. September 22, 2009

235. Robert K. Wylie was born in about 1849. U.S. Census Year 1880. Census Place Precinct 2, Denton, Texas. Roll: T9_1300. Family History Film. 1255300. p

89.1000. Enumeration District 104

236. John S. Chisum and Robert K. Wylie charged with rioting November 1878. Case #448. Dona Ana County, New Mexico. Haley Memorial Library & History Center.

237. Cramer, T. Dudley. 1996. *The Pecos Ranchers in the Lincoln County War.* Orinda California: Branding Iron Press. p 82

238. *Arizona Star* (Prescott). July 13, 1877

239. Atherton. *Cattle Kings.* p 127. Also see C.F. Ward. "John S. Chisum, Pioneer Cattleman of the Valley." Roswell, NM, *Daily Record.* October 7, 1937.

240. Agent Frederick C. Godfroy assumed charge of the Mescaleros Apache Indians on July 1, 1876. Many believe that Godfroy had fallen in league with the Murphy/Dolan faction. As cited earlier, the unpopular Godfroy had been labeled by many as the "Presbyterian Fraud" and was ousted from his position in 1879. Pat Coghlan, "The King of Tularosa", was born in Clonakilty, County Cork, Ireland on March 14, 1822. In 1845 he emigrated to the United States and joined the Army in 1847. Coghlan served in Texas and was honorably discharged in San Antonio in 1852. He farmed for a time, then moved to Mason County in 1862 where he was a storekeeper and cattle trader. He next moved to New Mexico where he was a cavalryman at Fort Stanton in Lincoln County in 1872. In 1874 Coghlan came to Tularosa. By that time he had acquired significant capital. He acquired town lots, built a store that covered an entire block, ran a hotel, a sawmill, a fruit farm and vineyard. Sonnichsen, Charles L..1973. *The Mescalero Apaches.* Norman, Oklahoma: University of Oklahoma Press. p 166. Also see O'Brien, Paul. 2009. *The Man From Clonakilty.* Unpublished Manuscript.

241. Cramer. *The Pecos Ranchers in the Lincoln County War.* p 85

242. District Court Records, Dona Ana County, New Mexico (Las Cruces) indicate that Chisum was involved in the following suits: five replevin suits Case Numbers 368–72; larceny Case Number 449; and rioting Case Number 448. This information was obtained in 1926 by Maurice G. Fulton and is on file in the Chaves County Historical Society.

243. Fort Craig was established in 1854. It was one of the largest and most important frontier forts in the west, and one of the eight forts situated along the primary north-south road in the Rio Grande Valley. Fort Craig played a crucial role in Indian campaigns and the Civil War. Military excursions from Fort Craig pursued such notable Apache leaders as Geronimo, Victorio and Nana. The fort was home to the 9th Cavalry and 38th and 125th Infantry.

244. *Mesilla Independent.* July 21, 1877. Also see Hinton. *John Simpson Chisum.* p 201

245. Sallie Lucy Chisum was born May 26, 1858 at Denton County, Texas.

246. Coe, George. 1984. *Frontier Fighter.* Chicago: Donnelley & Sons. p 142

247. HPH to CRC. September 22, 2009

248. Attributed to author and astronomer Cliff Stoll.

249. Montezuma Lodge was chartered May 8, 1851, by the Grand Lodge of Missouri. The charter went into practical effect with the institution of Montezuma Lodge

No. 109, August 12, 1851.

Many military, commercial and public leaders belonged to this lodge, among them were Kit Carson, Charles Bent, Ceran St. Vrain, Lafayette Head.

250. Hinton. *John Simpson Chisum.* p 194. Also *Mesilla News.* June 10, 24, 1876

251. In spite of continuing research Lawrence Gustave Murphy's origin remains something of a mystery. His obituary, published in the Santa Fe newspaper on October 26, 1878, states that he was born in County Wexford, Ireland in 1831. It goes on to claim that he was educated at Maynooth College in Kildare, Ireland, and that he had served United States Army at the rank of sergeant major. County Wexford has no record of his birth at that, or any other time. Maynooth College has no record of any student by that name ever attending that school. However, historian Charles Usmer has indicated that during a recent visit to the university he was able to locate evidence of Murphy's attendance. The Adjutant General of the United States Army has no record of any soldier by that name. Some believe that he had studied for the Episcopalian priesthood and had come to New Mexico from Canada, although scant documentation exists to support this belief. He did not come to New Mexico with the California Column as has so often been written. The first known historical record of L.G. Murphy is dated July 27, 1861. On that date he was commissioned a First Lieutenant in the 1st Regiment of the New Mexico Infantry. He soon transferred to the New Mexico Cavalry and was with Kit Carson during his expedition against the Navajos and the subsequent relocation of the tribe to Fort Sumner. Murphy was an excellent officer by all accounts and was eventually promoted to the rank of major for his meritorious service in the Navajo Wars and in controlling the Apaches at Bosque Redondo. In about 1868, in partnership with Lieutenant Colonel Emil Fritz who had been commander of the First Regiment California Cavalry, he established a brewery on the eastern edge of the Fort Stanton Indian Reservation. In the summer of 1870 the reservation was enlarged, and L.G. Murphy and Company became a privately owned island in the midst of government property. The partners made the most of their opportunity. In effect, they became both victualers (sellers of provisions to the military in the field) and Indian traders.

252. Miller, Darlis A.. 1982, *California Column in New Mexico*, Albuquerque, University of New Mexico, p 60,69,147. pp 218–219

253. Emil Christian Adolf Fritz was born at Eglosheim, Germany on March 3, 1832. At the time of his birth his father, Phillip Fritz, was the custodian of the Monrepose estate. Emil was the first of three Fritz children to immigrate to the United States. He probably came about the time of the California Gold Rush in 1849. Fritz enlisted in the U.S. First Dragoons in 1851 and saw service in the west. He mustered out on January 1, 1861 as a sergeant. Fritz was commissioned as a captain in Company "B" First California Cavalry on August 16, 1861. He led Union Troops into Tucson on May 20, 1862 just seven days after the town had been evacuated by Confederate forces. He reenlisted on August 1, 1864 at Fort Stanton, New Mexico as commanding officer and Brevet Lieutenant Colonel. It

was at Fort Stanton that he went into business with Lawrence G. Murphy.

254. Photo copy of discharge papers from Ft. Stanton of James J. Dolan shows his rank as "musician." He had been with General Hancock and the 37th. The original of this document is in Robert McCubbin collection.

255. Miller, Darlis A.. 1982. *The California Column in New Mexico.* Albuquerque: University of New Mexico

256. Miles Hood Swarthout. *The Shootist* (Dino De Laurentiis Company, 1976)

257. Haley Memorial Library & History Center. RNM II–D

258. Haley Memorial Library & History Center. RNM II–D. Records concerning the McSween marriage are confusing. The Probate Court marriage license shows the date as August 13, 1873, but a note from the clerk thereon indicates September 23, 1873. A check written by McSween to *The Atchison, Kansas Champion* on August 24, 1873 shows the date as being August 23, 1873, which is commonly held to be correct.

John Conklin Fraser was born on March 31, 1860, to Scottish parents in Chicago. Prior to becoming a Pinkerton Agent he was a plumber, printer and a telegraph clerk. In 1880 he was hired by the Pinkerton National Detective Agency, headquartered in Chicago. Fraser advanced rapidly in the organization, and by the end of the 1880s was transferred to the Denver branch office where he became assistant superintendent. In 1896 he was assigned to investigate the disappearance of Albert and Henry Fountain in New Mexico. A couple of years after his work on the Fountain case Fraser was advanced to the post of superintendent of the Denver office. In 1906 Fraser was transferred to San Francisco and promoted to manager of the Pinkerton's Pacific Coast Division. He relocated to Los Angeles in 1916 and maintained a home in Los Angeles as well as San Francisco. Fraser retired from the Pinkerton Agency in 1933. During his 53 years with the Pinkerton Agency Fraser developed a reputation as a first-class detective. He died on July 25, 1938.

259. Hough, Emerson. 1902. *The Story of the Outlaw.* New York: Grosset and Dunlap. p 203. Interestingly, Conway was a close friend and former classmate of Thomas Catron and Steve Elkins. Both men were staunch adversaries of John Chisum.

260. Baron, Robert M.. 2003. *Court of Inquiry, Lieutenant Colonel N.A.M. Dudley.* Fort Stanton, New Mexico: May, June, July 1879. Volume 1. Edina, Minnesota: Beaver Pond Press. pp 356–357 the testimony and map of Andy Boyle between pp 356–357.

261. Ibid

262. *The New Mexican.* August 10, 1878

263. Mehren, Lawrence Lindsay. 1969. *A History of the Mescalero Indian Reservations, 1869–1881.* Unpublished Manuscript. MA Thesis, Tucson: University of Arizona. p 84, pp 108–109

264. William Rosenthal was one of the largest beef contractors in the southwest at the time and was a member of the powerful Santa Fe Ring. He had come to New

Mexico in about 1870 and later became a United States assistant internal revenue collector.

265. George Coe interview with J. Evetts Haley. March 20, 1927. Haley Library & History Center. Midland, Texas. HHC

266. Wilson. *Merchants Guns & Money.* p 76

267. Maurice G. Fulton. Haley Memorial Library & History Center Library. RNM–VI–CC dated November 27, 1953

268. County of Dona Ana, New Mexico. *James Highsaw Indictment March 10, 1877.* Signed by Rynerson

269. The often maligned William Brady was born on August 16, 1829 in Cavan, County Cavan, Ireland. He left Ireland early in 1851, came to the United States and joined the Army on July 11, 1851. His enlistment was for five years, which he served in Texas where he was discharged at Fort Duncan. Brady reenlisted, and was next discharged in March 1861 at Fort Craig. He then joined the New Mexico Volunteer Infantry as a lieutenant, and eventually assumed command of Fort Stanton on May 14, 1864. Brady served with L.G. Murphy, and the two were extremely close friends. He was mustered out of the Army on October 31, 1866. Soon after, he became sheriff of Lincoln County, New Mexico succeeding George Peppin. On November 16, 1862 he married the widow Maria Bonifacia Chaves Montoya. Maria and William had eight children before he was killed, and Maria was pregnant with their ninth at the time of his slaying. An ill tempered man when drinking, which he reportedly did often, Brady is frequently portrayed as more of an evil man than might actually have been the case. Deeply indebted to Murphy, perhaps beyond all hope of recovery, Brady was fiercely loyal to Murphy and as such sealed his own fate. Brady was killed on April 1, 1878 by a group of the Regulators consisting of Jim French, Frank McNab, John Middleton, Fred Waite, Henry Brown and Billy Bonney and others. During his career as a lawman, Brady is not known to have killed anyone.

270. Nolan, Frederick. 2009. *The Life and Death of John Henry Tunstall.* Santa Fe: Sunstone Press. p 205

271. Wilson. *Merchants Guns and Money.* p 67

272. Ibid

273. Ibid. The exchange rate of the British Pound Sterling to U.S. Dollar in 1877 was roughly 5.076 U.S. Dollars to one Pounds Sterling.

274. Wilson. *Merchants Guns and Money.* p 67. Fulton papers. Box 12. Folder 4.

275. Nolan. *Tascosa.* p 45. Nolan attributes the financial backing for the formation of the Lincoln County Bank to John Chisum. He makes no mention of the backing of Robert D. Hunter in this enterprise. John Wilson, in *Merchants Guns and Money,* indicates that the proprietors of the bank were Colonel Robert D. Hunter, John S. Chisum, and Alexander A. McSween with John H. Tunstall as clerk. Two things are clear however; McSween had practically no financial resources of his own at the time and Colonel Hunter had provided financial backing.

276. Keleher. *The Fabulous Frontier.* pp 62–63

277. George Hogg was born about 1837. U.S. Census Year 1860. Census Place Albuquerque, Bernalillo, New Mexico Territory. Roll M653_712. p 200. Image 390.

278. Charlie Bowdre was born in 1848 in Wilkes County, Georgia and was the firstborn child of Albert and Lucy Bowdre. In 1853 the Bowdres moved to DeSoto County, Mississippi where they were farmers. The Bowdres had six more children; Eppie in 1854, Sallie in 1855, twins Volney and Benjamin in 1857, Willie in 1863 and Lucy Lee in 1863. Charlie left home sometime around 1870 and came to Lincoln County, New Mexico by way of Dodge City, then Fort Griffin and later Tascosa and Mobeetie, Texas. According to census records, Charlie married a Mexican girl named Manuela who was born 1855. The popularly believed theory is that Manuela was the daughter of Charlie's friend and colleague Fernando Herrera, but there are no records to prove this. It's unclear if Manuela's surname was Herrera or Gonzales, since when Charlie's estate was settled a Manuela Gonzales claimed it. Charlie Bowdre was killed by sheriff Pat Garrett's posse at Stinking Springs, New Mexico on December 23, 1880 and is buried along side Billy the Kid near Fort Sumner, New Mexico.

279. August M. "Gus" Gildea was born about 1854 in Texas. His wife's name was Mary.
U.S. Census Year 1880. Census Place San Antonio, Bexar, Texas. Roll: T9_1291. Family History Film 1255291. p 47.4000. Enumeration District 12.

280. Hinton. *John Simpson Chisum*. p 202

281. *Mesilla Independent*. September 1, 1877

282. O'Neal, Bill. 1979. *Encyclopedia of Western Gunfighters*. Norman: University of Oklahoma Press. p 42

283. *Mesilla Independent*. September 8, 1877

284. Frank Warner Angel. *Report on the Death of John H. Tunstall*. Department of Justice 1878. Records of the Department of Justice. NARS. p 24

285. *Las Cruces Echo Del Rio Grande*. January 19, 1878

286. Hinton. *John Simpson Chisum*. p 311

287. Ibid. p 312. Hinton cites Ayres, Adm'r v Pitzer Chisum et al. Certified Copy of Final Decree of Court in Chancery at Hillsboro, New Mexico, November 14, 1885. Copy in Deed Book A, pp 457–65, Chaves County, New Mexico. This decree was finally satisfied on August 25, 1897, in Fifth Judicial Court, Socorro, New Mexico.

288. Morton, who was called "Billy" or "Buck," was from Charlotte County, Virginia. He was orphaned shortly after the Civil War and headed west to make money to help support his five brothers and sisters. He is first recorded in Lincoln County on March 9, 1877 when he was known to be an employee of the Jas. J. Dolan & Company. On February 18, 1878 at approximately 5:30 PM he fired the first shot that, according to the postmortem examination would have ultimately killed John Henry Tunstall. He was killed by Regulators on March 9, 1878 in Agua Negra Canyon, New Mexico.

289. The attachment of Tunstall's assets grew from the false assertion that Tunstall and McSween were legally partners, and that as such the assets of the partnership could be attached in connection with McSween's alleged debts. Tunstall had indicated that such a partnership was anticipated for mid 1878, but it had not yet been legally formed.

290. Pajarito translates from Spanish to "small bird."

291. Tunstall was shot from some distance, and apparently from a point slightly lower than where Tunstall was seated on his horse. The approximate trajectory of the bullets were determined during the autopsy that was performed after Tunstalls death.

292. Tom Hill was originally from Texas, where he was known as Chelson, Chilson or Children. He has been described by Emerson Hough as being a *typical rough, dark, swarthy, low-breed, as loud mouthed as he was ignorant.* He was a braggart, but none the less a killer. Hill, along with Jessie Evans, had been charged with larceny in Lincoln County in 1876. He is believed by some to have been one of the killers of John Tunstall. Hill was killed by a half breed Cherokee sheepherder near Alamo Springs, Tularosa, New Mexico on March 9, 1878 while attempting to ransack a sheep camp. Jessie Evans was wounded in the wrist in the same exchange.

293. Frank Warner Angel. *Report on the Death of John H. Tunstall.* Department of Justice 1878. Records of the Department of Justice. NARS. Deposition of Florencio Gonzales.

294. Ash Upson was born in Connecticut and traveled most of the United States before landing in New Mexico and becoming the postmaster in Roswell. He was an educated man with a literary talent and aided Pat Garrett in writing the book *The Authentic Life of Billy the Kid.*

295. *The Mesilla News.* July 14, 1878

296. Affidavit by George Warden Peppin, sheriff of Lincoln County, which was enclosed in a letter to the United States Attorney General by the Commanding Officer at Fort Stanton, New Mexico, on August 15, 1878. In File No. 44-4-8. Record Group 60. Department of Justice Records. National Archives.

297. Immediately following Sheriff Brady in the line of succession, Peppin was appointed a Special Deputy U.S. Marshal as well as sheriff of Lincoln County following Brady's murder. George Peppin was born in Chittenden County, Vermont in 1838. By the time he was twenty he had already worked his way to Alleghany, California where on October 2, 1861 he enlisted in Company A, 5th Regiment of the California Infantry. He mustered out at La Mesilla, New Mexico on November 30, 1864. After a stint as a butcher at Fort Stanton in 1881 he drifted around Lincoln County taking jobs as a builder and a mason. He participated in the building of the Murphy store, McSween house, and the Lincoln jail. His first wife was Felipe Moya. They had three children. His second wife was Victoriana Salazar. They had five children. In August 1887 he lost the use of his right hand in an accident that severed the tendons in the right wrist. He died at home in Lincoln on September 18, 1904.

298. George Warden Peppin had been appointed sheriff after Brady's death. This in spite of three warrants out for him on three separate murders.

299. LeMay, John. 2006. *Roswell*. South Carolina: Arcadia. p 20

300. In spite of compelling evidence to the contrary, Tom Folliard's surname has been mistakenly spelled O'Folliard for decades. Practically every contemporary author has perpetuated this error. Numerous sources confirm the spelling as "Folliard", including U.S. CensusYear1870. Census Place Zavala, Texas. Roll M593_1597. p 551. Image 570. Also see Madasonian. July 23, 1881. See Governor Lew Wallace letter dated March 11, 1879 to Captain Henry Carroll, Commanding General Fort Stanton. See Pat Garrett's *The Authentic Life of Billy the Kid* in which he mentions Tom Folliard's name 30 times, and each time spells it "Foliard."

301. Poe, Sophie A.. 1936. *Buckboard Days*. Caldwell, Idaho: Caxton. p 162

302. Sallie Chisum "Journal." MSS in Chaves County Historical Society.

303. Nolan, Frederick. 2009. *The Lincoln County War, A Documentary History: Revised.* Santa Fe: Sunstone. pp 339–340

304. Cox. *Historical and Biographical Record.* p 330, p 365

305. Sallie Chisum. *Journals*

306. In 1878–79, Charley Nebo was with John Chisum's outfit as foreman/wagon boss. In a letter to Seymour on March 12, 1917 Charley wrote that "the Kid … stayed with me all the winter of 1878 in the Panhandle of Texas..." From the manuscript "The Genuine Cowboy Captured Alive, The Life of Charley Nebo". Lee, Jane Matson and Dworkin, Mark. *Western-Outlaw-Lawman History Association Journal.* Winter 2007. Vol. XVI. Number 4.

307. McCarty, John L. and Armstrong, Mel. Interview with Garrett H. Dobbs in 1942. Amarillo Public Library.

308. Sallie Chisum. *Journal*

309. WC to HPH. January 28, 1955

310. Fort Bascom was founded in 1863 during the Civil War on the south bank of the Canadian River in eastern New Mexico. The fort had a short but distinguished history. Troops from there helped control the Kiowas, Comanche, and other tribes inhabiting the Red and Canadian River region, watched over the Goodnight-Loving Cattle Trail as well as the Santa Fe Trail, and policed the activities of the "Comancheros." The fort also fielded several expeditions against the southern plains tribes. Fort Bascom was the base of one of the three columns deployed by General Sheridan in his 1868–69 campaign. At the time of the fort's abandonment in 1870, when the troops and stores were transferred to Fort Union, New Mexico, the poorly constructed post was still unfinished. It consisted of a sandstone officers' quarters and a few adobe buildings. No remains have survived.

311. Siringo, Charles A.. 2007. *Riata and Spurs*. Santa Fe: Sunstone Press

312. The plaza at Tascosa was known as Borrego Plaza, which translates from Spanish to English as "lamb".

Henry Franklin Hoyt was born January 30, 1854 at Saint Paul, Minnesota. He studied medicine at Rush Medical College and was tutored by Dr. John Henry Murphy. Nolan. *Tascosa.* pp 1–17

313. In 1939 Cal Farley established his Maverick Boys' Ranch at the old Tascosa town site, offering a home and training to underprivileged boys.

314. Rutherford B. Hayes was born in Ohio in 1822 and educated at Kenyon College and Harvard Law School. Hayes entered Congress in December 1865. Between 1867 and 1876 he served three terms as Governor of Ohio. He narrowly won the election of 1876 by a margin of one vote. The final electoral vote: 185 to 184. He was the country's 19th President, and served from 1877 to 1881. He had announced in advance that he would serve only one term, and retired to Spiegel Grove, his home in Fremont, Ohio at the end of his term in office. He died in 1893. Hayes's wife Lucy Ware Webb Hayes is said to hold the dubious distinction of being the First Lady who holds the record for taking the most belongings from the White House after leaving office.

315. For report on the Angel interview see Carl Schurz to Rutherford B. Hayes, August 31, 1878, in Hayes Memorial Library.

316. McKee, Irving. 1947. *Ben-Hur Wallace, The Life of General Lew Wallace* Berkeley: University of California Press. p 144. Also see Wallace, Lew 1906. *Lew Wallace, An Autobiography.* New York: Harper and Brothers Publishers. pp 914–915

317. The *Weekly New Mexican.* January 17, 1880 makes reference to Bonney as "The Kid". It was not until much later that he was given the appellation Billy the Kid by journalists and pulp fiction writers.

318. Huston Ingraham Chapman was Susan McSween's lawyer and was rumored to be romantically involved with her. On the evening of February 18, 1879 an unarmed Chapman was gunned down by a group of drunken revelers consisting of James Dolan, Jessie Evans and Billy Campbell. William Bonney witnessed the killing and would later testify against the murderers.

319. Hinton. *John Simpson Chisum.* p 329

320. The Governor left Santa Fe for Fort Stanton with General Edward Hatch, Commanding General of the Territory, on March 2, 1879. From the *Grant County Herald.* March 8, 1879.
Also see McKee. *Ben-Hur Wallace.* pp 147–150. Also see *Mesilla News.* May 17, 1879 for reference to the Troops being ordered into the field on March 11, 1879.

321. P. M. Chisum to Capt. H. Carroll, March 26, 1879

322. John S. Chisum to Governor Lew Wallace, April 15, 1879

323. WC to HPH. October 25, 1954
Also see Sallie Chisum. *Journal*

324. WC to HPH. April 5, 1954
This episode probably occurred during the spring of 1880. During that summer, and fall of 1880, William Bonney's rustling of Chisum cattle increased significantly.
Also see Anderson, George B.. *History of New Mexico.* New York: Pacific States Publishing Co.. I. p 227

325. Hinton. *John Simpson Chisum.* p 333

326. Nolan. *Tascosa.* p 46. Nolan reaffirms that William Bonney was not known as Billy the Kid until near the end of his last full year of life.

327. Ibid. p 44

328. Cox. *Historical and Biographical Record.* p 302

Statement is "On driving his herds back to the Pecos River from the Canadian, Mr. P. Chisum disposed of an interest to his brother James."

329. Brand change is from WC to HPH. March 9, April 3, 1954, and WC to Maurice G. Fulton. April 4, 1940. Date of brand registration from William M. Raine and Will C. Barnes 1930. *Cattle.* Garden City: Doubleday Doran and Company, Inc.. p 161

330. Cox. *Historical and Biographical Record.* p 302

331. After selling the Maxwell Land Grant and relinquishing his position as the largest private landholder in America, Lucien B. Maxwell retired to Fort Sumner, New Mexico. He purchased the buildings of the old fort for $5,000 and built a new twenty room mansion from what had been the officers' quarters. He also remodeled other buildings at the old fort to house the many Mexican-American and Indian employees who moved their families so they could remain with him. After Lucien Maxwell died, his Fort Sumner mansion became the home of his only son, Peter Maxwell. Pete continued managing the family's cattle and sheep ranching and was responsible for many employees, but he mostly lived quietly in the shadow of his then famous father.

It was during that time that Fort Sumner became a popular hangout for Billy the Kid, and "The Kid" knew Peter Maxwell quite well. More importantly, he knew Pete's sister Paulita even better. She is thought to have been the main reason Billy stayed so close to Fort Sumner even when he knew that Sheriff Pat Garrett was breathing down his neck. Often incorrectly mentioned as the daughter of Pete Maxwell, Paulita was Pete's younger sister and the eighth of nine children of Lucien and Ana Maria de la Luz Maxwell. She was born at Mora, New Mexico in 1864 and died December 17, 1929 at Fort Sumner, New Mexico.

332. Keleher. *The Fabulous Frontier.* p 65

333. Anderson. *History of New Mexico.* p 1025

334. Collinson, Frank and Clarke, Mary Whatley. 1997. *Life in the Saddle.* Norman: University of Oklahoma. p 145.

Keleher in *The Fabulous Frontier.* p 64. Keleher reports the quantity of Durham Shorthorn bulls as forty two.

335. Ibid

The shorthorn breed of cattle originated on the northeastern coast of England in the counties of Northumberland, Durham, York, and Lincoln. The first real development of the shorthorn breed took place in the valley of the Tees River. This river, the valley of which is so well known in the development of the breed, lies between Durham and York counties, and the large cattle that inhabited this fertile valley early became known as Teeswater cattle.

336. WC to HPH. March 22, April 9, May 3, 1954

337. Keleher, William A.. 1957. *Violence In Lincoln County: 1869–1881*. Albuquerque: University of New Mexico. p 49. The suit against John, James, Pitser and John's son-in-law William Robert was brought by William Rosenthal for a total of $20,370.68, Van C. Smith and A.O. Wilburn for $1,957.83, C.W. Lewis for $1,982.40, Luis Baca for $4,161.83, William Babb for $7,510.00, J.P. Chase for $426.50, Alexander Grzelachowski for $3,456.75, and Jose Perea for $437.88. All together this totals $57,030.86.

338. After Sallie and William divorced he continued in the ranching business and went into partners with H.G. Adams on the X I in Kansas.

339. Lathrop, Barnes F.. 1949. *Migration into East Texas, 1835–1860: A Study from the United States Census*. Austin: Texas State Historical Association

340. Roxburghshire, Scotland is of an irregular shape, with the greatest portion of it extending in every direction for about 30 miles. It is bounded on the north by Berwickshire; on the east and south by the English border; and on the west by Dumfries and Selkirkshires. It includes the ancient districts of Teviotdale and Liddisdale, which are named from the rivers Teviot and Liddal which run through them. The north and west portions of the county are mountainous, but the east and south are flat and fertile.

341. The portion of the Scottish Highlands, which now goes under the name of Strathglass, was once known as *Crom ghleann*. It is a valley that extends for twenty miles between two ridges of hills and is watered by the River Glass, which, at the lower end of the district, takes the name of the Beauly. There is a great deal of historical reference to some of the possible ancestors of Chisum in *Jennifer Stowell-Norris's article "The History of Strathglass Park." December 2, 2007.*

342. Although originally taken by force this Scandinavian colony soon became a part of the Frankish kingdom, and its Viking leader became a duke. As time went by the dukedom was enlarged, and the inhabitants became less and less Viking, and more Frankish in their way of life until eventually they became the people now known as the Normans.

343. The Domesday Book is a detailed survey of the land held by William the Conqueror and his people. It is the earliest surviving public record and a hugely important historical resource. The first draft was completed in August 1086 and contained records for 13,418 settlements in the English counties south of the rivers Ribble and Tees (the border with Scotland at the time).

344. Early attempts at Parish records keeping began as early as 1536 in England. Records were ordered to be kept by 1538, and by 1587 an order was issued that all records be copied.

345. Estimates place the death toll resulting from the Great Plague of 1665 in London at over 100,000. DeFoe, Daniel. 1722. *A Journal of the Plague Year*. The National Archives, Kew, Richmond, Surrey, England.

346. John Chisholm was the son of James Chisholm (and Ann Carter) who died in Maryland in 1698. James' father Richard may have been the first Chisholm to have

come to the Colonies from England. Richard was born in London in about 1613 and died in Lancaster, Virginia in about 1670. Richard married Margaret Isham of New Kent, Virginia.

347. The Chisholm Trail from Texas to Kansas was named for this Jesse Chisholm.
348. Steely. *Forty Seven Years.* p 377. Also see Pension application of Robert Hansley (Hensley) S4323. State of Tennessee. Hawkins County.
349. Ibid
350. Rebecca and Walter Robinson eventually inherited the Chisum home place.
351. Malinda Chisum was a daughter of Thomas Gibbons Chisum's Uncle John.
352. Andrew Turner was born in North Carolina April 5, 1762, and served from that state during the Revolutionary War. He died in Morgan County, Illinois, August 8, 1842, and is buried in the Rohrer cemetery.
353. Lucinda was actually a cousin. She died in Clarksville, Texas on October 31, 1837.
354. Steely. *Forty Seven Years.* p 324. Daniel Fitch Latimer II was born in 1810 and died May 30, 1836.
355. U.S. Census Year 1850. Census Place Precinct 9, Lamar, Texas. p 302a. December 15, 1850. Image 476. This source also shows a Robert Chisum born About 1842.
356. U.S. Census Year 1850. Census Place Precinct 9, Lamar, Texas. Roll M432_912. p 303. Image 183.
357. U.S. Census Year 1850. Census Place Precinct 9, Lamar, Texas. p 302a. December 15, 1850. Image 476. This source also shows a Robert Chisum born about 1842.
358. Some confusion exists regarding the given names of the Wilhite girls. The 1870 census shows only the initials of S.L. for Sallie and M.A. for Amanda. However, the 1860 Alabama census shows Sallie as Sarah E. and Amanda as Amanda H. U.S. Census Year 1870. Census Place Beat 1, Lamar, Texas. Roll M593_1594. p 192. Image 384. U.S. Census Year 1860. Census Place South West Division, Morgan, Alabama. Roll M653_19. p 409. Image 412.
359. Steely. *Forty Seven Years.* p 381
360. Steely, Skipper. *Forty Seven Years.*
361. Adams/Brown. *Three Ranches West.* pp 118–119
362. U.S. Federal Slave Schedule of 1850. Lamar County, Texas
363. Adams/Brown. *Three Ranches West.* p 82, p 90
364. Adams/Brown. *Three Ranches West.* p 83
365. U.S. Census Year 1850. Census Place Precinct 6, Lamar, Texas. Roll M432_912. p 296. Image 170.
366. Lamar County, Texas. Probate Records. *Will of John Johnson.* Mary Ann Johnson Stell was born December 14, 1827 and died June 1873. She married James W. Stell about 1847 in Tennessee.
367. U.S. Census Year 1850. Census Place Precinct 1, Lamar, Texas . Roll M432_912. p 270. Image 122.
368. Adams/Brown. *Three Ranches West.* p 166
369. Evidence seems to indicate that John Chisum left Jensie and the children in Bonham about 1863. Clarke, Mary W.. 1984. *John Simpson Chisum.* Austin. p 117

370. *Fort Worth Press*. October 6, 1963. Interview with Jinks and Emory.

371. Yvonne A. Jenkins 1976. *Ninety Years of Faith , An Interview with Eugie Jones Thomas,*

372. Leazur Alvis Jones was born May 28, 1822 and died March 30, 1877. He is buried at Greenwood, Arkansas.

373. Elizabeth Jones was born September 26, 1827 and died April 28, 1877. She is buried at Medlin Cemetery, Denton County, Texas.

374. The roots the Medlin Community, now called Trophy Club, run deep in the history of this area of North Texas. In 1847 Charles and Matilda Medlin, along with 20 other families from Missouri, settled along Denton Creek. Floods drove them to higher ground, to the area around present day Trophy Club. Much of the early history of the town is reflected in inscriptions on the tombstones in the cemetery that was designated a Texas historical landmark in 1977.

375. Born September 22, 1885 and died November 1985.

376. U.S. Census Year 1910. Census Place Justice Precinct 6, Lamar, Texas. Roll T624_1571. p 9A. Enumeration District 96. Image 1135.

377. U.S. Census Year 1920. Census Place Clarksville, Red River, Texas. Roll T625_1841. p 30A. Enumeration District 145. Image 190.

378. There is a record that has been submitted by an unidentified individual from New Mexico to the Latter Day Saints (hereinafter referred to as LDS) Church genealogical research center showing a Harriett Chisum and listing her father's name as John "Cow John" Chisum. This document, File# 2100212-0614108022844, is given no standing whatsoever considering that apart from the name "Harriet" there is no part of it that is correct and there are no documents supporting the file submission.

379. Phillip (spelled Philip) was originally left by John Johnson to his daughter Mary Stell in his will.

380. U.S. Census Year 1870. Census Place Beat 2, Lamar, Texas. Roll M593_1594. p 267. Image 534.

381. U.S. Slave Schedules 1860. Provo, Utah. Washington, District of Columbia. National Archives and Records Administration. 1860. M653. 1438 rolls.

382. John Johnson. U.S. Slave Schedule 1860. Western Division. Robertson, Tennessee.

383. LDS Church File #1887968-0124103150910.

384. James Chisum died on March 12, 1908 in Artesia, Eddy, New Mexico and is buried there.

385. Walter married Inez V. Simpson on November 15, 1887 in Chavez County, New Mexico.

386. *The Southwestern Dispatch*. August 3, 1928. James Mullens

387. Ibid

388. Nolan, Frederick. 2009. *The Lincoln County War*. Santa Fe: Sunstone Press. p 58

389. *The Southwestern Dispatch*. August 3, 1928. James Mullens

390. Nolan. *The Lincoln County War*. p 58

391. Cunningham, Eugene. "Fought With Billy the Kid: Florencio Chavez." *Frontier Times*. Volume IX, March 1932. p 243

392. Coe. *Frontier Fighter.* p 142

393. Utley, Robert M.. 1989. *Billy the Kid, A Short and Violent Life.* Lincoln: University of Nebraska Press. p 86

394. Scattered entries in Sallie Chisum's diary from July and August 1878 clearly suggest more than a casual relationship. Historical Center for Southeast New Mexico, Roswell.

395. Sallie Chisum Robert Stegman Diaries. Artesia Historical Museum & Art Center. Artesia, New Mexico. p 137

396. U.S. Census Year 1900. Census Place Cimarron, Meade, Kansas. Roll T623_490. p 1. Enumeration District 154.

397. RNM 252. Haley Memorial Library & History Center

398. Redfield, George B., January 28, 1937. *Interview, Comanche Indians On Chisum Cattle Trail.* In own words of Sallie Chisum Robert. Transcribed by Lucius Dills, Roswell Historian.

399. Most of the surviving Sallie Chisum Robert Diaries are housed at the Artesia, New Mexico Historical Museum & Art Center.

400. U.S. Military Service Records of Pitser Miller Chisum. National Park Service Records of Civil War Soldiers and Sailors. Confederate. Texas.

401. Steely. *Forty Seven Years.* p 673

402. Steely Collection. *Mary V. Daniel Papers.* p 263

403. Lamar County Marriage Book 9. p 358. February 18, 1884

404. Some sources have cited Angie's middle name as Isabella.

405. William James Chisum. California Death Index. 1940 through 1997.
Date of birth August 7, 1864. Place of birth listed as Texas.
Date of death June 12, 1956 at Los Angeles, California.

406. Klasner. *My Girlhood Among Outlaws.* pp 224–225

407. Jeff Chisum Military Service Record. National Park Service Records of Civil War Soldiers and Sailors. Confederate. Texas.

408. Steely. *Forty Seven Years.* p 487

409. Steely. *Neville Papers.* p 1206
Turner Edmundson is mentioned in the "First Church of Paris," where Edmundson and his wife are noted as having made a donation of land for the Shady Grove Camp Ground to a Methodist congregation. See Fuller, Benjamin Franklin. 1900. *History of Texas Baptists.* Louisville, Kentucky: Baptist Book Concern. pp 403–404

410. Steely. *Forty Seven Years.* p 639

411. Many Chisum family genealogists have incorrectly reported Jeff's date of death as 1865 and his place of death as Lamar County, Texas.

412. Ara and Oscar were twins. The 1900 Chaves County, New Mexico census shows both Ara and Oscar as having been born on June 9, 1892. Other accounts, including multiple family genealogy records such as the George Family Genealogy Files.

413. U.S. Selective Service Draft Records. Santa Ana, Orange County, California. June 1, 1917. Roll 1531223

414. U.S. Social Security Death Index. Social Security Number 540-28-2844. Baker City, Baker County, Oregon. Oregon Death Index. 1903 through 1998. Certificate 7874.

415. U.S. Social Security Death Index. Social Security Number 560-22-8327. State of California. Issue Date Before 1951.

416. U.S. Social Security Death Index. Social Security Number 541-78-7480. Last Residence Baker City, Baker County, Oregon.

417. U.S. Social Security Death Index. Social Security Number 540-26-8481. Last Residence Klamath Falls, Klamath County, Oregon. Date of birth February 12, 1924.

418. U.S. Social Security Death Index. Social Security Number 541-12-5929. Last Residence Clackamas, Clackamas County, Oregon. Date of birth February 6, 1923. Date of death August 28, 1998.

419. U.S. Census Year 1920. Census Place Los Angeles Assembly District 73, Los Angeles, California. Roll T625_114. p 15B. Enumeration District 398. Image 257.

420. U.S. Census Year 1930. Census Place Los Angeles, Los Angeles County, California. Roll 163. p 21B. Enumeration District 723. Image 992.0.

421. California Birth Index. 1905 through 1995. Sacramento, California. California Department of Health Services. Center for Health Statistics.

422. Some sources have Nancy Epps Chisum Bourland's date of death as January 6, 1869.

423. Some sources have recorded her name as Sarah. The 1870 census simply has the initials S.A. for her, and M.A. for her sister Amanda. U.S. Census Year 1870. Census Place Beat 1, Lamar, Texas. Roll M593_1594. p 192. Image 384. However, the 1860 census is far more clear in that it shows her name as Sarah and not Sallie. U.S. Census Year 1860. Census Place South West Division, Morgan, Alabama. Roll M653_19. p 409. Image 412.

424. Some sources record a son named Ernest C. as well as a daughter named Sallie. Thus far daughter Sallie is unconfirmed by the author.

425. Fleming, Elvis E.. 2003. *Treasures of History VI, Historical Events of Chaves County, New Mexico.* New York: iUniverse. p 3

426. U.S. Census Year 1860. Census Place Denton, Texas. Roll M653_1292. p 451. Image 378.
U.S. Census Year 1910. Census Place Roswell Ward 3, Chaves County, New Mexico. Roll T624_913. p 4B. Enumeration District 23. Image 686.
U.S. Census Year 1920. Census Place South Roswell, Chaves County, New Mexico. Roll T625_1074. p 4B. Enumeration District 2. Image 667.

427. U.S. Federal Salve Census 1860. Census Place Fairfield, Freestone County, Texas.

428. Collinson/Whatley. *Life in the Saddle.* p 145

429. Anderson. *History of New Mexico: its resources and people, Volume I.* p 1025

430. Territory of New Mexico, County of Chaves. Application for Marriage License.

Marriage License. Marriage Certificate. Marriage Record Book B. p 449. B.F. Chisum/Jane Allen

Also see State of New Mexico, County of Chaves. Application for Marriage License. Marriage License. Marriage Certificate. Marriage Record Book L. p 2,240. B.F. Chisum/Jennie Brown Also see Caldwell Files. *Frank Chisum.*

431. U.S. Census Year 1870. Census Place Coleman, Texas. Roll M593_1579. p 308. Image 8.

432. Fleming. *Treasures of History.* p 6. Fleming attributes the claim that Chisum gave Frank (rather than sold him) 200 head of cattle to a local rancher named James Miller who later wrote of this event in one of his manuscripts. Miller indicates that the date was 1880, which does not fit the other associated facts and thus gives rise to the concern that either or both claims by Miller may be inaccurate. The fact remains that Sallie Chisum's diaries are quite clear on the dates of her arrival and departure from Tascosa and the fact that Frank accompanied the the group. Further, while camped along the Canadian at Tascosa Frank Chisum attended school with the children of James Chisum and learned how to read and write.

433. Pearce, W.M.. 1964. *The Matador Land and Cattle Company.* Norman: University of Oklahoma Press. pp 6–8

434. Fleming. *Treasures of History.* p 5. Fleming claims that J. Evetts Haley mentioned this with regard to his interview(s) with Frank Chisum.

435. Frank may have been married before he wed Jane Allen in 1909 giving him a total of three marriages in all. There is a record of a Frank Chisum having married a Harriet Berry on January 17, 1884 at Falls, Texas. All of the information seems to match up with our Frank Chisum. Harriet was born in Texas in about 1855 and it appears as though she had been married to Jiles Berry. In the interest of completeness I am offering the foregoing information, but can not fully attest to its accuracy at this writing.

See LDS Church Records. Batch M591743. Source Call Number 0895641-V.1. Also see U.S. Census Year 1880. Census Place Precinct 1, Harrison, Texas. LDS Church Records 1255310 NA File T9-1310. p 563 B

436. U.S. Census Year 1910. Census Place Roswell Ward 3, Chaves, New Mexico. Roll T624_913. p 4B. Enumeration District 23. Image 686. Also see Chaves County, New Mexico records of marriage license of Frank Chisum and Jane Allen . Copy in Caldwell Files. *Chisum*

437. Jane is believed to have been born Jane Deams in Richmond, Virginia in 1859. Her parents were Jim Phillips and Antoinette Deams. She had a brother, Jerrell Deams, who lived in Texas.

438. Jennie was born May 5, 1859 in Georgia. Her father's name was Henry Wright. Mother's name unknown.

439. Entry in the diary of Sallie Chisum dated September 14, 1928 "dear old Frank came to say goodbye. He leaves to make his home with his brother in Wichita Falls, Texas."

440. U.S. Census Year 1900. Census Place Decatur, Wise, Texas. Roll T623_1680. p 10b. Enumeration District 136.

441. Lakeview Cemetery, Wichita Falls, Texas. Index Number 332-5875. Block 6 Plot 015

442. Massey, Sara R.. 2000. *Black Cowboys of Texas*. Texas A&M University Press. p 317

443. It was not until 1867 that the state of Texas required former slaves to select a last name.

444. U.S. Census Year 1900. Census Place: Decatur, Wise, Texas. Roll T623_1680. p 10B. Enumeration District 136.

445. The spelling of the surname Hembry is believed to be incorrect. There were no Hembry families in Missouri at the time, but there are at least four slave owning families that have surnames spelled in a very similar way to Hembry.

446. U.S. Census Year 1870. Census Place Precinct 1, Denton, Texas. Roll M593_1582. p 128. Image 256.

447. U.S. Census Year 1880. Census Place Denton, Denton, Texas. Roll T9_1300. Family History Film 1255300. p 31.2000. Enumeration District 102.

BIBLIOGRAPHY

REFERENCE MATERIAL

Adams, Clarence S. and Brown, Tom E.. 1972. *Three Ranches West.* New York: Carlton Press

Anderson, George B.. 1907. *History of New Mexico: Its Resources and People,* Volume 2. Los Angeles New York Chicago: Pacific Publishing Company

Atherton, Lewis. 1967. *The Cattle Kings.* Indiana University Press

Baron, Robert M.. 2003. *Court of Inquiry: Lieutenant Colonel N.A.M. Dudley, Fort Stanton, New Mexico, May, June, July 1879, Volume 1 & 2.* Edina, Minnesota: Beaver Pond Press.

Bates, Edward F. Bates. 1918. *History and Reminiscences of Denton County.* Denton: McNitzky Printing Company

Bonney, Cecil. 1971. *Looking Over My Shoulder, Seventy Five Years in the Pecos Valley.* Roswell: Hall-Poorbaugh Press, Inc.

Burns, Walter Noble. 1926. *The Saga of Billy the Kid.* University of New Mexico Press

Chrisman, Harry E.. 1990. *Lost Trails of the Cimarron.* Athens: Swallow Press

Collinson, Frank and Clarke, Mary Whatley. 1997. *Life in the Saddle.* Norman: University of Oklahoma

Clarke, Mary W.. 1984. *John Simpson Chisum.* Austin

Clark, Pat B.. 1937. *The History of Clarksville and Old Red River County.* Dallas: Mathis Van Nort & Co

Cox, James. 1895. *Historical and Biographical Record of the Cattle Industry.* New York: Antiquarian Press, Ltd.

Cramer, T. Dudley. 1996. *The Pecos Ranchers in the Lincoln County War.* Orinda, California: Branding Iron Press

DeArment, Robert K.. 2007. *Deadly Dozen, Twelve Forgotten Gunfighters of the Old West, Volume 1.* Norman: University of Oklahoma Press

Dobie, J. Frank. 1964. *Cow People.* Boston: Little Brown & Company

Dunham, Philip and Jones, Everett L.. 1983. *The Negro Cowboys.* University of Nebraska Press

Erwin, Allen A.. 1965. *The Southwest of John Horton Slaughter.* Arthur H. Clark Co.

Fleming, Elvis E.. 2003. *Treasures of History VI. Historical Events of Chaves County, New Mexico.* New York: iUniverse Inc.

Fuller, Benjamin Franklin. 1900. *History of Texas Baptists.* Louisville, Kentucky: Baptist Book Concern

Garrett, Patrick Floyd. 2007. *The Authentic Life of Billy the Kid.* Santa Fe: Sunstone Press

Goodnight, Charles. *The Tragic Death of Oliver Loving.* Manuscript

Haley, J. Evetts. 1936. *Charles Goodnight, Cowman and Plainsman.* Norman: University of Oklahoma

Hinton, Dr. Harwood P. New Mexico Historical Review Vol. XXXI July 1956 Number 3 *John Simpson Chisum*

Hough, Emerson. 1902. *The Story of the Outlaw.* New York: Grosset and Dunlap

Hunter, John M.. 1925. *The Trail Drivers of Texas.* Nashville: Cokesbury Press

Johnson, M. L.. 1935. *Trail Blazing: A True Story of the Struggles with Hostile Indians on the Frontier of Texas.* Dallas: Mathis Publishing Company

Kenner, Charles L.. 1969. *The Comanchero Frontier: A history of New Mexican, Plains Indian Relations.* Norman: University of Oklahoma Press

Keleher, William A.. 2008. *The Fabulous Frontier.* Santa Fe: Sunstone Press

Keleher, William A.. 2009. *Violence In Lincoln County: 1869–1881.* Santa Fe: Sunstone Press

Klasner, Lily. 1972. *My Girlhood Among Outlaws.* Tucson: University of Arizona

Lathrop, Barnes F.. 1949. *Migration into East Texas, 1835–1860: A Study from the United States Census.* Austin: Texas State Historical Association

LeMay, John. 2006. *Roswell.* South Carolina: Arcadia

McLean, William Hunter. 1978. *From Ayr to Thurber: Three Hunter Brothers and the Winning of the West.* Fort Worth Genealogical Society

McCoy, Joseph G.. 1940 (Ralph P. Bieber editor). *Historic Sketches of the Cattle Trade of the West and Southwest* , Glendale California

McKee, Irving. 1947. *Ben-Hur Wallace: The Life of General Lew Wallace* Berkeley: University of California Press

Miller, Darlis A.. 1982. *The California Column in New Mexico.* Albuquerque: University of New Mexico

Nolan, Frederick. 2007. *Tascosa.* Lubbock: Texas Tech University Press.

Nolan, Frederick. 2009. *The Life and Death of John Henry Tunstall.* Santa Fe: Sunstone Press

Nolan, Frederick. 2009. *The Lincoln County War, A Documentary History.* Santa Fe: Sunstone Press

O'Neal, Bill. 1979. *Encyclopedia of Western Gunfighters.* Norman:University of Oklahoma Press

Oden, Bill. 1966. *Early Days on the Texas New Mexico Plains.* Canyon, Texas

Pearce, W.M.. 1964. *The Matador Land and Cattle Company.* Norman: University of Oklahoma Press

Petersen, Paul R.. 2007. *Quantrill in Texas: The Forgotten Campaign.* Cumberland House Publishing

Poe, Sophie A.. 1936. *Buckboard Days.* Caldwell Idaho: Caxton

Redfield, George B. *Comanche Indians On Chisum Cattle Trail.* Checked by Lucius Dills, Roswell Historian. Paraphrased by C. W. Barnum. In the words of Sallie Chisum Roberts

Siringo, Charles A.. 2007. *Riata and Spurs.* Santa Fe: Sunstone Press

Strickland, Rex W.. 1937. *Anglo-American Activities in Northeastern Texas, 1803–1845.* (Ph.D. dissertation, University of Texas)

Taylor, Thomas Ulvan. 1936. *The Chisholm Trail and Other Routes.* San Antonio: Printed for Frontier Times

Thrapp, Daniel L.. 1991. *Encyclopedia of Frontier Biography.* University of Nebraska

Utley, Robert M.. 2002. *Lone Star Justice:The First Century of the Texas Rangers.* Oxford: Oxford University Press

Wallace, Lew. 1906. *Lew Wallace, An Autobiography.* New York: Harper and Brothers Publishers

Wallis, George W.. 1964. *Cattle King of the Staked Plains.* Denver: Adams

Wilbarger, J.W.. 1889. *Indian Depredations in Texas.* Austin: Hutchings Printing House

Wilson, John P.. 1987. *Merchants Guns and Money, The Story of Lincoln County and Its Wars.* Santa Fe: Museum of New Mexico Press

ARCHIVED MATERIALS

J. Evetts Haley Memorial Library and History Center. Midland, Texas
- The Robert N. Mullin Collection
- The J. Evetts Haley Collection
- The Philip J. Rasch Collection
- Tapes Nos. 1 through 9, from recordings of interviews between William

Chisum and Allen A. Erwin during the summer of 1952 in the Arizona
Pioneers' Historical Society, Tucson
New Mexico Historical Museum & Art Center Archives. Artesia, New Mexico.
Sallie Chisum Robert Collection
Texas A & M University, Gee Library, Commerce Texas - Steely, Skipper. *Forty Seven Years*
Texas A & M University, Gee Library, Commerce Texas - Steely, Skipper Collection

UNPUBLISHED MATERIAL

Frank Warner Angel. *Report on the Death of John H. Tunstall*. Department of Justice 1878. Records of the Department of Justice. NARS
Cooke County Texas Deed Book 4, 105
The Diamond Jubilee Historical Souvenir Program. Coldwater, Kansas. 30 August through 2 September 1959
Dunnahoo, Rufus H.. *Interview on 19 March 1937*. Roswell, NM
Jenkins, Yvonne A.. 1976. *Ninety Years of Faith - An Interview with Eugie Jones Thomas*.
Lamar County, Texas Genealogy and History Volume 8 and 9. May 1990 through February 1992
Lamar County, Texas Genealogy and History Volume 22. 2004
Mehren, Lawrence Lindsay. 1969. *A History of the Mescalero Indian Reservations, 1869–1881*. Unpublished Manuscript. MA Thesis, Tucson: University of Arizona
Sanders, Charles O.. *Research Papers on Tom Folliard and George Hindman*. December 2007 and January 2008

MAGAZINES AND PERIODICALS

Clark, Mary W. "History of Clarksville." *Paris News*. December 7, 1943. Neville. Backward Glances
Cunningham, Eugene. "Fought With Billy the Kid: Florencio Chavez." *Frontier Times*. Volume IX. March 1932
Mehren, Lawrence L.. "Scouting for Mescaleros: The Price Campaign of 1873." *Journal of the Southwest*. 1968
Nelson, Morgan. "First among the first." *Wild West History Journal*. Volume II Number 5. October 2009

Redfield, George B.. "Chisum Makes a Trail." *The New Mexico Sentinel.* December 8, 1939

Taylor, Taylor U., *Trailing John Chisum to New Mexico,* Frontier Times. Volume 13 Number 8. June 1936

Lee, Jane Matson and Dworkin, Mark. "The Genuine Cowboy Captured Alive." *The Life of Charley Nebo.* Western Outlaw Lawman History Association Journal, Winter 2007. Volume XVI. Number 4

INDEX

Do not stand on my grave and weep; I am not there.
I do not sleep. I am a thousand winds that blow.
I am the diamond glints on snow. I am the sunlight on ripened grain.
I am the gentle autumn's rain.
When you awaken in the morning's hush,
I am the swift uplifting rush
Of quiet birds in the circled flight.
I am the soft stars that shine at night.
Do not stand at my grave and cry; I am not there. I did not die.

—Mary Elizabeth Frye

www.ingramcontent.com/pod-product-compliance
Lightning Source LLC
LaVergne TN
LVHW051146240125
801989LV00003B/476